Towards an Anthropology of Data

Journal of the Royal Anthropological Institute Special Issue Series

The *Journal of the Royal Anthropological Institute* is the principal journal of the oldest anthropological organization in the world. It has attracted and inspired some of the world's greatest thinkers. International in scope, it presents accessible papers aimed at a broad anthropological readership. All of the annual special issues are also available from the Wiley-Blackwell books catalogue.

Previous special issues of the *JRAI*:

Mind and Spirit: A Comparative Theory, edited by T.M. Luhrmann

Energy and Ethics, edited by Mette M. High and Jessica M. Smith

Dislocating Labour: Anthropological Reconfigurations, edited by Penny Harvey and Christian Krohn-Hansen

Meetings: Ethnographies of Organizational Process, Bureaucracy, and Assembly, edited by Hannah Brown, Adam Reed, and Thomas Yarrow

Environmental Futures, edited by Jessica Barnes

The Power of Example: Anthropological Explorations in Persuasion, Evocation, and Imitation, edited by Andreas Bandak and Lars Højer

Doubt, Conflict, Mediation: The Anthropology of Modern Time, edited by Laura Bear

Blood Will Out: Essays on Liquid Transfers and Flows, edited by Janet Carsten

The Return to Hospitality: Strangers, Guests, and Ambiguous Encounters, edited by Matei Candea and Giovanni da Col

The Aesthetics of Nations: Anthropological and Historical Approaches, edited by Nayanika Mookherjee and Christopher Pinney

Making Knowledge: Explorations of the Indissoluble Relation between Mind, Body and Environment, edited by Trevor H.J. Marchand

Islam, Politics, Anthropology, edited by Filippo Osella and Benjamin Soares

The Objects of Evidence: Anthropological Approaches to the Production of Knowledge, edited by Matthew Engelke

Wind, Life, Health: Anthropological and Historical Perspectives, edited by Elisabeth Hsu and Chris Low

Ethnobiology and the Science of Humankind, edited by Roy Ellen

TOWARDS AN ANTHROPOLOGY OF DATA

EDITED BY RACHEL DOUGLAS-JONES,
ANTONIA WALFORD and NICK SEAVER

This edition first published 2021
© 2021 Royal Anthropological Institute

Registered Office
John Wiley & Sons Ltd, The Atrium, Southern Gate, Chichester, West Sussex PO19 8SQ, UK

Editorial Offices
350 Main Street, Malden, MA 02148-5020, USA
9600 Garsington Road, Oxford OX4 2DQ, UK
The Atrium, Southern Gate, Chichester, West Sussex PO19 8SQ, UK

For details of our global editorial offices, for customer services, and for information about how to apply for permission to reuse the copyright material in this book, please see our website at www.wiley.com/wiley-blackwell.

The right of Rachel Douglas-Jones, Antonia Walford and Nick Seaver to be identified as the authors of the editorial material in this work has been asserted in accordance with the UK Copyright, Designs and Patents Act 1988.

Library of Congress Cataloging-in-Publication Data

CIP data requested

9781119816768

A catalogue record for this book is available from the British Library.

Journal of the Royal Anthropological Institute.
Incorporating MAN
Print ISSN 1359-0987
All articles published within this special issue are included within the ISI Journal Citation Reports® Social Science Citation Index. Please cite the articles as volume 27(Supp) of the Journal of the Royal Anthropological Institute.

Cover image: An aisle of server cabinets in a London data centre, copyright: A.R.E. Taylor

Cover design by Ben Higgins

Set in 10 on 12pt Minion by Aptara Inc.

Printed in the UK by Hobbs the Printers Ltd.

1 2021

Contents

Notes on contributors   7

Rachel Douglas-Jones, Antonia Walford & Nick Seaver
Introduction: Towards an anthropology of data   9

1   Vijayanka Nair *Becoming data: biometric IDs and the*
    individual in 'Digital India'   26

2   Nick Seaver *Everything lies in a space: cultural data and*
    spatial reality   43

3   Tahani Nadim *The datafication of nature: data formations*
    and new scales in natural history   62

4   A.R.E. Taylor *Future-proof: bunkered data centres and the*
    selling of ultra-secure cloud storage   76

5   Cori Hayden *From connection to contagion*   95

6   Hannah Knox *Hacking anthropology*   108

7   Antonia Walford *Data – ova – gene – data*   127

8   Sarah Blacker *Strategic translation: pollution, data, and*
    Indigenous Traditional Knowledge   142

9   Rachel Douglas-Jones *Bodies of data: doubles,*
    composites, and aggregates   159

Bill Maurer *Data forward: an afterword*   171

Index   176

Notes on contributors

Sarah Blacker is a SSHRC Postdoctoral Research Fellow in the Department of Anthropology at York University in Toronto, and a guest scientist at the Museum für Naturkunde Berlin. *Kaneff Tower, 4700 Keele Street, Toronto, Ontario, Canada, M3J 1P3. sblacker@yorku.ca*

Rachel Douglas-Jones is an Associate Professor of Anthropological Approaches to Data and Infrastructure at the IT University of Copenhagen. She heads the Technologies in Practice research group, and co-directs the ETHOS Lab. *Technologies in Practice, IT University of Copenhagen, Rued Langgaards Vej 7, 2300, Copenhagen, Denmark. rdoj@itu.dk*

Cori Hayden is Associate Professor of Anthropology at the University of California-Berkeley and the UC Berkeley-UC San Francisco Joint Ph.D. Program in Medical Anthropology. *Department of Anthropology, University of California, Berkeley, 232 Kroeber Hall, Berkeley, CA 94720-3710, USA. cphayden@berkeley.edu*

Hannah Knox is Associate Professor of Anthropology at University College London. *Department of Anthropology, University College London, 14 Taviton Street, London WC1H 0BW, UK. h.knox@ucl.ac.uk*

Bill Maurer is Professor of Anthropology and Law, and Dean of the School of Social Sciences, at the University of California, Irvine. *Department of Anthropology, 3203 Social & Behavioural Sciences Gateway, University of California-Irvine, Irvine CA 92697-5100, USA. wmmaurer@uci.edu*

Tahani Nadim co-heads the department Humanities of Nature at the Museum für Naturkunde Berlin and is a Junior Professor of Socio-Cultural Anthropology at the Institute for European Ethnology at the Humboldt-Universität zu Berlin.

Journal of the Royal Anthropological Institute (N.S.) 27, 7-8
© Royal Anthropological Institute 2021

Museum für Naturkunde, Leibniz-Institut für Evolutions- und Biodiversitätsforschung, Invalidenstraße 43, 10115 Berlin, Germany. tahani.nadim@hu-berlin.de

Vijayanka Nair is Assistant Professor, San Diego State University. *Department of Anthropology, San Diego State University, 5500 Campanile Drive, San Diego, CA 92182-6040, USA. vnair@sdsu.edu*

Nick Seaver is Assistant Professor of Anthropology at Tufts University, in Medford, Mass. *Department of Anthropology, Tufts University, 5 The Green, 311A Eaton Hall, Medford, MA 02155, USA. nick.seaver@tufts.edu*

A.R.E. Taylor is a social anthropologist based at the University of Cambridge. *Department of Social Anthropology, University of Cambridge, Free School Lane, Cambridge CB2 3RF, UK. aret2@cantab.ac.uk*

Antonia Walford is a Lecturer in Digital Anthropology at University College London. *Department of Anthropology, University College London, 14 Taviton Street, London WC1H 0BW, UK. antonia.walford@ucl.ac.uk*

Introduction: Towards an anthropology of data

Rachel Douglas-Jones *IT University of Copenhagen*

Antonia Walford *University College London*

Nick Seaver *Tufts University*

The world is talking 'data'. The early cross-disciplinary, business-orientated hype around the potential of 'big' data, with its promises of unprecedented insight into social life, has given way. Data now motivates a sweep of dystopian visions, from rampant commodification to the invasion of privacy, political manipulation, and shadowy data doubles. Yet anthropologists have been cautious in taking data itself as their object, even as the social life of data practices becomes manifest in our ethnographies. In this introduction, we argue for an anthropology of data that is ethnographically specific and theoretically ambitious, putting forward a case for why anthropological engagements with the data moment might be not only politically important but also conceptually generative.

Among experts and amateurs, from the spectacular to the mundane, something called 'data' has permeated the ethnographic field. In Yogyakarta, Indonesia, a taxi driver tells an anthropologist how he puzzles over the booking apps that allocate rides to him; he considers putting his accounts into 'therapy', strategically accepting and declining requests so that he will have 'better data' (Sandbukt 2018). On the border between Kyrgyzstan and Russia, an ethnographer studying seasonal migrant labour finds herself concerned by data gathered into the 'black list', a tool used by Russian immigration services to make migrants deportable (Reeves 2016). In the United States, a grieving daughter describes how a personal database of memories appears to bring her mother back to life (Hales 2019). From conflicting data about voter turnout in the 2019 Indian elections, apparitions of 'ghost voters' emerge (*India Today* 2019). As a viral pandemic encircles the globe, data about infection and mortality rates becomes a matter of international public dispute (Street & Kelly 2020). Anthropologists find themselves needing to make sense of 'data' – and not only their own – as an emergent ethnographic object.

Journal of the Royal Anthropological Institute (N.S.) **27**, 9-25
© Royal Anthropological Institute 2021

At a moment when 'data' commonly implies a universalizing epistemology, the essays in this volume attend to data's multiplicity and particularity, relocating it in diverse local worlds. The growing presence of data in our fieldsites demands this traditional ethnographic work, which foregrounds the practical existence of data, in small forms that complicate and exceed its 'big' reputation. This collection starts from the popular association of 'data' with digital technologies – networked computing systems that register, store, and analyse ever more information about ever more aspects of life – but it also expands the frame, looking to data's relations with existing informational forms, such as documentation and accounting, to find continuity, rather than disjuncture. The work collected here charts a course between hailing data as a radical rupture with the past, and recognizing data as simply a continuation of familiar practices of social ordering, by attending to how discourses, practices, and imaginaries of data are configuring and inflecting the familiar in unfamiliar or surprising ways.

In this special issue, we draw data's apparent novelty into conversation with many of anthropology's central concepts, from kinship to value to personhood. This introduction demonstrates the necessity of this theoretical project, describing one shape it could take. Our first section is diagnostic, disambiguating different ways that data is talked about and done. We illustrate data's charismatic hold and review key approaches to its study within anthropology so far. Looking to an earlier period of technological and conceptual innovation – the advent of new reproductive technologies and the anthropological response to them – we identify areas of analytical interest we might attend to in the present data moment. By treating data as at once an empirical concern for ethnographers and an opportunity to revisit key anthropological concepts, the pieces collected in this volume show the potential for a transformative anthropology of data – one that goes beyond updates to the ethnographic record and uses data as a generative site of anthropological theory building.

Diagnosis and disambiguation in the data moment

Data, despite its apparent simplicity in common use, is not simply 'given' (as the word's etymological roots might suggest). What it is, and what it means, shifts. Everyday definitions of data start with the familiar: documents, numbers, building blocks of quantification, governance, and analysis. However, borrowing charisma from computation, data has also acquired a more revolutionary reputation: a powerful entity that shapes commercial futures; an engine of growth that drives institutions to 'datafy' themselves in pursuit of profit or efficacy (Fourcade & Healy 2017). To make sense of data, we need to first disambiguate the many uses of the term.

Knowing data

One reaction to data's ubiquity and polysemy is to insist on its material specificity. 'Data' continues to designate concrete, straightforward, empirical stuff (Dourish 2017). It takes the form of spreadsheets, .csv files, digitized archives, hand drawings and notes, or graphs on laptops; it is collected through sensors, database entries, mobile phones, and census work, from questionnaires to clicks. Thus understood, we can trace a decades-long history of ethnographic work on data, including the nature of evidence (Engelke 2008; Hastrup 2004); governmental practices of quantification and accounting (Maurer 1997; Nelson 2015); and the production of indicators by international non-governmental organizations and experts (Merry 2016; Murphy 2017). Data has appeared in the ethnographic record in analyses of 'audit culture' in the

1990s (Power 1997; Strathern 2000); studies of the charismatic role of documents in bureaucracy (Hull 2012; Riles 2006); and the seductive power of the numerical (Merry 2016; Porter 1995; Verran 2010).

Anthropologists and historians have also drawn out the importance of colonial bureaucratic practices of enumeration, which underpinned territorial dispossession and enforced a violent legibility on colonized peoples (Appadurai 1993; Scott 1998); more broadly, European empire building relied foundationally on quantification and the 'avalanche of numbers' that captured the eighteenth- and nineteenth-century European imagination, as well as the standardization, classification, and accounting that it permitted (Hacking 1990; Poovey 1998).[1] These continuities suggest that data is in fact a familiar concern for anthropologists, knowable through already-existing frames. The data revolution may not be so revolutionary after all (cf. Pfaffenberger 1988).

However, data has come to signify and act beyond these earlier practices. As people around the world reckon with data's significance, we reopen the definitional question as an ethnographic problem: what is data? As an object of ethnographic scrutiny, data is not merely varied, it is mercurial. What it is can change depending on the use to which it is put, or when one asks (Star & Ruhleder 1996). Data might be a store or source of value, an asset or a liability. Data for the taxi driver in Yogyakarta is not the same thing – either as an object or as meaning – as data for a worker placed on a Russian 'black list'. Tom Boellstorff and Bill Maurer describe this mercurial character as a consequence of data's sociality: '[D]ata is formed through relations that extend beyond 'data' itself; ... what counts as data (and data's referent) is a social process with political overtones; and ... data is always in real-time transformation in ways that cut across notions of nature and culture' (2015: 3-4). These relations, processes, and transformations are at the heart of this special issue. Understanding data as socially constituted has consequences for how we understand both academic disciplinary and public responses to data's growing prominence.

Data and disciplines

For many, 'data' appears to transcend old disciplinary boundaries and to promise new synthetic knowledges.[2] For others, this universalist drive represents a threat to the particularity of disciplinary expertise. Sociologists have described the growth of 'social' big data collection by commercial firms as a threat to their empirical authority (Savage & Burrows 2007); geographers worry about being 'left behind as others leverage insights from the growing data deluge' (Kitchin 2013: 262); social scientists have pursued data as a means to know the social (e.g. Marres 2017; Tinati, Halford, Carr & Pope 2014); historians have set about applying digital methods such as text mining, visualization, and mapping techniques to their topics (Mullaney 2019a; 2019b); and humanists continue to pursue digital, data-driven projects (Gardiner & Musto 2015; Terras, Nyhan & Vanhoutte 2013). These responses continue a history of promise and threat that dates back at least to the advent of computing itself (see Seaver, this volume).

What, then, of anthropologists? With some exceptions (e.g. Crowder, Fortun, Besara & Poirier 2019; Knox & Nafus 2018; Madsen, Blok & Pedersen 2018), anthropology has largely responded to the data moment by figuring ethnographic fieldwork as a necessary or more sensitive qualitative complement to large-scale data collection and analysis. It has done so in two senses. The first positions ethnography as a counterpart to data, what Boellstorff (2013) has noted as the presentation of '"ethnography" as the Other to big data'. From a position that takes data to be a competitor epistemology, ethnography is either at risk of losing its epistemic territory or an under-appreciated corrective that can balance out the reductionism of large-scale, quantitative methods. A now familiar critical stance is that big data simply misses out all that is human, and embodied, about living in the world. For example, the tech ethnographer Tricia Wang (2016) has argued, within the corporate context, that 'big data needs thick [ethnographic] data', drawing on conventional arguments in favour of mixed-methods research (cf. Seaver 2015).

The second approach finds anthropologists attending ethnographically to data practitioners themselves. We can already point to detailed analyses of the work and worlds of data scientists (Lowrie 2018; Williams 2018), Quantified Self trackers (Lupton 2013; Nafus & Sherman 2014; Ruckenstein & Schüll 2017), border management regimes (M'charek, Schramm & Skinner 2014), and global health experts (Biruk 2018). With these ethnographies come methodological challenges. Taking their first steps into the field, ethnographers find that their fieldsites are often distributed, access is ethically fraught, and technical practices are opaque (Knox & Nafus 2018; Seaver 2017). Nonetheless, fieldsites for those who seek to study communities and practices data continue to multiply around the world: Quantified Self communities, data mining start-ups, clandestine data centres, biometric infrastructures, and more.

Many other contemporary ethnographers may be more accurately described as accidental ethnographers of data. They do not set out to study data, but rather find it central in the lives of the people with whom they work. To study the nation-state, health systems, judicial systems, the economy, or scientific communities is to come up against infrastructures, practices, and discourses of data. A study of indigenous kinship might lead one to a genetic database, and from there into issues of sovereignty, ownership, and biocapital (Reardon 2017; TallBear 2013). An analysis of courtrooms might lead to software developers developing predictions of recidivism or newly spatialized carceral imaginations (Benjamin 2016; 2019). These accidental ethnographers of data will find it tightly knitted to core anthropological themes: kinship, economy, religion, law, and so on. Data cannot be set aside, because it is bound up with the development of new norms, with changing ideas of personhood, place, kin, and more. Encountering data requires anthropologists to revisit their theoretical commitments.

Data as theory
The rise of data has troubled settled agreements and reopened normative discussion about matters of long-standing anthropological interest. When people turn to data to know themselves and their world, we find the meaning of social concepts changing. To make visible some of these transformations, we draw a parallel between the current data moment and an earlier moment where new technologies opened up and challenged the meaning of core anthropological concerns. The technologies and discussion around New Reproductive Technologies (NRTs) constitute a prior moment of transformative technological change which gave rise to broad anthropological re-theorizing. By reading through that moment, we set out to identify similar themes critical to the current juncture.

A brief recapitulation of NRTs – both their technical capacities and the resulting work in anthropology – is useful. As the now familiar account goes, in the early 1990s, the development of in vitro fertilization techniques led to new possibilities for human procreation, and reopened public discussions about how kin could be conceptualized. This sudden prominence of NRTs in Euro-American consciousness demanded that the public – and anthropologists – reconsider a fundamental and taken-for-granted aspect of life: reproduction. From conception to parenthood, in vitro new technologies challenged understandings of the artificial and the natural, and assumptions about what is available for human intervention (Wagner 1977; 2016 [1975]); in so doing, they undid the very grounds upon which such categories organized and shaped the world in the first place (Strathern 1992*a*; 1992*b*). As legal cases made their way through different national courts, and teams of lawyers debated the new meanings of parent and child, in anthropology, two moves followed.

First, new technologies meant new fieldsites: kinship was no longer the domain of the domestic, nor the way to characterize the exoticized other – it was in laboratories, hospital waiting rooms, and, more recently with the advent of consumer genetics, corporate boardrooms (Franklin & McKinnon 2001; Reardon 2017). The entities that populated these fieldsites – such as cell lines, embryos, technologies, technical procedures – shifted in and out of existing categorizations, creating a need for conceptual re-theorization (e.g. Thomson 2007). Second, kinship was suddenly once again a lively vernacular social category, giving it a new hold on the anthropological imagination (Franklin & McKinnon 2001: 173). A shared public and academic question emerged: how would people orientate themselves to what seemed to be a tectonic shift in how they conceived life, and yet was, at the same time, uncannily familiar in the social forms it reproduced? (Franklin 2013).

Today, we see 'data' moving research similarly in both of these registers: it opens up fieldsites, and it prompts questions about what is new (and what is not) in the way it reproduces the social. While the former is reflected in ethnographies of data practice, the latter, more theoretical, concern is still emerging. Drawing from the legacies of NRTs, we reflect on what an anthropology of data which is both attentive to shifting tectonics and similarity of form might attend to. In what follows, we tack back and forth between ethnographic and theoretical work on data, and critical commentaries on NRTs, using the comparison to draw out categories troubled, presumptions that no longer hold, and novel contours to social life.

Calculative compositions

Like NRTs, data collection opens up new aspects of life for intervention and manipulation. The body is an ideal example: iris scans, facial recognition, gait analysis, voiceprints, and even analprints (Park *et al.* 2020) make new markers of identity accessible and claim to surface deeper meanings about people. There is also the routine but voracious collection of mundane data online – data on everyday intimate, personal, private activity – framed as a source of valuable insight (Couldry & Mejias 2019; Zuboff 2019). Where NRTs stressed the binary between the natural and artificial, these data practices draw into dispute the interior and exterior, the intimate and the productive, and the private and the public.

These new forms of visibility are also new arenas for calculation. The presence of data asks people to reinvest in the power of numbers (Porter 1995): the idea that nothing can escape quantification and ceaseless calculation. Consequently, the data moment also asks us to refocus our anthropological attention on social practices of quantification and measurement. While quantification and numbers have often been analysed (and thoroughly critiqued) as being seductive because they simplify and reduce social life (Merry 2016), we frequently find data used to figure life as extremely complex. From the neuroscientists in Rayna Rapp's examination of big data neuroscience who end up looking for a 'needle in a haystack' (Sullivan 2013, cited in Rapp 2016: 8) to the government officials in Louise Amoore's (2006) accounts of new forms of data-driven securitization who warn that there are untold threats knowable through the data, big data is understood by many of its practitioners to replicate the messiness and complexity of life; renowned MIT computer scientist Alex Pentland calls his work with big data 'reality mining' (Eagle & Pentland 2006). But we might say, as Franklin said of IVF, that data is both 'like and unlike what it imitates' (2013: 8). The 'insight' data gives works through the collapse of the tension between entities and their representation in data, such that its proponents can claim that 'your data' knows you better than you know yourself (Douglas-Jones, this volume). In so doing, however, it also makes 'yourself' newly available for reworking, re-assimilating, reconfiguring, re-evaluating. 'Deeper insight' is revealed as, in fact, dependent on creative acts that make people (or communities, or things) tractable to emergent forms of governance, from state interventions to grassroots appropriations to self-directed bodily optimization (Nafus & Sherman 2014; see also Nair, this volume). Within the representational logic of many big data practices there are therefore simultaneous enactments of both conservation and transformation. This demands an equal sensitivity to the constitutive tension between these two qualities in our critical approaches. This is apparent in, for example, Simone Browne's analysis of biometric data collection, in which she takes Frantz Fanon's notion of 'epidermalization', employed to describe the 'marking of the racial Other' as a fractured 'body out of place' (Browne 2010: 134), and reworks it as 'digital epidermalization', in order to take account of how the apparently disembodied and neutral technologies of contemporary biometric data collection operate to profoundly destabilize the ontological security of black bodies (see also Nair, this volume). Here, technologies that are claimed to be beyond race (Browne 2010: 143) are revealed as the mechanisms of racialization itself.

Thus the challenge arises: how to handle the tension between the claims made on behalf of data, and the realities of data's effects? This is one of the pressing questions for an anthropology of data. Scholars across disciplines have remarked on shifts or displacements in the idea of knowledge production at work in the way people make claims with data, particularly big data (Walford 2020), as, for example, when practitioners suggest that aggregate units such as 'class' or 'gender' are no longer relevant in the face of the hyper-granularity of big data (cf. Cheney-Lippold 2011). Shifts such as these move knowledge production into familiar but not quite recognizable epistemological terrain. Natasha Dow Schüll notes that Quantified Self practitioners reach uneasily for terms such as 'quantitative autobiography' (2019: 31) in order to capture the way their self-knowledge slips between fact and fiction. In a different context, Orit Halpern uses the term 'communicative objectivity', to signal a 'new aesthetic and practice of truth; a valorization of analysis and pattern seeking' (2014: 15) discernible in the construction of 'smart' data-driven environments. Catelijne Coopmans's description of data mining as a form of 'artful revelation' (2014: 37) plays exactly with the trope of hidden depths and visible surfaces experienced by analysts of data sets. Similarly, Louise Amoore characterizes the practices employed by the US government to 'flag' the presence of terrorists 'in the data' as working through an 'ontology of association' (2011: 27), in which disparate data points are connected up temporarily in order to create a fleeting, but potentially life-changing, risk-based and often racialized identity. In these examples, key epistemological principles that have commonly been ascribed to scientific knowledge – universality, replicability, objectivity, stability through time – no longer fully apply to the claims being made, and yet the resulting analyses are taken as truth.

While pattern analysis, temporary association, and revelation are familiar to Euro-American sensibilities, they also lead to conclusions that are difficult to fully recognize, not just analytically, but in terms of their representational construction, legal status, and social and ethical implications. In data's torqued extensions of what is already known, then, quantification and measurement are not just social practices, they are constitutive of specific forms of sociality that claim to reach beyond the social categories that social scientists are fluent in. Anthropologists of data need both to develop a sensitivity to the claims made of data's capacity to reshape the world, and to keep a firm grip on the tools at hand to anchor those claims in specific histories of practice and thought.

Retention and reinvention of form
Drawing on such histories will allow anthropologists to nuance the wider debate on data, which often relies on an overly simplified relationship between the old and the new. Numbering and enumeration are powerful, and as we have mentioned, data belongs to calculative regimes that rest on prior histories of listing, counting, and specifying (Porter 1995). The creation of data by nation-states to tell stories about people and place is rightly analysed and critiqued as today being in continuity with colonial violence (Couldry & Mejias 2018; Kukutai & Cormack 2019; Thatcher, O'Sullivan & Mahmoudi 2016), retaining administrative legacies stark in national statistics (Isin & Ruppert 2019; cf. Hull 2012). Biometrics, Simone Browne (2015) points out forcefully, is a direct descendant of Victorian practices of anthropometry and, before that, the practice of branding slaves, which coerced the body's surface into a determination of their identity as property (see also Chun 2009). But these are not the only histories to tell of data. Halpern (2014) argues that it makes little sense to consider imaginaries of data-driven self-regulating 'smart cities' without simultaneously drawing links to cybernetic imaginaries that accompanied earlier eras of computational dreaming. Anthropologists need to look to such histories; but they also need to ethnographically trace out the means by which the contemporary data moment is reworking and reshaping such histories in ways that have yet to be fully understood.

Here, we take inspiration from critical archivist Ann Laura Stoler, who asks how imperial legacies of inequality endure so recognizably and yet, at the same time, so invisibly – not as 'mimetic versions of earlier imperial incarnations' but 'refashioned' to be 'ineffably threaded through the fabric of contemporary life forms [such that] they seem indiscernible as distinct effects, as if everywhere and nowhere at all' (2016: 4). For example, if the legacies of quantification, and the concomitant 'birth of statistics', can be credited with inventing the idea of the 'normal' (Hacking 1990; cf. Foucault 1977) – and, of course, the 'abnormal' – which has subsequently woven itself into the way many people now conceptualize the world, then the turn to big data might be seen as permitting the exploration of other charismatic and emergent forms of social distribution, perhaps along the lines of what Michelle Murphy (2015) calls 'phantasmagrams … intangible form[s] brought into sensibility as a palpable presence with the help of quantitative practices' (see also Murphy 2017). Murphy is here thinking specifically of economic forms, but we might also think of the way recommendation algorithms draw on vast amounts of consumer data to redistribute people according to logics of 'likeness' and 'liking' (Lury & Day 2019; Seaver 2012). Whilst there is no doubt that contemporary data practices are forms of 'infopower' (Koopman 2019), it is an open ethnographic question as to what specific shapes these forms are taking.

As Minna Ruckenstein and Natasha Dow Schüll argue, ethnography here becomes a means to negotiate the complex power dynamics that are woven through datafication, 'by revealing how data and its technologies are taken up, enacted, and sometimes repurposed' (2017: 265). Whilst contemporary data practices often present familiar power dynamics, people are also taking hold of data in projects of refusal and resistance, whether Data for Black Lives (Watson-Daniels *et al.* 2020) or the enlisting of citizens in scientific initiatives (Gabrys, Pritchard & Barratt 2016). As Dana Greenfield suggests, following Michelle Murphy's lead, self-tracking data practices might also be seen as a form of 'counter-conduct' (Murphy 2012), in the vein of the consciousness-raising activities of feminists in the 1960s and 1970s, in which women appropriated speculums to do their own vaginal examinations (Greenfield 2016: 134). Stories told with and about data matter: both histories of specific data forms and the knowledge that is folded into contemporary data-driven practices and discourses produce specific configurations of resistance and assimilation.

Anthropology has much to offer current critical engagement with data, not least by decentring the focus on Euro-America, which at present dominates the scholarly literature on the subject. Established anthropological debates around personhood, relations, society, nature, the state, and value are all valuable tools with which to theorize the emergent phenomenon of 'data' as we have described it. However, it is also clear that an anthropological engagement with data demands that anthropologists develop and modify these theoretical approaches in order to take account of the only partially recognizable social and cultural forms that data practices are producing. This will require an openness to other disciplines as much as a consolidation and extension of our disciplinary conventions. Aptly, it is in this spirit of conservation and transformation that we approach an anthropology of data.

Essays in this volume
The pieces collected here explore a range of possible directions for an anthropology of data that is attentive to historical continuities and disjunctions, and to the conditions for thought that the present data moment has engendered. They explore these broad concerns in particular locations, drawing out the significance of data for topics of long-standing anthropological concern. Here we introduce and gather them together in four thematic areas: aesthetics, temporality, economy, and composition.

Data aesthetics
We begin with Vijayanka Nair's detailed ethnography of *Aadhaar*, the nation-wide biometric identity programme of the Government of India. Tracing the project from its policy inception into registration offices and, eventually, to the courts, Nair observes a shift in the programme's purpose. Early in its history, *Aadhaar* was framed as a tool to help citizens prove that they were indeed who they said they were, merely registering an already existing social identity. Yet, as the system took shape, the programme's central task turned from verifying 'are you who you say you are' to the much more vexed question of 'who are you?' Moving back and forth between the database and its reception, Nair finds that various technical aspects of *Aadhaar*, from the shape of the registration interface to the construction of the database, re-stage the broader tension between individuality and dividuality in which Indian citizens have often found

themselves caught as they negotiate their political agency. Paying attention to the aesthetic 'surface' of the database – the literal, bureaucratic form through which data is made – Nair demonstrates that 'being translated into data was a complex *process*' (original emphasis).

Contemporary data discourses often claim for data a privileged access to deeper social reality; through attention to the process of 'becoming data', as Nair puts it, we see the contingencies and flaws inherent in 'dataism' (van Dijck 2014). There is more to data than representational adequacy, as Nair's ethnography demonstrates. Data's aesthetic form, whether in the design of interfaces or the shape of visualization, elicits social effects. In Nick Seaver's essay, we encounter a form of data aesthetics endemic to contemporary machine learning: the representation of culture as a mathematized, mappable space. To make sense of contemporary music recommender systems, which analyse user interaction data to create 'music spaces' full of users and music to be recommended, Seaver tells the history of a related technique with roots in anthropology: multidimensional scaling. Tracing the interlinked history of anthropology and computing through the 1960s and 1970s, Seaver finds that spatializing practices are used by post-war cognitive anthropologists to grant elusive 'cultural' phenomena a sense of reality by borrowing from the world of physical objects and geographical distance. Spatializing data creates new surfaces, transforming sparse and discrete data points into apparently continuous cultural environments. Nair's and Seaver's essays suggest the importance of a move away from a representational critique of data; their analyses demonstrate the effects that data has in the world irrespective of its accuracy. An aesthetic sensibility, and attention to the persuasiveness of form (Strathern 2005: 10; cf. Riles 1998), opens up critical readings of data beyond representational paradigms.

Data times
Several essays in this collection attend to the ways that data is caught up in temporalizing projects. In conventional critiques, data's apparent fixity contrasts with the dynamic world it is marshalled to represent. Anthropological approaches to data recognize, as Tom Boellstorff (2013) has argued, that 'data is always a temporal formation' – it is *dated*, sampled from a particular moment in time. But anthropologists can do more than relocate data in its proper temporal context: we can examine how data is enlisted in efforts to produce new temporalities.

Data times are diverse, competing, and often contradictory temporal frames. In Tahani Nadim's analysis of the material stuff of natural history archives, she reads digitized and physical records of biological species together, finding the temporalities of both data collection and storage entangled with the history of colonialism. Nadim's essay expands our temporal horizon, spanning from early pen-and-paper days to new methods of DNA barcoding. Those new methods, like many data initiatives, distinguish themselves not only by their 'bigness', but also by their claims to speed. Advocates for new techniques bemoan the 'taxonomic impediment' – the slowness of conventional methods for collecting, analysing, and classifying biodiversity data – and promise a future in which DNA sequencing data will provide a total archive of earth's animals, plants, and fungi. The speed of this new data is not only a resource, but also a demand: this digital salvage taxonomy requires urgent action before the anticipated decimation of earthly biodiversity arrives. If the future can be caught in data before it is destroyed, it can also be reshaped to retell the past. Nair asks what it means for postcolonial India to be a world 'leader' in biometrics-based governance, as both people and technologies are enrolled making the data cosmopolis of Digital India.

The relationship between data and imagined futures takes on a new concreteness in the 'data bunkers' described in A.R.E. Taylor's contribution: here, data is not fundamentally static and durable, but rather a vulnerable collection of networked traces, always at risk of being wiped out of existence by catastrophic events. Anxieties about future data loss manifest in a concern for the physical arrangement of information, the location of backups and of the wires along which data flows, when every connection is a potential risk. These bunkers, often repurposed Cold War bomb shelters, reach forward and backward in time for their meaning, showing what happens when the protection of data and its integrity displaces the now-dated image of the family hunkering down with canned food. Data times appear in myriad forms across these essays, unsettling accepted genealogies and taken-for-granted futures of the data present.

Data economies

Given the entanglement of data and capital described above, it is not surprising to find concerns about economy threaded through the essays. In 2016, the Financial Accounting Standards Board declared that data should potentially be listed as a separate 'tangible corporate asset' on balance sheets, though as yet with no agreed means of calculating 'fair value' (Monga 2016). But across the essays in this collection, data is made valuable in diverse ways, entering economies not always recognizable as financial. Hannah Knox, in her essay on the careful and hopeful acts of energy trackers, shows how the value of data is both about saving money on heating bills and about a new understanding of the home gained through working with the data sets over large coffee shop tables at meet-ups. At a moment when 'data-driven' decisions are commonly valorized, Knox's ethnography of environmental data presents the complex unfolding of this drive, as people work to make sense of data produced by sensors in their homes. A concern for data – and for giving data force – draws people into new relations, and data generates forms of relationality that challenge conventional ethnographic imaginaries. Knox puts forward the 'hack' as a method for anthropological engagement with data practices – one which takes data 'not just as a stable representation that we need to deconstruct, but also as a means of engaging with relations that are imprecise and unknown'. Situating anthropology in data streams and assemblies as people worry and wonder about their home's energy consumption, Knox asks: how can we think data with and through capitalism?

Antonia Walford's essay about environmental data collaborations in the Brazilian Amazon presents another setting where the value of data is multiple. The data economies of the Large-Scale Biosphere-Atmosphere project are those of scientific collaboration, belonging to complex relations and socialities. Walford's close attention to how data is made, and its capacities for transformation, gives us insight into its conceptual flexibility as it moves between people with different relations both to it and to each other. For some, data is valuable because it takes work to collect, but for others, it has value because it can be made into something else, used and used again in future research collaborations internationally, beyond Brazil. By foregrounding the labour involved in the generation and reproduction of data's social value – nuancing the alienation, ownership, and rights in and for data – Walford's analysis demonstrates that to consider data as merely a commodity or currency is to overdetermine what else it might be. These details offer ethnographic differentiation to imaginaries of a global data economy, and provide a counterpoint to the clean association of data with financial value.

Data compositions

Nair's and Knox's essays illustrate how data imaginaries can serve to compose and recompose 'publics' in different forms, through the centralized operations of a government database or the distributed interpretative work of local enthusiasts. Rachel Douglas-Jones's essay zooms in on the act of composition itself, tracing how 'bodies' of data come to refer both to physical bodies and to bodies politic; examining how data is thought of as a means to knowledge about such bodies. How might data collection be shaped to invoke new knowledges, and to what ends? Douglas-Jones begins with data on and for the physical body, looking at Scandinavian communities convened around the use of everyday tracking devices. She examines the cultural understandings of the body that underlie efforts to compose sovereign individuals who are coextensive with their 'personal' data. Moving from the sovereign body to the sovereign people, she shifts the site of analysis to Indigenous Data Sovereignty movements. Here, what data is, and is about, becomes a matter of how stories are told and how prior modes of collecting data (though government statistics) give shape to what data will be, and how those peoples will be known.

Such data analytic practices appear to validate long-held anthropological ideas about persons and groups (Strathern 1992c): datafied persons are conspicuously partible, decomposed into collections of interests for the purposes of advertising and reaggregated into countless new collectives along axes of partial connection. But the power to aggregate and disaggregate – to classify or to individuate – is not evenly distributed. These questions of the power to define come forward in Sarah Blacker's account of a report on the environmental and health effects of toxins flowing through Lake Athabasca in Alberta, Canada. The object at the centre of Blacker's analysis is a technique known as the 'three-track methodology', which was designed to allow the inclusion and recognition of Indigenous knowledge within official policy-making. Put to use under fraught political conditions, the methodology represents an attempt to compose data in such a way that it can be legible to Western science, recognizable as policy-relevant. Blacker analyses how different kinds of knowledge are made into data, working through the aesthetic, temporal, and incommensurable dimensions present in the making of contamination evidence. Her essay suggests that data cannot be read without its national and historical framing – framings which become part of the question 'what is data?'

In both Blacker's and Douglas-Jones's essays, data shows its capacity for composition, bringing persons and data into new social and political formations. Both accounts refuse the spatialization of a technological timeline (Fabian 1983) when considering the uses to which indigenous knowledge and data will be put. An anthropology of data works towards developing theory to accommodate data's compositional capacity, and, we suggest, contributes to re-composing anthropological attention at the same time.

Cori Hayden's contribution turns to another form of composition, analysing how concerns about connection and contagion from late nineteenth-century crowd theory have become newly relevant with the emergence of online 'crowds' that are at once the subjects and objects of massive data production. As she writes, '[C]rowd theory's distinctive preoccupations, from the potentially destructive but also generative force of emotional contagion and suggestibility, to the peculiarly more-than-human heterogeneity of crowds, to a concern with how ineffable energetic forces travel, have come so alive in recent discussions'. Where the power of 'big data' is conventionally associated with its size and scope, Hayden traces an argument for attending to the modes of connection within the crowd, the shape of the network through which social intensities flow and act. Through a careful reappraisal of work by notorious theorists like Gustave Le Bon, Hayden demonstrates the value of expanding our theoretical frames of reference when working to understand such apparently novel dynamics as social action in online spaces. The presence, availability, and behaviour of data in these spaces prompts the revisitation of questions central to the crowd theory of the nineteenth century.

In his afterword, Bill Maurer recognizes across these essays a concern for data's transformative potential – for its capacity to produce new social compositions while indexing the old. In spite of its association with static records and fixity, data is lively. In asking how we might apply this insight to the systemic inequalities reinscribed by many of the data practices we encounter in this special issue, and in our everyday, Maurer turns our attention to the politics of data. How might a 'machine ethnography' (Kockelman 2020: 351), learning from data activists, generate an alternate data politics, using the instabilites within systems of inequality to chart through them 'new paths' of transformation? (Milner 2019).

Conclusion

Data is generated for and drawn into existing social worlds and problems. In data practices, we recognize continuities with deeper pasts, with projects of society making and attempts at 'managing' people and their worlds. How it will come to speak to and shape those worlds and problems cannot be known in advance. The anthropological capacity to critically regard the claims of the new, and to see how old ideas appear in new guises, is necessary at a juncture where new injustices emerge in the name of new freedoms.

As a powerful generic, linking widely varying practices and objects to each other through its apparently modest epistemic form, an anthropology of data should, following Marilyn Strathern (2014), recover the specifics of this generic, locating 'data' in its contexts. But, as the essays in this collection demonstrate, it remains necessary and generative to think data across sites. From the informatic rendering of genomics (Tutton & Prainsack 2011) to the citizen as a digitally rearticulated configuration of domination and resistance (Lyon 2008; Ruppert 2012), or the vast Earth BioGenome project as systems of exchange flourishing through data, social practices are valued on data markets that exist at the edges of conventional regulatory apparatuses (Gerlitz & Helmond 2013; Maurer 2015). Much is being worked out. These studies, and many others like them, demonstrate the immense intellectual potential of the social study of data. We close with a call for further work that thinks across sites and settings to produce concrete theoretical formulations. An anthropology of data provides ethnographic thickness and sited-ness to counter data's ideologies of objectivity; it can also open up new conceptual approaches for thinking with and about social worlds, as they are used, made, and done through data. For data makes relations, and it is the careful analysis of the consequences of this capacity to mould and reshape hoped-for futures towards which an anthropology of data should direct itself.

Journal of the Royal Anthropological Institute (N.S.) **27**, 9-25
© Royal Anthropological Institute 2021

NOTES

The authors thank the reviewers of this collection. We learned after the fact that the late Sally Engle Merry had provided insightful comments which helped us reshape our arguments. Thanks are due also to Katie Smith and Nayanika Mathur for their critical readings of work in progress, and to Jessica Turner and Lara Tatiana Reime for their support of the editorial process. We thank the participants of the seminar that gave rise to this collection, in particular discussants Haidy Geismar and Marilyn Strathern.

[1] For work that directly draws such comparisons between contemporary datafication and colonialism, see Couldry & Mejias (2018); Dourish & Mainwaring (2012); Isin & Ruppert (2019).

[2] Out of cross-disciplinary engagements, the reflexive field of critical data studies has emerged as a transdisciplinary formation (Dalton & Thatcher 2014; Kitchin & Lauriault 2014).

REFERENCES

AMOORE, L. 2006. Biometric borders: governing mobilities in the war on terror. *Political Geography* **25**, 336-51.

————— 2011. Data derivatives: on the emergence of a security risk calculus for our times. *Theory, Culture & Society* **28**: 6, 24-43.

APPADURAI, A. 1993. Number in the colonial imagination. In *Orientalism and the postcolonial predicament: perspectives on South Asia* (eds) C.A. Breckenridge & P. van der Veer, 314-37. Philadelphia: University of Pennsylvania Press.

BENJAMIN, R. 2016. Catching our breath: critical race STS and the carceral imagination. *Engaging Science, Technology and Society* **2**, 145-56.

————— (ed.) 2019. *Captivating technology: race, carceral technoscience and liberatory imagination in everyday life*. Durham, N.C.: Duke University Press.

BIRUK, C. 2018. *Cooking data: culture and politics in an African research world*. Durham, N.C.: Duke University Press.

BOELLSTORFF, T. 2013. Making big data, in theory. *First Monday* **18**, 10 (available online: *https://doi.org/10.5210/fm.v18i10.4869*, accessed 13 January 2021).

————— & B. MAURER 2015. Introduction. In *Data: now bigger and better!* (eds) T. Boellstorff & B. Maurer, 1–6. Chicago: Prickly Paradigm Press.

BROWNE, S. 2010. Digital epidermalization: race, identity and biometrics. *Critical Sociology* **36**, 131-50.

————— 2015. *Dark matters: on the surveillance of blackness*. Durham, N.C.: Duke University Press.

CHENEY-LIPPOLD, J. 2011. A new algorithmic identity: soft biopolitics and the modulation of control. *Theory Culture & Society* **28**: 6, 164-81.

CHUN, W.H.K. 2009. Introduction: Race and/as technology; or, how to do things to race. *Camera Obscura* **24**: 1, 7-35.

COOPMANS, C. 2014. Visual analytics as artful revelation. In *Representation in scientific practice revisited* (eds) C. Coopmans, J. Vertesi, M. Lynch & S. Woolgar, 36-58. Cambridge, Mass.: MIT Press.

COULDRY, N. & U. MEJIAS 2018. Data colonialism: rethinking big data's relation to the contemporary subject. *Television and New Media* **20**, 336-49.

————— 2019. *The costs of connection: how data is colonizing human life and appropriating it for capitalism*. Stanford: University Press.

CROWDER, J.W., M. FORTUN, R. BESARA & L. POIRIER 2019. *Anthropological data in the digital age: new possibilities, new challenges*. London: Palgrave Macmillan.

DALTON, C. & J. THATCHER 2014. What does a critical data studies look like, and why do we care? Seven points for a critical approach to 'Big Data'. *Society & Space*, 12 May (available online: *https://www.societyandspace.org/articles/what-does-a-critical-data-studies-look-like-and-why-do-we-care*, accessed 18 January 2021).

DOURISH, P. 2017. *The stuff of bits: an essay on the materialities of information*. Cambridge, Mass.: MIT Press.

————— & S. MAINWARING 2012. Ubicomp's colonial impulse. *Proceedings of UbiComp '12*, 133-42 (available online: *https://www.dourish.com/publications/2012/ubicomp2012-colonial.pdf*, accessed 13 January 2021).

EAGLE, N. & A. PENTLAND 2006. Reality mining: sensing complex social systems. *Personal and Ubiquitous Computing* **10**, 255-68.

ENGELKE, M. (ed.) 2008. The objects of evidence: anthropological approaches to the objects of knowledge. *Journal of the Royal Anthropological Institute* (N.S.) **14**: S1.

FABIAN, J. 1983. *Time and the other: how anthropology makes its object*. New York: Columbia University Press.

FOUCAULT, M. 1977. *Discipline and punish* (trans. A. Sheridan). New York: Pantheon.

FOURCADE, M. & K. HEALY 2017. Seeing like a market. *Socio-Economic Review* **15**, 9-29.

Franklin, S. 2013. *Biological relatives: IVF, stem cells, and the future of kinship*. Durham, N.C.: Duke University Press.

———— & S. McKinnon 2001. *Relative values: reconfiguring kinship studies*. Durham, N.C.: Duke University Press.

Gabrys, J., H. Pritchard & B. Barratt 2016. Just good enough data: figuring data citizenships through air pollution sensing and data stories. *Big Data & Society* **3**: 2 (available online: *https://journals.sagepub.com/doi/full/10.1177/2053951716679677*, accessed 29 January 2021).

Gardiner, E. & R.G. Musto 2015. *The digital humanities: a primer for students and scholars*. Cambridge: University Press.

Gerlitz, C. & A. Helmond 2013. The like economy: social buttons and the data-intensive web. *New Media & Society* **15**, 1348-65.

Greenfield, D. 2016. Deep data: notes on the *n of 1*. In *Quantified: biosensing technologies in everyday life* (ed.) D. Nafus, 123-46. Cambridge, Mass.: MIT Press.

Hacking, I. 1990. *The taming of chance*. Cambridge: University Press.

Hales, M.K. 2019. Animating relations: digitally mediated intimacies between the living and the dead. *Cultural Anthropology* **34**, 187-212.

Halpern, O. 2014. *Beautiful data: a history of vision and reason since 1945*. Durham, N.C.: Duke University Press.

Hastrup, K. 2004. Getting it right: knowledge and evidence in anthropology. *Anthropological Theory* **4**, 455-72.

Hull, M. 2012. *Government of paper: the materiality of bureaucracy in urban Pakistan*. Berkeley: University of California Press.

India Today 2019. Ghosts didn't vote in Lok Sabha polls, all were humans, says EC rubbishing claims on data mismatch. *India Today*, 1 June (available online: *https://www.indiatoday.in/india/story/ghosts-did-not-vote-2019-lok-sabha-polls-data-mismatch-election-commission-1540291-2019-06-01*, accessed 13 January 2021).

Isin, E. & E. Ruppert 2019. Data's empire: postcolonial data politics. In *Data politics: worlds, subjects, rights* (eds) D. Bigo, E. Isin & E. Ruppert, 207-28. London: Routledge.

Kitchin, R. 2013. Big data and human geography: opportunities, challenges and risks. *Dialogues in Human Geography* **3**, 262-7.

———— & T.P. Lauriault 2014. Towards critical data studies: charting and unpacking data assemblages and their work. *The Programmable City Working Paper* **2** (available online: *http://papers.ssrn.com/sol3/papers.cfm?abstract_id=2474112*, accessed 13 January 2021).

Knox, H. & D. Nafus (eds) 2018. *Ethnography for a data-saturated world*. Manchester: University Press.

Kockelman, P. 2020. The epistemic and performative dynamics of machine learning praxis. *Signs and Society* **8**, 319-55.

Koopman, C. 2019. *How we became our data: a genealogy of the informational person*. Chicago: University Press.

Kukutai, T. & D. Cormack 2019. Mana motuhake ā-rarauna: datafication and social science research in Aotearoa. *Kōtuitui: New Zealand Journal of Social Sciences Online* **14**: 2 (available online: *https://doi.org/10.1080/1177083X.2019.1648304*, accessed 13 January 2021).

Lowrie, I. 2018. Becoming a real data scientist: expertise, flexibility and lifelong learning. In *Ethnography for a data-saturated world* (eds) H. Knox & D. Nafus, 62-81. Manchester: University Press.

Lupton, D. 2013. Quantifying the body: monitoring and measuring health in the age of health technologies. *Critical Public Health* **23**, 393-403.

Lury, C. & S. Day 2019. Algorithmic personalization as a mode of individualization. *Theory, Culture & Society* **36**: 2, 17-37.

Lyon, D. 2008. Biometrics, identification and surveillance. *Bioethics* **22**, 499-508.

Madsen, M., A. Blok & M. Pedersen 2018. Transversal collaboration: an ethnography in/of computational social science. In *Ethnography for a data-saturated world* (eds) H. Knox & D. Nafus, 183-211. Manchester: University Press.

Marres, N. (ed.) 2017. *Digital sociology: the reinvention of social research*. Oxford: Wiley.

Maurer, B. 1997. *Recharting the Caribbean: land, law and citizenship in the British Virgin Islands*. Ann Arbor: University of Michigan Press.

———— 2015. Principles of descent and alliance for big data. In *Data: now bigger and better!* (eds) T. Boellstorff & B. Maurer, 67-86. Chicago: Prickly Paradigm Press.

M'CHAREK, A., K. SCHRAMM & D. SKINNER 2014. Topologies of race: doing territory, population and identity in Europe. *Science, Technology, and Human Values* **39**, 468-87.

MERRY, S.E. 2016. *Seductions of quantification: measuring human rights, gender violence and sex trafficking.* Chicago: University Press.

MILNER, Y. 2019. Abolition means the creation of something new: the history of big data and a prophecy for big data abolition. *Medium*, 31 December (available online: *https://medium.com/@YESHICAN/abolition-means-the-creation-of-something-new-72fc67c8f493*, accessed 18 January 2021).

MONGA, V. 2016. Accounting's 21st century challenge: how to value intangible assets? *The Wall Street Journal*, 21 March (available online: *https://www.wsj.com/articles/accountings-21st-century-challenge-how-to-value-intangible-assets-1458605126*, accessed 13 January 2021).

MULLANEY, T. (ed.) 2019*a*. *The Chinese deathscape: grave reform in modern China.* Stanford: University Press.

——— 2019*b*. No room for the dead: on grave relocation in contemporary China. Stanford University blog, 14 March (available online: *https://stanfordpress.typepad.com/blog/2019/03/no-room-for-the-dead.html*, accessed 13 January 2021).

MURPHY, M. 2012. *Seizing the means of reproduction: entanglements of feminism, health and technoscience.* Durham, N.C.: Duke University Press.

——— 2015. Phantasmagrams of population: *Histories of the Future* (available online: *http://histscifi.com/essays/murphy/phantasmagrams-of-population*, accessed 13 January 2021).

——— 2017. *The economization of life.* Durham, N.C.: Duke University Press.

NAFUS, D. & J. SHERMAN 2014. Big data, big questions: this one does not go up to 11: the Quantified Self movement as an alternative big data practice. *International Journal of Communication* **8**, 1784-94.

NELSON, D.M. 2015. *Who counts? The mathematics of death and life after genocide.* Durham, N.C.: Duke University Press.

PARK, S., D.D. WON, B.J. LEE, *et al.* 2020. A mountable toilet system for personalized health monitoring via the analysis of excreta. *Nature Biomedical Engineering* **4**, 624-35.

PFAFFENBERGER, B. 1988. The social meaning of the personal computer: or, why the personal computer revolution was no revolution. *Anthropological Quarterly* **61**: 1, 39-47.

POOVEY, M. 1998. *A history of the modern fact: problems of knowledge in the sciences of wealth and society.* Chicago: University Press.

PORTER, T. 1995. *Trust in numbers: the pursuit of objectivity in science and public life.* Princeton: University Press.

POWER, M. 1997. *The audit society: rituals of verification.* Oxford: University Press.

RAPP, R. 2016. Big data, small kids: medico-scientific, familial and advocacy visions of human brains. *BioSocieties* **11**, 1-21.

REARDON, J. 2017. *The post-genomic condition.* Chicago: University Press.

REEVES, M. 2016. The black list: on infrastructural indeterminacy and its reverberations. In *Infrastructures and social complexity* (eds) P. Harvey, C. Bruun Jensen & A. Morita, 296-308. London: Routledge.

RILES, A. 1998. Infinity within the brackets. *American Ethnologist* **25**, 378-98.

——— (ed.) 2006. *Documents: artifacts of modern knowledge.* Ann Arbor: University of Michigan Press.

RUCKENSTEIN, M. & N.D. SCHÜLL 2017. The datafication of health. *Annual Review of Anthropology* **46**, 261-78.

RUPPERT, E. 2012. The governmental topologies of database devices. *Theory, Culture & Society* **29**: 4-5, 116-36.

SANDBUKT, S. 2018. *The future of digital payments: the impact of disintermediated and decentralised financial technologies in Indonesia.* Work in Progress paper, IT University of Copenhagen.

SAVAGE, M. & R. BURROWS 2007. The coming crisis of empirical sociology. *Sociology* **41**, 885-99.

SCHÜLL, N.D. 2019. Self in the loop: bits, patterns and pathways in the quantified self. In *A networked self and human augmentics, artificial intelligence, sentience* (ed.) Z. Papacharissi, 25-38. London: Routledge.

SCOTT, J.C. 1998. *Seeing like a state: how certain schemes to improve the human condition have failed.* New Haven: Yale University Press.

SEAVER, N. 2012. Algorithmic recommendations and synaptic functions. *Limn 2: Crowds and Clouds* (available online: *https://limn.it/articles/algorithmic-recommendations-and-synaptic-functions/*, accessed 13 January 2021).

——— 2015. Bastard algebra. In *Data: Now bigger and better!* (eds) T. Boellstorff & B. Maurer, 27-45. Chicago: Prickly Paradigm Press.

Journal of the Royal Anthropological Institute (N.S.) **27**, 9-25
© Royal Anthropological Institute 2021

―――― 2017. Algorithms as culture: some tactics for the ethnography of algorithmic systems. *Big Data & Society* **4**: 2 (available online: *https://journals.sagepub.com/doi/full/10.1177/2053951717738104*, accessed 29 January 2021).

Star, S. & K. Ruhleder 1996. Steps toward an ecology of infrastructure: design and access for large information spaces. *Information Systems Research* **7**, 111-34.

Stoler, A.L. 2016. *Duress: imperial durabilities of our times.* Durham, N.C.: Duke University Press.

Strathern, M. 1992a. *Reproducing the future: essays on anthropology, kinship and the new reproductive technologies.* Manchester: University Press.

―――― 1992b. *After nature: English kinship in the late twentieth century.* Cambridge: University Press.

―――― 1992c. Parts and wholes: refiguring relationships in a post-plural world. In *Conceptualizing society* (ed.) A. Kuper, 74-104. London: Routledge.

―――― (ed.) 2000. *Audit cultures: anthropological studies in accountability, ethics, and the academy.* London: Routledge.

―――― 2005. *Partial connections.* Oxford: AltaMira Press.

―――― 2014. Reading relations backwards. *Journal of the Royal Anthropological Institute* (N.S.) **20**, 3-19.

Street, A. & A. Kelly 2020. Counting coronavirus: delivering diagnostic certainty in a global emergency. *Somatosphere*, 6 March (available online: *http://somatosphere.net/forumpost/counting-coronavirus-diagnostic-certainty-global-emergency/*, accessed 13 January 2021).

TallBear, K. 2013. *Native American DNA: tribal belonging and the false promise of genetic science.* Minneapolis: University of Minnesota Press.

Terras, M., J. Nyhan & E. Vanhoutte (eds) 2013. *Defining digital humanities: a reader.* Farnham, Surrey: Ashgate.

Thatcher, J., D. O'Sullivan & D. Mahmoudi 2016. Data colonialism through accumulation by dispossession: new metaphors for daily data. *Environment and Planning D: Society and Space* **34**, 990-1006.

Thomson, C. 2007. *Making parents: the ontological choreography of reproductive technologies.* Cambridge, Mass.: MIT Press.

Tinati, R., S. Halford, L. Carr, & C. Pope 2014. Big data: methodological challenges and approaches for sociological analysis. *Sociology* **48**, 663-81.

Tutton, R. & B. Prainsack 2011. Enterprising or altruistic selves? Making up research subjects in genetic research. *Sociology of Health and Illness* **33**, 1081-95.

van Dijck, J. 2014. Datafication, dataism and dataveillance: Big Data between scientific paradigm and ideology. *Surveillance & Society* **12**, 197-208.

Verran, H. 2010. Number as an inventive frontier in knowing and working Australia's water resources. *Anthropological Theory* **10**, 1-8.

Wagner, R. 1977. Scientific and indigenous Papuan conceptualizations of the innate. In *Subsistence and survival* (eds) T.P. Bayliss-Smith and R.G. Feachem, R.G. &. New York: Academic Press.

―――― 2016 [1975]. *The invention of culture.* Chicago: University Press.

Walford, A. 2020. Data aesthetics: rethinking the materiality of information. In *Lineages and advancements in material culture studies: perspectives from UCL* (eds) T. Carroll, A. Walford & S. Walton, 205-17. London: Bloomsbury.

Wang, T. 2016. Why big data needs thick data. *Ethnography Matters*, 20 January (available online: *https://medium.com/ethnography-matters/why-big-data-needs-thick-data-b4b3e75e3d7*, accessed 13 January 2021).

Watson-Daniels, J., Y. Milner, N. Triplett, *et al.* 2020. *Data for Black Lives COVID-19 Movement Pulsecheck and Roundtable Report,* April (available online: *https://communityresourcehub.org/resources/data-for-black-lives-covid-19-movement-pulse-check-and-roundtable-report/*, accessed 13 January 2021).

Williams, K. 2018. Engineering ethnography. In *Ethnography for a data-saturated world* (eds) H. Knox & D. Nafus, 82-104. Manchester: University Press.

Zuboff, S. 2019. *The age of surveillance capitalism: the fight for a human future at the new frontier of power.* London: Profile.

Introduction : Vers une anthropologie des données

Résumé

« Données » : le mot est sur toutes les lèvres. L'engouement initial, interdisciplinaire et à vocation commerciale, autour du potentiel des « mégadonnées », et leurs promesses d'éclairage inédit de la vie sociale, est retombé. Les données inspirent désormais une déferlante de visions dystopiques, de la marchandisation effrénée à l'invasion de la vie privée, en passant par les manipulations politiques et

Journal of the Royal Anthropological Institute (N.S.) **27**, 9-25
© Royal Anthropological Institute 2021

les mystérieux doubles numériques. Les anthropologues, cependant, sont prudents lorsqu'il s'agit de prendre les données elles-mêmes comme objet d'étude, alors même que leur place dans la vie sociale devient manifeste dans nos travaux ethnographiques. Cette introduction défend une anthropologie des données ethnographiquement spécifique et théoriquement ambitieuse, expliquant pourquoi l'intérêt des anthropologues pour l'ère des données pourrait s'avérer non seulement politiquement important, mais aussi conceptuellement constructif.

1

Becoming data: biometric IDs and the individual in 'Digital India'

VIJAYANKA NAIR *San Diego State University*

Aadhaar (literally 'foundation') is the largest national biometric identification drive the world has witnessed. An *Aadhaar* is a twelve-digit ID number linked to its holder's iris scans, fingerprints, facial photograph, and demographic information in a centralized database. In but a decade, India has expeditiously enrolled over 90 per cent of its billion-strong population into a Central Identities Data Repository. This essay is an ethnographic consideration of the processes by which *Aadhaar* enrollees become data, focusing on the sociopolitical valence of biometric data. It argues that the datafication of the body via *Aadhaar* occasions re-examinations of – and contestations over – the idea of the individual in postcolonial India, a country often deemed sociocentric in popular and scholarly discourse alike. Further, it suggests that biometric socialization facilitates belonging in a 'Digital India', often rendered as a data cosmopolis in emergent technocratic imaginations.

In 2009, the Unique Identification Authority of India (UIDAI) was instituted by executive order and directed to generate unassailable unique IDs for all of India's population. Roughly a decade later, this task has been all but accomplished: India's controversial *Aadhaar* (literally 'foundation' or 'support' in several Indian languages) ID programme is now the world's largest national biometric identification system. To date, the UIDAI has enrolled over 90 per cent of India's residents into its Central Identities Data Repository (CIDR) and has generated more than 1.25 billion *Aadhaar* IDs.[1] An *Aadhaar* is a randomly generated unique twelve-digit identification number, linked to its holder's iris scans, fingerprints, facial photograph, and demographic details in the CIDR.[2] In the absence of universal birth registration, Indians had previously used state-issued eligibility documents like ration cards and driver's licences as proofs of identity.

The ruling political coalition in 2009 observed that in postcolonial India, those who most needed robust proof of identity (PoI) in fact had the least access to it. A serviceable ID, they reasoned, would allow marginalized populations and those living in poverty to access welfare programmes as well as private sector services. An attendant challenge facing the government was that existing welfare delivery databases in India – teeming as they were with 'fake', 'duplicate', and 'ghost' identities – were inefficient and susceptible to being mercilessly defrauded by middlemen and unscrupulous officials

Journal of the Royal Anthropological Institute (N.S.) **27**, 26-42
© Royal Anthropological Institute 2021

(UIDAI 2010: 2-3).[3] After much deliberation, the UIDAI reached the conclusion that an 'innovative' biometric ID infrastructure would solve both these problems in one fell swoop.[4] *Aadhaar*'s ID system would deploy bodily indices to incontrovertibly stabilize, and subsequently verify online as needed, whether 'you are who you say you are' (UIDAI 2010: 25). The UIDAI is described by its first Director General as a 'unique public-private partnership' comprising 'private sector employees and government sector employees'. It brought together seasoned government bureaucrats and private sector players, most notably India's IT and marketing networks. Experts from these distinct sectors shared the goal of creating a foolproof national ID system (Sharma 2020: 42).

The UIDAI invited anyone who had resided in India for over six months to voluntarily acquire an *Aadhaar*, free of cost. *Aadhaar*'s versatility putatively derived from its singular purpose. *Aadhaar* would 'guarantee identity' but not rights, benefits, services or citizenship (UIDAI 2010).[5] Its restrained design, however, would allow for seamless access to goods and services issuing from the public and private sectors alike. Storing a 'minimal' amount of personal data, this token-less ID – merely a number unencumbered by a card – was built to support limitless applications. *Aadhaar*'s technology architects rightly predicted that it would, in time, become the one universal, nationally accepted ID in India. In 2021, *Aadhaar* serves as one of the 'central pillars' of 'Digital India', an endeavour 'to transform India into a digitally empowered society and knowledge economy'.[6] This initiative aims to foster digital literacy, increase internet connectivity across India, make all government services available via online or mobile platforms, and accelerate 'financial inclusion' programmes.[7]

Aadhaar was presented as being perfectly innocuous – it was and would always be devoid of intelligence. *Aadhaar*'s gargantuan and globally unparalleled biometric ID infrastructure was to pave the way for India to join the coterie of 'developed' nations (Jha 2017). Critics warned, however, that this cheerful rhetoric was obscuring concerted efforts to establish a surveillance state in India (Ramanathan 2010). They stressed that Indian residents enrolled in the *Aadhaar* programme not because it offered a bouquet of possibilities but because it became de facto mandatory to possess a biometric ID. For welfare departments, cellphone companies, and banks, *Aadhaar* soon became the only acceptable form of ID.[8] What both advocates and sceptics assumed, however, is that there existed an easily delineable 'individual' to whom an *Aadhaar* number could be assigned using technology.

In this essay, I argue that it is fruitful to think about what it means for India's billion-strong population to become individualized, instantaneously retrievable bodily data. I regard the process of becoming data – most crucially biometric data – as an experiment in rethinking both personhood and belonging.

Based on fieldwork in New Delhi, this essay tracks how *Aadhaar*'s blueprint is brought to life in Enrolment Centres. I then contemplate how *Aadhaar*'s CIDR informs technocratic imaginations of a 'Digital India'. 'Digital India' is often construed as what I am calling a 'data cosmopolis', a place indifferent to collective identities. In the last section of the essay, I briefly discuss objections to *Aadhaar* presented in India's highest court. I conclude that *Aadhaar*'s attempt to anchor the 'individual' in bodily data unleashed a kaleidoscopic rendering of the 'individual' as many things: a unique body; the legal subject of the Constitution; the inhabitant of a borderless digital world; the consumer of goods and services; and the *aam aadmi* (common man) from whom collective identities could not be alienated. The chief protagonist of this essay is the elusive individual in India.

Finding the individual in the state[9]

Bernard Cohn contended that as targets of the nineteenth-century colonial Census, Indians were faced with the complicated question of 'who they were' (1987: 248). This prompted 'objectification', wherein Indians stood back and looked at 'themselves, their ideas, their symbols and culture', viewing them as 'things' or 'entities' (1987: 229). I propose that *Aadhaar*, as a form of identification, precipitated various moves to objectify the idea of the individual in India. While the individual is the principal bearer of rights and responsibilities in India's Constitution (Béteille 1986), scholarly and popular discourse has often suggested – if not without controversy (see, e.g., Mines 1988) – that in India the individual doesn't quite exist. If at all discernible, the individual is subordinate to variously defined groups or collectives, or so the argument goes. Writing on the eve of independence about India's enduring 'social structure', Jawaharlal Nehru – India's first Prime Minister – pointed to the importance of the institutions of village, caste, and joint family, adding that 'in all these three it is the group that counts: the individual has a secondary place' (Cousins 1951: 248). Sociologist Louis Dumont argued that caste, as an instantiation of the principle of hierarchy, largely precluded the possibility of manifest individualism (Dumont 1970).[10] Ethnosociologist McKim Marriott argued that Indian individuals are 'composite and divisible' and thus better thought of as 'dividuals' (1989: 17). Political theorist Sunil Khilnani observes that even as postcolonial India bestowed upon the individual many rights and duties traditionally 'anchored in collectivities', the individual does not have a strong social or political presence in the country (1997: 59).[11] Anthropologist Thomas Blom Hansen judiciously maintains that Indian democracy 'means competing communities, where the paradigm of rights is translated into community assertion and notions of collective entitlements' (1999: 57). I suggest that *Aadhaar* is a fraught postcolonial endeavour to curate an 'individual' who 'counts'.[12] I examine how the datafication of the body and 'squeaky-clean' – in the words of an official – databases are implicated in a bid to render the 'individual' materially and conceptually separable from the imagined collective. This effort, however, is shot through with ambiguity, uncertainty, and contestation.[13]

  Striking to me, over the course of my research on *Aadhaar*, has been UIDAI officials' constant invocation of the notion of the 'individual'. A senior official at the UIDAI, in one of our very first conversations, explained *Aadhaar* to me thus: 'Identity always existed', he said, in a carefully considered way. '*Aadhaar*', he continued, 'allows the individual to stand out in a crowd'. The UIDAI's first strategy document similarly emphasized, in its closing statement, that *Aadhaar* would 'empower the individual' (UIDAI 2010). I contend that these formulations are neither accidental nor without consequence. *Aadhaar* – a complex assemblage of people and things – symbolically removed persons from the grip of their social worlds, translated them into unique biometric data, transported them to a database, and was to lay the foundation for them to 'stand out' in a crowd.

  If the purpose of the Census was, and continues to be, the synoptic classification and categorization of India's population based on information pertaining to 'social, demographic, economic and other related aspects',[14] one might argue that the purpose of the *Aadhaar* database was to find and create a record of the 'somatic singularity' (Foucault 2006) of every Indian resident. Attempts at objectifying the individual

Journal of the Royal Anthropological Institute (N.S.) **27**, 26-42
© Royal Anthropological Institute 2021

through *Aadhaar* chiefly consisted in tying the notion of the individual to bodily signatures – unique data to be stored in a database – that could circumvent the thorny questions of religious, caste, class, or tribal identity.[15] Yet becoming data was both saturated with familiar sociality and the basis for imagining new modes of belonging. A multiplicity of actors – vocal relatives of the Enrollee, opinionated bystanders – crowded the spaces producing the individual. These actors did not just mediate questions of social classifications but also made themselves relevant through touch and physical presence. Equally, the datafication of the individual allowed for an efflorescence of technocratic modes of imagining new collectives and affinities.

Becoming data

Aadhaar enrolment made clear to me that one is not born, but rather must become, data (following Beauvoir 2009 [1949]).[16] Most straightforwardly, I use the coinage 'becoming data' to emphasize that being translated into data was a complex *process*. It bears mentioning that while the English word 'data' derives from the Latin *datum* '(thing) given', in several Indian languages, the familiar word *dātā* means giver or donor, and is often used to describe charitable actors. This common word comes from the Sanskrit root '*dā*', which means 'to give'. In the context of *Aadhaar*, the giver (the Enrollee who submits data to *Aadhaar*) quite literally becomes the given (data). Biometric signatures were to be the basis for establishing oneself as an 'individual'.

Over the following pages, I describe how a resident is enrolled in the central ID database and is subsequently issued an *Aadhaar* number (see also Nair 2018).

The UIDAI designed its *Aadhaar* Enrolment Client Multi-Platform software 'in-house'. *Aadhaar* would collect minimal data; recipients were reassuringly told that the ID's 'dumbness' was its veritable strength (Nilekani 2018). Certified Enrolment Agencies (these could be either public or private entities) were charged with setting up Enrolment Centres and collecting resident data via UIDAI software. *Aadhaar*'s blueprint was operationalized by a legion of personnel: over 800,000 trained 'Operators' were employed by Enrolment Agencies to 'capture' demographic and biometric data (UIDAI 2012*a*). Enrolment Agencies were responsible for assembling infrastructure, Enrolment Stations, and staff. Operators entered the resident data into Enrolment software and sent it to the CIDR, where information was 'de-duplicated' (checked against existing data). The resident was then issued a randomly generated twelve-digit unique identification number. The UIDAI made clear that '*Aadhaar* is designed to include, but not depend on, demographic data for the purpose of establishing unique identity via de-duplication' (UIDAI 2014*a*: 24).

The Enrolment Centre I spent the most time in was run by a private company in New Delhi. The company described itself as one of the chief financial groups in India and had been awarded a contract as an Enrolment Agency. The high-rise that housed its office was a grey building on one of the premier streets of New Delhi, dotted with government and cultural establishments. *Aadhaar* enrolment was one of many things that this company did. It held a few other government contracts and also undertook data management, market research, and wealth management in the private sector.

Two cubicles in the company's brightly lit 50 × 20 feet office were devoted to *Aadhaar* enrolment. An Enrolment Station comprised two computer monitors, set up back-to-back on a rectangular table. The resident sat on a chair against a white screen at one end of the table and the Operator sat on the opposite side of the table. The arrangement of the monitors was deliberate – it was to allow the resident to see exactly what the

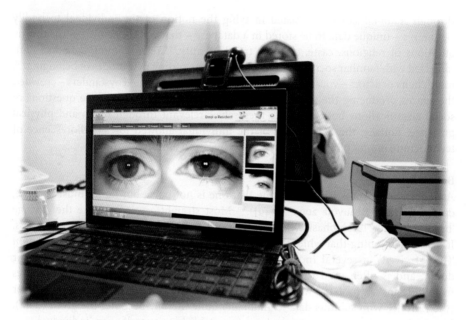

Figure 1. Iris scanning. (Photo by the author.)

Operator saw. A tangle of wires connected a keyboard, a printer, an iris scanner, a fingerprint scanner, and a camera to the Operator's computer.

I spent several months sitting beside two Operators called Shreya and Adil,[17] both in their early twenties and tasked with entering resident data into *Aadhaar* software. 'I've enrolled so many people, I now dream in *Aadhaar* Enrolments', Shreya once said to me as her trained hands glided across the keyboard and expertly adjusted an iris scanner to biometrically 'capture' the irises of a resident (Fig. 1). Her supervisor casually dropped by. Assuming the stance of an Enrollee, he in turn authoritatively declared, 'No one who has been biometrically enrolled by us can possibly forget the experience'. Shreya had started working soon after graduating from school, and would always dress in jeans and T-shirt. Adil had a college degree, and would usually also wear 'Western' clothes.

The two Operators had a good rapport. There was healthy competition between the two, both striving to enrol more people than the other. '*Tune kitne banaa liye?*' (How many [*Aadhaars*] have you made?), they'd ask each other periodically. Often Shreya would tease Adil, calling him *dheelu* (lackadaisical). He, in turn, would call her a *kaamchor* (shirker). Neither seemed to have much evidence on their side. While *Aadhaar* manuals present enrolment as an engagement between a single resident and a trained enumerator, it is more often than not a collaborative affair involving family members, curious onlookers, and bored office staff. Operators were expected to be *vinamra* (pleasant) at all times – they had learned this from Enrolment Manuals, and during their 'Operator training'. They did take pleasure, however, in exchanging notes about the *paagal log* (mad people) they encountered over the course of the day. Notably, the Enrolment Centre wasn't quite a rule-adhering space that churned out 'docile bodies' through verbal injunctions and engagements that might recall Foucauldian 'cellular' disciplining (Foucault 1995 [1975]). Enrolment was, on

Journal of the Royal Anthropological Institute (N.S.) 27, 26-42
© Royal Anthropological Institute 2021

the contrary, understood to be a collective, improvised, and occasionally raucous affair.

Demographic data collection

One of the UIDAI's biometric co-ordinators, Brajesh, described to me pitched battles in the early days of the UIDAI over what demographic data *Aadhaar* ought to collect. The private sector imports disagreed with veteran bureaucrats. The latter wanted to collect more demographic data than was strictly necessary. A settlement between the two was reached in the form of making certain demographic data part of an 'optional' field. This was viewed as a momentous victory by Brajesh. 'You must have noticed that father, mother, guardian, husband, or wife's details – previously required on all *sarkari* [government] forms – is optional for *Aadhaar* Enrolment', he said enthusiastically. I *had* noticed this. Other engineers similarly reminded me that *Aadhaar* collected 'minimal data' and could technically have collected *only* biometric data for the purposes of identification. The sanctity of *Aadhaar* derived from its indifference to collective identities. If it weren't for the recalcitrance of the bureaucracy, the 'one body, one number' dream might have been realized. Even one's given name, indexing as it does collective identities in the South Asian context, could have reasonably been deemed superfluous in the context of this project.

As it happened, when a resident entered an Enrolment Centre, their first task was to fill in a demographic Enrolment Form. The form collected 'demographic data', and had four required fields: name, gender, contact details (address), and age/date of birth. The resident would fill in the form by hand. To enrol for *Aadhaar*, the resident was also required to provide the government with copies of existing forms of identity proof they already had. The 'resident needs to carry original documents and a photocopy of Proof of Identity (PoI), Proof of Address (PoA), Date of Birth (DoB), Proof of Relationship (PoR) documents for verification', the UIDAI underlined (2012a: 6). The Enrolment Agency was, in turn, required to verify these original documents. As part of the enrolment process, the Operator typed into the client software demographic information from the Enrolment Form (Fig. 2).

At the Enrolment Centre in Delhi, both Operators *and* residents were unwaveringly committed to furnishing the 'details' of relatives. Hardly ever was this opportunity to establish familial ties forgone. The UIDAI was one of the first government bodies, also, to include transgender as a gender category, but as Brajesh admitted to me, this option was woefully under-utilized. When Shreya was filling in the name of a person's 'relation', she would sometimes face the wrath of Enrollees who wanted their deceased relatives to be mentioned online, and indeed with the honorifics 'Late' or 'In heaven'. Some women would insist that both their maiden 'caste' and their post-marriage one be included in the database. The Operators' inability to do so would leave Enrollees indignant. One might say that the datafied Indian was wary of digital isolation, and that in many ways, *Aadhaar* enrolment undermined the project of producing an individual *sans* collective affiliation. Anthropologists like Gabriella Coleman (2010), Christopher Kelty (2008), and Nick Seaver (2017) who study algorithms and software have argued that these 'stable objects' are the consequence of, and animated by, human practice. Nowhere was this more in evidence than in the engagements of Enrollees and Operators with the *Aadhaar* demographic software. Even as the *Aadhaar* project assigned demographic

Journal of the Royal Anthropological Institute (N.S.) **27**, 26-42
© Royal Anthropological Institute 2021

Figure 2. Demographic data entry. (Photo by the author.)

details and group identities secondary significance in the *Aadhaar* software, they more often than not were of utmost importance to Enrollees.

Biometric socialization

Biometric data capture was the next step in the 'data entry' process. This portion of the enrolment was bewildering to many: '*Meri Mrs ko khud aana pageda?*' [Will my Mrs (wife) have to come *herself* (to register)?], harried men would ask incredulously. Amused, the Operators would explain that every discrete body had to be individually recorded in the CIDR. I use the term 'biometric socialization' to describe the interactions through which people are introduced to biometrics, and, in turn, how biometrics become part of everyday life.[18] Operators were entrusted with capturing a facial photograph, fingerprints, and iris scans for all residents over 5 years old, and recording 'biometric exceptions' in cases where biometrics could not be adequately recorded (UIDAI 2012a: 17). The socialization of Enrollees into the biometric arena also involved a visual prompt that encouraged the linking of 'identity' to fragments of the body. As the resident was enrolled, they beheld their eyes magnified manifold, their fingerprints come into relief, their face looking back at them from a computer monitor. The process made explicit the ordinarily 'tacit body' (Leder 1990): immediate, fragmented, and visually imposing. Simone Browne's concept of 'digital epidermalization' is helpful here. According to Browne, this 'is the exercise of power cast by the disembodied gaze of certain surveillance technologies (for example, identity card and e-passport verification machines) that can be employed to do the work of alienating the subject by producing a "truth" about the body and one's identity (or identities) despite the subject's claims' (2009: 135).

Aadhaar exemplifies how this disembodied gaze could not exist without the embodied, tactile co-optation of a slew of people. There is a way in which the collective

Journal of the Royal Anthropological Institute (N.S.) **27**, 26-42

Figure 3. Fingerprinting. (Photo by the author.)

is indispensable to the making of the biometric person – biometric datafication in enrolment centres was almost always a group activity. Led by the Operator, entire families, even strangers, would gamely – or grudgingly – participate in enrolment, their efforts meeting with varying degrees of success.

Nikolas Rose and Peter Miller (2010) argue that government 'in the present' is dependent upon technologies for 'governing at a distance'. Official UIDAI documents reflect this analysis, asserting that they are building an apparatus that will allow the 'government a clear view of India's population' through the generation of data (UIDAI 2010: 5). Yet touch seems overwhelmingly to be the condition of possibility for the state to 'see' its subjects via the *Aadhaar* database. The collection of biometric data was a challenging process, as fingers and irises frequently resisted 'capturing' (Figs 3 and 4). During my fieldwork on *Aadhaar*, I came to appreciate how much 'hand-holding' was literally required to accomplish biometric enrolment. Rarely did an unaided fingerprinting attempt succeed. Operators would routinely leave their seats and cross over to the resident's side, pressing fingers onto the fingerprint scanner with just the right amount of pressure, often with help from family members.

Operators I spoke to insisted that '*chuachut ki problem*' (the problem of 'untouchability') had no place within the Enrolment Centre. They observed that '*log apni jaat line mein dikhaatein hain*' (people might assert their caste position in queues [outside the Centres]) by not wanting to stand behind – or in close proximity to – a person of a 'lower caste', for example. Collective identities and indeed blatant casteism hovered about the Centre and could not entirely be banished as idea or practice, the Operators acknowledged.

Most people who entered the Enrolment Centre did not know how to handle biometric devices. The Operator's touch shielded them from the potential embarrassment of being defeated by a machine. The very young and very old

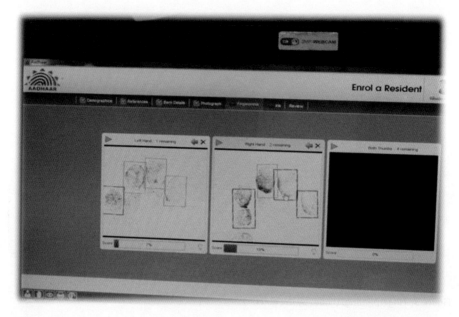

Figure 4. Fingerprints that cannot be 'captured' are outlined in red. (Photo by the author.)

often found themselves being part of elaborate, trying choreographies. However, they were by no means the only demographic whose bodily impressions biometric machines routinely spurned. The UIDAI had initially sought to use only fingerprinting for biometric identification but found that with a considerable segment of India's population engaged in manual labour, fingertips were usually too worn to meet required biometric quality 'measured using standardized automated algorithms and thresholds' (UIDAI 2012b:13). It thus introduced iris scanning, which, in turn, engendered another set of dextrous manoeuvres.

In the context of *Aadhaar*, one might suggest that there was no such thing as 'untouched' data. Even as the language of cleanliness used by UIDAI officials obscured the tactile processes that went into the making of *Aadhaar* data, the sequestering of the individual in a database was a distinctly collaborative, touchy process. This was the sort of group activity, however, that is liable to be written out of history. While the UIDAI considered its data to be standardized and otherwise unsullied by variation in human judgement, this assumption was belied by how much Operators and Enrollees shaped the working of the software, the database, and indeed the answer to the question of who the Indian individual is. Some scholars go so far as to suggest that 'raw data' is an oxymoron (Gitelman 2013), others that *all* data is 'cooked by the processes and practices of production' (Biruk 2018: 4).

At the end of the day, the Centre I stationed myself at would upload data packets to the UIDAI's data repository. Agencies were required to back up data and export data packets to the CIDR regularly. At the CIDR, a person's data was de-duplicated. According to the UIDAI, the

> process of establishing the identity of a person who has enrolled for an *Aadhaar* number through
> the Enrolment process wherein his/her data (demographics and biometrics) is compared against the

entire gallery of residents who have been enrolled thus far is called de-duplication. De-duplication, hence, involves 1:n comparisons where 'n' represents the total gallery size (UIDAI 2014*b*).

If and when the data was confirmed as being 'unique', the UIDAI issued an *Aadhaar* number (UIDAI 2012*a*: 28). Once it exited the Enrolment Centre, 'data' was subjected to the technocratic grip, the noisy Enrolment process being translated into zeros and ones to be stored in the *Aadhaar* database.

A digital passage to a data cosmopolis?

Anthropologists have observed that social and material infrastructures are inextricably linked, and that to study infrastructure is to explore forms of belonging (Anand 2011). 'Data entry' and the *Aadhaar* database were seen to afford 'entry' into a certain formation, the contours of which I discuss here. *Aadhaar* was the key to 'transforming' India into 'Digital India'.

What was 'Digital India', and what was its relation to the *Aadhaar* holder?

Aadhaar was inaugurated by the United Progressive Alliance, a coalition led by the centrist Indian National Congress. 'Digital India' was inaugurated by the National Democratic Alliance, led by the Hindu nationalist Bharatiya Janata Party. This coalition came to power in 2014 and endorsed *Aadhaar*, launched by its arch political rival, as passionately as it had previously opposed it.

Anthropologists have long been interested in the initiation ritual as a mode of selecting and grooming potential members to be ushered into the fold of a 'group', variously defined. I suggest that biometric initiation was a means of entering not just a database, but Digital India. Integration into a Digital India mirrored anthropological descriptions of initiation ceremonies, complete with 'tests' and 'ordeals' (*pace* Turner 1969) such as producing the right papers and making one's body compatible with biometric devices. The initiate would regularly fail and retake these 'tests'. In order to qualify as an ID-brandishing member of 'Digital India', the initiate was required to prove their worthiness. The Operator and family members who participated in enrolment shared the duty of nudging and guiding the initiate into the community of the biometricized. Biometric technologies served as tools for a purifying ritual – once truth had been extracted from the surface of the body, the initiate was ripe for assimilation into a 'clean' 'Digital India'.

Enrolment incorporated a fleeting moment of the ritual inversion of roles. We could also apply the language of 'liminality' to biometric enrolment. Victor Turner argues that 'the liminality of the permanently structural inferior contains as its key social element a symbolic or make-believe elevation of the ritual subjects to the positions of eminent authority' (1969: 168). The setting of the Enrolment Station served as a liminal venue where the 'characteristics of the ritual subject (the "passenger") were ambiguous' (1969: 94). The arrangement of computers quite plainly allowed the Enrollee to see like a state, and, in a sense, experience and transiently possess the power of the state, as held by its agents.

There are, however, limits to a Turnerian analysis of *Aadhaar*. Turner argues that after reincorporation,

The ritual subject, individual or corporate, is in a relatively stable state once more and, by virtue of this, has rights and obligations vis-à-vis others of a clearly defined and 'structural' type; he is expected to behave in accordance with certain customary norms and ethical standards binding on incumbents of social position in a system of such positions (1969: 95).

An Enrollee's (re)aggregation into India does not merely imply a settling into an established system of structural positions in society. It is simultaneously implicated in the reconstitution of India as 'Digital India'.

In the imaginations of many of *Aadhaar*'s architects, 'Digital India' would be a place where *Aadhaar* would enable a 'voluntary' association between the UIDAI, the ID holder, and service providers; each identity authentication would be 'purpose blind', the state would serve merely as the 'custodian' of data, and the UIDAI would 'maintain' the Identities Repository. In this ecosystem, meddling touts, middlemen – and the corruption they engaged in under the auspices of the state – would be things of the past. I suggest that *Aadhaar*'s designers often saw biometric IDs as an 'identity gateway' to what I will provisionally call a 'data cosmopolis'.[19] 'Digital India' inheres in the continuum between the offline and online, the virtual and the actual.[20] This 'data cosmopolis' confounds received understandings of the immaterial and the material, identity and recognition, the 'pure' and the 'impure', and citizenship and residence. In part, I mobilize the idea of a cosmopolis because *Aadhaar* was informed by the neoliberal, market-orientated cosmopolitanism of many of its designers.[21] Nandan Nilekani and Viral Shah predicted that soon 'Government will disappear from people's everyday lives; instead of taking the physical form of offices and bureaucrats, government will now be evident only through the delivery of its services and their outcomes' (2015: 281). In the 'data cosmopolis', the state would be but one of a range of vendors.[22] Importantly, *Aadhaar*-based 'Digital India' was also a 'cosmopolis' because it performed a flattening of caste, class, religion, and other markers of group and collective identities.

Aadhaar's data cosmopolis was envisioned as ever expanding, constantly in a state of becoming. *Aadhaar* was its foundational 'soft infrastructure', characterized by flexibility, and the potential to create 'virtual' highways and extensive webs of communication. Once part of *Aadhaar*'s database, one was expected to eventually consume goods and services from both the private and public sectors using *Aadhaar*. This biometric data-based ID could, in other words, generate more data: a data 'footprint'. In this data cosmopolis, 'data is power', the UIDAI's first Chairman confirmed (Nilekani 2018). The matter of who held this power, however, was to become the subject of vociferous debate. Intriguingly, once you entered *Aadhaar*'s database, there was no readily available 'opt-out' option. The *Aadhaar* database held one's biometric information 'forever'. There was no leaving this cosmopolis. As a UIDAI architect joked with me, 'to become immortal, all you have to do is to register with *Aadhaar*'.

After the Cambridge Analytica scandal broke, Nandan Nilekani (2018) advocated for an approach to the internet that would 'empower users with the technical and legal tools required to *take back* control of their data' (emphasis added). He continued: 'The Internet, it has become clear, is not so free, after all; users are paying in the form of personal information, which is collected by "data brokers" and sold to third parties'. Nilekani now travels the globe, popularizing the idea of 'data fiduciaries' who might act on behalf of the 'individual' on the Internet. India, he promises, will lead the charge in creating these fiduciaries. In this context of India's data cosmopolis, Ruha Benjamin's warning is worth remembering. 'Algorithmic neutrality', she tells us, 'reproduces algorithmically sustained discrimination' (2019: 140).

Contesting datafication

After 2012, *Aadhaar* began to be seriously challenged through 'Public Interest Litigation' cases (PILs) in the Supreme Court of India. The UIDAI had statedly collected the biometric signatures of each of India's residents in order to fortify their individuality. No sooner had it started its project than sceptics, however, charged that this move was in fact desecrating individuality by trampling on the liberal tenets of equality, freedom, and personal liberty.

On a crisp winter morning, in Court No. 4, a Senior Advocate, arguing on behalf of the petitioners against *Aadhaar*, claimed that *Aadhaar* contravened Articles 14 (Equality before law), 19 (Protection of certain rights regarding freedom of speech), and 21 (Protection of life and personal liberty).

In his rousing oral submissions, the Senior Advocate time and again went back to a stock phrase. '*Aadhaar*', he would say, 'violates the integrity of my body'. The most basic aspect of rights, he insisted, is that 'no one can interfere in my body'. Biometrics were posed in this debate as 'intimate', 'unique', and 'distinctive' personal information that could not be wrested from a person. 'Sweeping up biometrics of tens and thousands of people is a transgression of the right to life', the Senior Advocate claimed. He accused the government of stealing information from India's residents, liberally using the terms 'deception' and 'purloining' in his description of *Aadhaar* Enrolment. The litigants' affidavit similarly argued that the government had extracted information from 'unsuspecting individuals' (Puttaswamy 2012). While the UIDAI had zealously recorded biometric information apparently to dignify and animate the 'individual', *Aadhaar*'s opponents excoriated the UIDAI for successfully subduing the 'individual' via its process of enumeration. As the Senior Advocate put it:

> I will begin with the preamble, the primary bright line that has been crossed. It [*Aadhaar*] alters the relationship between individual and the state. There are many rights given to citizens … Bright lines cannot be crossed. This is one such … It is the domination of the state over the individual. The individual then doesn't really remain an individual; the state dominates.

The Senior Advocate painted a picture of how all devices used by an individual might, in the future, be made to communicate with the UIDAI's database. This would enable centralized surveillance and ensure the 'complete destruction of personal autonomy'. Once personal devices became dependent on their links to a centralized database rather than discrete silos, an individual would be unable to maintain control over their data. Their freedom would be irreparably undermined. The Senior Advocate went to great lengths to highlight this 'mundane' aspect of surveillance, creating scenarios to illustrate how no aspect of a person's existence would be left untouched by 'Big Brother'. His submission also warned that under the auspices of *Aadhaar*, state surveillance would undergo rapid and exponential expansion. He argued that traces of the body hoarded by the state had been unconstitutionally made central to the smooth functioning of everyday life. The state's use of *Aadhaar* was characterized as being autocratic rather than democratic. The alienation of bodily information and its insertion into a centralized database was compromising the very idea of the individual, *Aadhaar*'s opponents charged.

The portrait of the person the UIDAI chose to forward in response was that of the '*aam aadmi*', or the 'common man'. A government official read to me from the response petition filed by the Solicitor General:

> The object and purpose of the UID (*Aadhaar*) project is to promote inclusion and benefit marginalized sections of the society who have no formal proof of identity vis-à-vis the State and hence experience difficulties in accessing various welfare schemes that are implemented by the Government of India

and State Governments. The key role of the UID (Unique ID) number is that of an enabler (Solicitor General of India 2012: 155).

An official told me that 'a rickshaw *wallah* would be willing to give much more than his fingerprints to get services. "*Woh haath kaatke de dega*" [he will cut off his hand and give it to you]. He doesn't even get four *rotis* [unleavened bread] a day'.

Symptomatic of a complex historical juncture in India's history, competing – if incomplete – models of the Indian 'individual' emerged in the case against *Aadhaar*. The story of this Supreme Court trial closes with *Aadhaar* being ruled constitutional. The written judgment returned to the trope of the ill-treated common man and combined it with a celebratory discourse on technology. 'It [*Aadhaar*] has become a symbol of the digital economy and has enabled multiple avenues for a common man' (Supreme Court of India 2018: 4), one of its preliminary pages declared.

Conclusion

To conclude this discussion, I want to briefly return to the idea of *becoming* data. Focusing on the notion of becoming data allows one to recognize the widespread conflation – in official and everyday discourse – of 'identity' with *Aadhaar*. Indeed, in UIDAI discourse, *Aadhaar* was sometimes figured as identity guarantor and at other times as *being* one's identity. The terms 'identity', 'ID', and 'identification' were often used interchangeably. This jumbling was reflected in the changing national slogans for *Aadhaar*. While the first 2010 slogan was '*Aadhaar: Aam Aadmi ka Adhikaar'* (*Aadhaar: The Right of the Common Man*), in 2016, this was changed to '*Mera Aadhaar, Meri Pehchaan'* (*My Aadhaar, My Identity*). The latter slogan melds the notion of identity with an ID number linked to a specific set of data. In Hindi, it seems to propose that my *Aadhaar is* my identity. Lastly, the phrase 'becoming data' acknowledges the expectation of the UIDAI that residents keep it abreast of their activities. The data the government held was to be continually refreshed through data 'updation' (UIDAI 2010). Residents were to update their biometrics, if and when required. They were to inform the government if they got married. They were to voluntarily report to the government if they moved home. A data relation with the UIDAI was envisioned as a lifelong interaction. An *Aadhaar* holder was thus continually in a process of becoming data – and this data was not limited to biometric data.[23] Mirroring the lives of residents, the database was consequently itself in a constant state of becoming, never was it to be static. The 'foundation' – *aadhaar* – was mutable.

It may be safe to say that 'Digital India' and its individual members, far from being stable entities, are currently in a febrile state of becoming.

In this article, I have discussed how India's *Aadhaar* database was assembled through intricate processes of data entry, and how the datafication of unique bodies through biometric technologies became grounds for revisiting and reckoning with governance lexicons and practices in present-day India.[24] *Aadhaar* brought to the fore the question of who the Indian 'individual' might be. The promise of *Aadhaar* had been that it would identify and emancipate the 'individual', rescuing them from the clutches of middlemen and demands made by collectives. And yet groups and collectives, as I have shown, continually overrun the space of the 'individual', not least during the process of *Aadhaar* enrolment. The ritual of enrolling for *Aadhaar* facilitates a movement into what is imagined by many a technocrat as the 'data cosmopolis' of Digital India; a cosmopolis indifferent to miscellaneous collective identities and dependencies of yore. In recent times, however, the project's architects have sought to re-embed the 'individual' in a matrix that makes them dependent on a new set of mediators. Perhaps *Aadhaar* ultimately succeeds in forging what we might call *para individuals*. These para individuals are recognized, but not as citizens; they enjoy 'access', but not to rights; they exist, but only in the space between the online and the offline.

India is setting a global precedent for the large-scale use of biometric-based digital governance. Indeed, *Aadhaar* architects regard themselves as the digital ID vanguard of the world. The scale and success of India's biometric identification programme was designed to destabilize the language and logics of translation that undergird commonly recognized North-South, centre-periphery, developed-developing distinctions. But as Anthony Appiah reminds us, in their 'ruthlessly utopian varieties', cosmopolitanisms can easily turn 'toxic' (2005: 220). While biometrics are used for border security and immigration in many countries, projects such as the national United Kingdom Identity Cards Act 2006 were withdrawn on the grounds that they compromised civil liberties. If science and technology were used in the colonial moment to both contain and 'civilize' the 'natives', and were part of the strategy of colonial power (Prakash 1999), we might ask what it means for postcolonial India to be a world 'leader' in biometrics-based governance.

NOTES

I am extremely grateful for the feedback I received on this essay from Thomas Blom Hansen, Sarah Igo, Marc Galanter, Mitra Sharafi, Maria Lepowsky, Moyukh Chatterjee, Alison Cool, and the Editors of this special volume.

[1] Press Information Bureau of India, 'Now 125 crore residents of India have Aadhaar', 27 December 2019 press release (*https://pib.gov.in/PressReleseDetailm.aspx?PRID=1597768*, accessed 26 January 2021).

[2] The UIDAI would store the name, date of birth, father's/husband's/guardian's name or mother's/wife's/guardian's name (optional for adult residents), address, all ten fingerprints, facial photograph, scans of both irises, and the unique identification (UID) number of each of India's residents (UIDAI 2010: 3).

[3] With the 2010 general elections round the corner, the United Progressive Alliance fervently promoted *Aadhaar*.

[4] 'Biometrics' for most of the twentieth century referred to 'the statistical science of biological data analysis', but now popularly refers to 'the automated recognition of individuals based on precisely measured features of the body' (Breckenridge 2014: 11).

[5] See Cohen (2019) for more on *Aadhaar* and the idea of the 'social' in relation to 'service delivery'.

[6] *https://www.digitalindia.gov.in/* (accessed 1 February 2021).

[7] I treat 'Digital India' as a concept that existed long before it was officially adopted in 2014.

[8] The legal status of *Aadhaar* has been very unsteady. To give it legal sanction, the National Identification Authority of India Bill 2010 was first introduced to the Rajya Sabha (Upper House of Parliament) on 3 December 2010 by the majority Indian National Congress government. It was opposed by the Bharatiya Janata Party. Under the BJP government, the *Aadhaar* bill was re-scripted. This overhauled bill was reintroduced to Parliament in 2016 and passed as a Money Bill: the *Aadhaar* (Targeted Delivery of Financial and Other Benefits, Subsidies and Services) Bill, 2016. In India, a Money Bill relates to public spending and taxation and thus need be passed only by the Lower House of Parliament in the bicameral legislature. *Aadhaar*'s constitutionality was challenged in the Supreme Court but it was declared legal in 2018 (Supreme Court of India 2018).

[9] This is a reference to Brown (1992).

[10] Das and Oberoi (1971: 43) argue that several axiomatic principles are not 'properly established' by Dumont. They challenge the notion that caste is central to Hinduism; that the sacred is all-encompassing and the non-sacred incidental; and that there is a necessary correlation between hierarchy and separation. They also contest the idea that there is an absolute separation between the pure and the impure. They argue, instead, that transmutation and relationalism are central to these ideas. States that are neither pure nor impure, they add, are equally important to Hinduism.

[11] André Béteille asserts that baked into the Constitution is a contradiction of sorts: its

design may be said to put equality in the place of hierarchy and the individual in the place of caste. Hierarchical values are repudiated, and the commitment to equality is strongly asserted; but the repudiation of collective identities of the kind on which the traditional hierarchy rested is not as clear as the repudiation of hierarchy itself (1986: 123).

This is on account of the fact that the Constitution deals in 'concessions' for 'collective identities' (1986: 124) and has promoted 'compensatory discrimination' (Galanter 1986).

[12] Scholars have pointed out that as an analytic category, 'identity' means both too much and too little (Brubaker & Cooper 2000). For the designers of *Aadhaar*, identity, first and foremost, meant a biological selfsameness that could be translated into data. This data would be a resource for curating an 'individual'.

[13] It is generative to think about *Aadhaar* alongside Adriana Petryna's concept of 'biological citizenship', which she uses to illuminate how in the aftermath of the Chernobyl disaster, 'the injured biology of a population has become the basis for social membership and for staking claims to citizenship', under circumstances 'where democratization is linked to a harsh market transition' (2004: 261). The *Aadhaar* system, based as it is on biological features, precludes the possibility of direct claim-making.

[14] *http://censusindia.gov.in/* (accessed 26 January 2021).

[15] Even though caste is notoriously hard to define anthropologically, it is an immensely important vector in everyday life across India (see Das 2015).

[16] See Colin Koopman (2019) on data and the 'informational person'.

[17] I use pseudonyms in this article except for instances in which I am referring to a public figure.

[18] In crafting the notion of 'biometric socialization', I follow Don Kulick and Bambi Schieffelin, who underline that 'all interactions are potentially socializing contexts' (2004: 350), and far from unidirectional.

[19] The idea of the data cosmopolis draws on Pollock (2006).

[20] Along with Tom Boellstorff, I see 'the gap between online and offline' not as 'a suspect intellectual artefact to be blurred or erased' but as politically constitutive (2008: 50).

[21] See Sharma (2020) for the difference between how the public sector and private sector recruits at the UIDAI approached the problem of generating a unique identification number for every Indian resident.

[22] For more on how *Aadhaar* temporalizes the state by reconfiguring it as a 'start-up state', see Nair (2019).

[23] For writings in the 'anthropology of becoming', see Biehl & Locke (2017).

[24] I use Partha Chatterjee's definition of governance, which he describes as 'the body of knowledge and set of techniques used by, or on behalf of, those who govern' (2004: 4).

REFERENCES

ANAND, N. 2011. Pressure: the politechnics of water supply in Mumbai. *Cultural Anthropology* **26**, 542-64.
APPIAH, K.A. 2005. *The ethics of identity*. Princeton: University Press.
BEAUVOIR, S. DE 2009 [1949]. *The second sex* (trans. C. Borde & S. Malovany-Chevallier). New York: Random House.
BENJAMIN, R. 2019. *Race after technology: abolitionist tools for the New Jim Code*. Cambridge: Polity.
BÉTEILLE, A. 1986. Individualism and equality. *Current Anthropology* **27**, 121-34.
BIEHL, J. & P. LOCKE (eds) 2017. *Unfinished: the anthropology of becoming*. Durham, N.C.: Duke University Press.
BIRUK, C. 2018. *Cooking data: culture and politics in an African research world*. Durham, N.C.: Duke University Press.
BOELLSTORFF, T.D. 2008. *Coming of age in Second Life: an anthropologist explores the virtually human*. Princeton: University Press.
BRECKENRIDGE, K. 2014. *Biometric state: the global politics of identification and surveillance in South Africa, 1850 to the present*. Cambridge: University Press.
BROWN, W. 1992. Finding the man in the state. *Feminist Studies* **18**, 7-34.
BROWNE, S. 2009. Digital epidermalization: race, identity and biometrics. *Critical Sociology* **36**, 131-50.
BRUBAKER, R. & F. COOPER 2000. Beyond 'identity'. *Theory and Society* **29**, 1-47.
CHATTERJEE, P. 2004. *The politics of the governed: reflections on popular politics in most of the world*. New York: Columbia University Press.
COHEN, L. 2019. The 'social' de-duplicated: on the *Aadhaar* platform and the engineering of service. *South Asia: Journal of South Asian Studies* **42**, 482-500.
COHN, B. 1987. *An anthropologist among the historians and other essays*. Oxford: University Press.
COLEMAN, G. 2010. Ethnographic approaches to digital media. *Annual Review of Anthropology* **39**, 1-19.

Journal of the Royal Anthropological Institute (N.S.) **27**, 26-42
© Royal Anthropological Institute 2021

COUSINS, N. 1951. *Talks with Nehru: India's Prime Minister speaks out on the crisis of our time*. New York: Victor Gollancz.

DAS, V. 2015. Caste. In *International encyclopedia of the social & behavioral science* (Second edition) (ed.) J.D. Wright, 223-7. Oxford: Elsevier.

————— & J.S. UBEROI 1971. On the nature of caste in India: A review symposium on Louis Dumont's *Homo hierarchicus*: 6 The elementary structure of caste. *Contributions to Indian Sociology* **5**, 33-43.

DUMONT, L. 1970. *Homo hierarchicus: the caste system and its implications* (trans. M. Sainsbury, L. Dumont & B. Gulati). Chicago: University Press.

FOUCAULT, M. 1995 [1975]. *Discipline and punish: the birth of the prison* (trans. A. Sheridan). London: Vintage.

————— 2006. *Psychiatric power: lectures at the Collège de France, 1973-74* (ed. J. Lagrange; trans. G. Burchell). Basingstoke: Palgrave Macmillan.

GALANTER, M. 1986. The 'compensatory discrimination' theme in the Indian commitment to human rights. *India International Centre Quarterly* **13**: 3/4, 77-94.

GITELMAN, L. (ed.) 2013. *'Raw data' is an oxymoron*. Cambridge, Mass.: MIT Press.

HANSEN, T.B. 1999. *The Saffron Wave: democracy and Hindu nationalism in modern India*. Princeton: University Press.

JHA, L.K. 2017. Aadhaar helped Indian government save $9 billion, says Nandan Nilekani. *Livemint*, 13 October (available online: *https://www.livemint.com/Politics/6NgxeSDqmL6BgrLoFS6RRI/Aadhaar-helped-Indian-government-save-9-billion-says-Nanda.html*, accessed 26 January 2021).

KELTY, C.M. 2008. *Two bits: the cultural significance of free software*. Durham, N.C.: Duke University Press.

KHILNANI, S. 1997. *The idea of India*. London: Hamish Hamilton.

KOOPMAN, C. 2019. *How we became our data: a genealogy of the informational person*. Chicago: University Press.

KULICK, D. & B.B. SCHIEFFELIN 2004. Language socialization. In *A companion to linguistic anthropology* (ed.) A. Duranti, 349-68. Oxford: Blackwell.

LEDER, D. 1990. *The absent body*. Chicago: University Press.

MARRIOTT, M. 1989. Constructing an Indian ethnosociology. *Contributions to Indian Sociology* **23**, 1-39.

MINES, M. 1988. Conceptualizing the person: hierarchical society and individual autonomy in India. *American Anthropologist* **90**, 568-79.

NAIR, V. 2018. An eye for an I: recording biometrics and reconsidering identity in postcolonial India. *Contemporary South Asia* **26**, 143-56.

————— 2019. Governing India in cybertime: biometric IDs, start-ups and the temporalized state. *South Asia: Journal of South Asian Studies* **42**, 519-36.

NILEKANI, N. 2018. Data to the people: India's inclusive internet. *Foreign Affairs* **19** (available online: *https://www.foreignaffairs.com/articles/asia/2018-08-13/data-people*, accessed 1 February 2021).

————— & V. SHAH 2015. *Rebooting India: realizing a billion aspirations*. Gurgaon: Penguin Books India.

PETRYNA, A. 2004. Biological citizenship: the science and politics of Chernobyl-exposed populations. *OSIRIS* **19**, 250-65.

POLLOCK, S. 2006. *Language of the gods in the world of men: Sanskrit, culture, and power in premodern India*. Berkeley: University of California Press.

PRAKASH, G. 1999. *Another reason: science and the imagination of modern India*. Princeton: University Press.

PUTTASWAMY, K.S. 2012. Justice K.S.Puttaswamy (Retired) & another versus Union of India & Others. Writ Petition (Civil) No. 494 of 2012.

RAMANATHAN, U. 2010. A unique identity bill. *Economic and Political Weekly* **30**, 10-14.

ROSE, N. & P. MILLER 2010. Political power beyond the state: problematics of government. *British Journal of Sociology* **61**, 271-303.

SEAVER, N. 2017. Algorithms as culture: some tactics for the ethnography of algorithmic systems. *Big Data & Society* **4**: 2 (available online: *https://journals.sagepub.com/doi/full/10.1177/2053951717738104*, accessed 26 January 2021).

SHARMA, R.S. 2020. *The making of Aadhaar: world's largest identity platform*. New Delhi: Rupa.

SOLICITOR GENERAL OF INDIA 2012. Response Petition to Writ Petition (Civil) No. 494 of 2012 Justice K.S. Puttaswamy (Retired) & another versus Union of India & Others.

SUPREME COURT OF INDIA 2018. Judgment Civil Original Jurisdiction Writ Petition (Civil) No. 494 of 2012.

TURNER, V.W. 1969. *The ritual process: structure and anti-structure*. London: Routledge.

UIDAI (Unique Identification Authority of India) 2010. *Strategy overview: creating a unique identity number for every resident in India*. New Delhi: Government of India.

Journal of the Royal Anthropological Institute (N.S.) **27**, 26-42
© Royal Anthropological Institute 2021

———— 2012*a*. Enrolment process essentials. New Delhi: Government of India. Version: 2.0.0.6 Release date: 13 December.

———— 2012*b*. Role of biometric technology in Aadhaar enrollment. New Delhi: Government of India.

———— 2014*a*. Aadhaar product document. New Delhi: Government of India.

———— 2014*b*. Report on *Aadhaar*-enabled de-duplication & verification exercise. New Delhi: Government of India.

Devenir une donnée : individu et biométrie dans l'« Inde numérique »

Résumé

Aadhaar (littéralement « foundation ») est la plus grande campagne nationale d'identification biométrique que le monde ait jamais vue. Un *Aadhaar* est un numéro d'identification à douze chiffres, lié aux données de son possesseur – iris, empreintes digitales, image faciale et informations démographiques – stockées dans une base de données centralisée. En l'espace d'une décennie, l'Inde a inscrit de manière expéditive plus de 90 % de son milliard d'habitants au Registre central des données sur l'identité. Cet article consiste en un examen ethnographique des processus par lesquels les personnes fichées par *Aadhaar* deviennent des données. Se concentrant sur la valence sociopolitique des données biométriques, l'autrice avance que la « donnéification » du corps via *Aadhaar* donne lieu à une remise en question – et à une contestation – de la notion d'individu dans l'Inde postcoloniale, que la littérature populaire comme scientifique a souvent présentée comme sociocentrique. Elle suggère par ailleurs que la socialisation biométrique facilite l'appartenance à une « Inde numérique » que les imaginations technocratiques émergentes décrivent souvent comme une cosmopole de données.

2

Everything lies in a space: cultural data and spatial reality

NICK SEAVER *Tufts University*

This essay examines the use of spatializing techniques for analysing cultural data, drawing on fieldwork with developers of music recommender systems in the United States. Comparing these practices with related analytic techniques developed by post-war cognitive anthropologists, it explores three broad topics: how such techniques engender a sense of continuous, enveloping milieu from discrete and often sparse data; how spatialization is used to grant culture a kind of reality rooted in pragmatic action and scientific quantification; and how spatial representations of culture are essentially anticipatory for the people who make them, transforming the near future into the nearby.

> Similarity is an institution.
> Mary Douglas (1986: 55)

The music space

'Imagine', the start-up founder instructs me, 'that we know what music you like right now'. Jason holds one hand in front of his body, indicating a point in the space between us. 'And we also know', he continues, 'who has already been listening to that music'. His other hand indicates another point, further away.

We are chatting in a San Francisco bar at a happy hour for music technologists, and I have accidentally overdressed. The 'tech' people, like the founder I call Jason, are wearing T-shirts with company logos on them, picked up for free from their employers or event sponsors. My button-front shirt and jacket mark me as a non-coder, which means I must be 'biz': someone who can't make software, but who might provide access to resources, computational or monetary. I try to clarify what I'm doing in this humid bar; I'm a graduate student studying music recommender systems; I'm interested in how technologists like him make sense of cultural phenomena like music and taste. Jason, an autodidact coder, is sceptical: 'Ah, Ph.D.s are worthless! You should quit!'

Nevertheless, he continues his pitch, hands out, marking a pair of invisible points in the air. 'If we know where you are, and who was here before you, we could build a service that lets you see where *those* people' – he wiggles one hand – 'the people who were *here* three months ago' – he wiggles the other hand – 'we could show you where they are now, what they're listening to'. Jason's hands draw a path between us, along which I might travel as my taste evolves. A good music recommender, he suggests, would help

Journal of the Royal Anthropological Institute (N.S.) **27**, 43-61

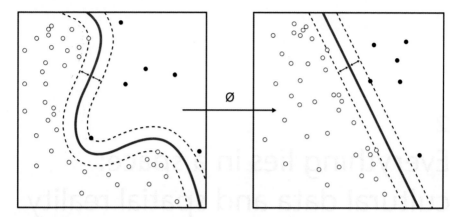

Figure 1. A classifying boundary in data space. (Credit: Alisneaky, Wikimedia Commons, CC BY-SA 4.0)

me catch up with the listeners whose taste is, in some vaguely geographical sense, ahead of my own.

Bodied forth into the area between us, navigated by gestures and populated by brief pinches in the air, is the music space. The music space is an abstraction: an idealized vision of all the world's music, arranged by similarity. If you find yourself within such a space, you will be surrounded by music that you like; to find more of it, you only need to look around and move. In the music space, genres are like regions, playlists are like pathways, and tastes are like drifting, archipelagic territories. Your new favourite song may lie just over the horizon.

'Similarity spaces' like these are ubiquitous in conversations among the people who make music recommender systems and in the broader world of machine learning, of which algorithmic recommendation is a prominent part. They ground talk about similarity and difference in a shared spatial imaginary, manifested in gesture, speech, or illustration. They provide a setting in which diverse entities might be drawn together, revealing new forms of relatedness. I may live far away from someone who shares my musical taste, but in the music space, we can nonetheless be 'neighbours'.[1]

In machine learning, these spaces are not only metaphorical abstractions used in conversation; they are also technical abstractions, implemented in software. Look up 'data science' on Wikipedia, for instance, and you may find it illustrated by a diagram showing black and white points distributed in space, separated by a bright red line (Fig. 1)[2]. That line represents a classifying boundary between two subsets of data (e.g. in a common pedagogical example, between medical images of cancerous and non-cancerous tumours). The work of machine learning involves making procedures to locate points in space and finding some boundary that adequately separates them; the resulting model can then be used to classify new points according to their positions on either side of the line.

Spatial understandings of data move through technical infrastructures and everyday conversation; they are at once a kind of metaphor and a concrete computational practice. In other words, 'space' here is both a formalism – a restricted, technical concept that facilitates precision through abstraction – and an *informalism* (Helmreich 2016: 468) – a less disciplined figure that travels alongside formal techniques. In practice, it is often hard or impossible to separate technical specificity from its metaphorical accompaniment. When data scientists speak of space, they speak at once figuratively and technically.[3] Thus, the start-up founder who constructs similarity spaces in computational substrates also speaks casually as though we already live in these landscapes.

While many cultural critics are comfortable using informal spatial metaphors to describe social life, the mathematization of data science often seems anathema to 'culture' per se: it quantifies qualities, rationalizes passions, and plucks cultural objects from their everyday social contexts to relocate them in the sterile isolation of a computational grid. In the geographer Henri Lefebvre's terms, data scientific spaces are a clear example of 'abstract space': a kind of conceptual space in which everything is measurable and quantified, controlled by central authorities in the service of capital (Lefebvre 1991; Prey 2015). For Lefebvrians, like other critics, the proliferation of such spaces under capitalism represents 'the devastating conquest of the lived by the conceived' (Wilson 2013) – an incursion of 'data' into the world of culture.

Yet the spatializing techniques of data science, which increasingly lay claim to knowledge about something they call 'culture' (Savage & Burrows 2007; Striphas 2015), are not strangers to anthropology. While contemporary cultural anthropologists may encounter data science as an unfamiliar encroachment on their disciplinary territory, many of machine learning's statistical techniques have their origins in the human and behavioural sciences, deriving from methods designed to measure human cognition, preference, or culture. In this essay, I trace the branching genealogies of academic kinship, returning to the point where the lineages of present-day data science and cultural anthropology meet and split: in the post-war 'cognitive turn' across the social sciences. Techniques embraced and developed by Cold War cognitive anthropologists are ancestors of today's data scientific practices.

Comparing anthropology's own history of formal spatializing methods with the spaces of recommender systems suggests three persistent and significant features of spatializing techniques and their attendant informalisms. First, they grant culture a kind of reality often reserved for physical objects, not only by reifying culture as 'data' but also by rendering that data into spatial form. Second, they engender a sense of continuous, enveloping milieu from discrete and often sparse data, producing spaces that feel like given, natural environments to their makers, despite their radical reconfigurability. Third, while often critiqued as static, synchronic, or detemporalizing, these spatial models are essentially anticipatory for the people who make them, serving as tools for predicting the near future by turning it into the nearby.

As Antonia Walford (2017) has argued, an anthropology of data can do more than re-establish the basic fact that data is always created, and never simply 'raw', 'objective', or 'natural'. Here, my interest is in what people *do* with data – how particular data practices have reality-producing effects. If culture has always been an unsteady object for its analysts, often threatening to vanish into unreality, how is data marshalled to prop it up, and to what ends? Answering this question requires us to attend more closely to the relationship between anthropologists and computational methods.

The data of anthropology

In 1962, the Wenner-Gren Foundation hosted a symposium on 'The Use of Computers in Anthropology'. In his introduction to the symposium proceedings, Dell Hymes described the appeal of computational techniques for the anthropologist: 'Computer processing, properly prepared, can enable us to see relations and patterns in masses of data previously too large to comprehend' (1965: 30). While some anthropologists feared computing 'as alien or inimical to a humane intellectual outlook', Hymes argued that it promised to transcend the divide between anthropology's 'humanistic' and 'scientific' modes (1965: 25). The challenge was to begin producing data that was precise and formal enough to be analysed by computers. Although fieldworkers might resist it, Hymes thought this was a salutary challenge, which would force researchers to make their mysterious empiricism and sometimes vague theory more explicit.

But the promise of computing was also a threat. Presciently, Hymes wrote: 'Our society, and the sciences adjacent to anthropology, are such that it seems inevitable that the computer will be used extensively, willy-nilly, so that the choice is only whether in the immediate future the computer will be used well or ill' (1965: 29). Although the digital computer was relatively new, it was already being taken up by disciplines like sociology, psychology, and linguistics; if anthropologists neglected computation, they risked losing their 'present status as a peer among the human sciences' (Hymes 1965: 30). The symposium proceedings reflected this pressure, dominated by techniques from adjacent fields, with anthropologists figured primarily as novices who might want to learn about the workings of computer memory or computational lexicography.

But only eight years after the Wenner-Gren symposium, the state of computing in anthropology had apparently changed. A 1970 review of 'computer applications in cultural anthropology' declared that 'most of the material which appeared in that volume [Hymes' proceedings] is now obsolete' (Burton 1970: 37). Computer hardware and mathematical models had already advanced, and 'computer applications in anthropology have expanded greatly' (Burton 1970: 37), becoming – at least for some anthropologists – so ordinary that they were casually used for exploratory data analysis without being mentioned in publications.

The author of that review was Michael Burton, a new assistant professor in the School of Social Sciences at the University of California, Irvine. His view of computing's prevalence was likely shaped by this unusual setting: the school had no departments, with anthropologists, psychologists, economists, and sociologists working together in an 'organized anarchy' (Kavanagh 2010: 17). What united them was a shared commitment to quantitative, computational, and cognitive approaches to the problems of social life. Irvine would become a key location in the development of cognitive anthropology, which was defined not only by its interest in culture as a mental phenomenon, but also by an interest in computational methods (D'Andrade 1995).

According to Burton, 'one of the most important reasons for anthropologists to use computers' was a new 'breakthrough' technique called 'non-metric multidimensional scaling' (1970: 42). Multidimensional scaling (MDS) was a data analysis technique that had originated in psychology, growing from that field's interest in producing measurement scales for concepts like intelligence or personality traits. Non-metric MDS, developed by researchers at Bell Labs (Kruskal 1964; Shepard 1962), diverged from its predecessor in that it did not require strictly quantified measurements as input data. As Burton put it, non-metric MDS provided a way 'to measure phenomena which have previously seemed too soft and elusive to express quantitatively' (1970: 37) – namely culture.

For example, in a chapter on the 'semantic dimensions of occupation names' (1972), Burton analysed data that had been collected from fifty-four Harvard students. Given sixty cards with occupation names on them, the students were instructed to sort the cards into piles. This pile sorting technique was also borrowed from psychology, and

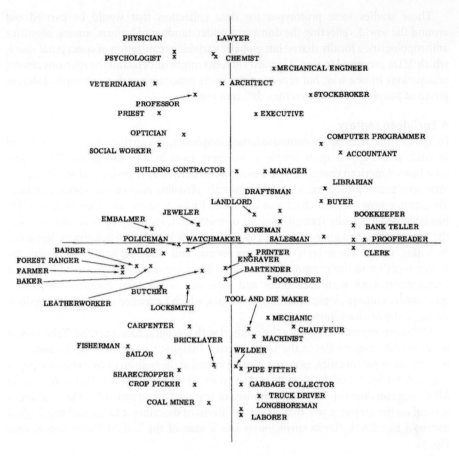

Figure 2. Two-dimensional scaling of occupation terms. (Burton 1972: 63; courtesy of the Center for Advanced Studies in the Behavioral Sciences.)

the organization of the piles was treated as similarity data: the more often occupations were sorted into the same pile, the more similar they were. A non-metric MDS algorithm could transform this coarse data about the similarity of concepts or objects into a quantified, computational representation of space (Fig. 2). Clusters of points in this space might represent categories reflected in the informants' piles; lines through the space might indicate important dimensions along which the sorted items were understood to vary.

Non-metric MDS was computationally intensive, requiring so many iterated calculations that it was practically impossible to perform without the aid of a digital computer. It would also become one of cognitive anthropology's signature techniques, and Irvine a key site in its development for anthropological use. In 1969, an advanced research seminar was held near the campus, co-organized by Roger Shepard – one of the originators of non-metric MDS – and A. Kimball Romney – who had earlier co-organized the Wenner-Gren symposium. The seminar's proceedings featured a range of MDS applications, from Burton's scaling of occupation terms to scalings of nations and snack foods.

These studies were prototypes for data collection that would be carried out around the world, reflecting the dominant understanding of 'culture' among cognitive anthropologists: a locally shared but globally variable organization of conceptual space, which MDS promised to map. Harvard students might understand the relations among occupations in one way, but repeating the same procedure with a culturally different group of people was likely to return different results.

A Euclidean fantasy

In spite of the technique's computational complexity, the spatial diagrams produced by MDS could appear quite simple to interpret, even by non-specialists. They relied on a Euro-American common-sense association between proximity and similarity (cf. Strathern 2020), presenting a straightforwardly plausible map of conceptual relations. To examine how such an effect was achieved, I now turn my attention to how MDS has been pedagogically framed, in a set of methods texts sampled from the 1970s to the present (Bernard 2006; Davison 1983; Kruskal & Wish 1978; Schiffman, Reynolds & Young 1981). These texts show how formal and informal senses of 'space' are woven together in the pursuit of plausibility. They are remarkably consistent in their presentation, both with each other and with one of the final iterations of Irvine's quantitative anthropological methods seminars, which I attended as a graduate student, co-taught by Michael Burton.

MDS texts typically introduce the method with a geographical exercise. Take a set of locations, like major cities in the United States. Imagine a table showing the distances between each pair of cities, as is sometimes printed at the bottom of conventional paper maps. What MDS can do is create a map from just these distances. Precisely how an MDS program does this is typically omitted or reserved for an appendix. The texts focus instead on the output: a plot that, as Russell Bernard describes it in his anthropological methods handbook, 'looks suspiciously like a map of the United States' (2006: 684; Fig. 3).

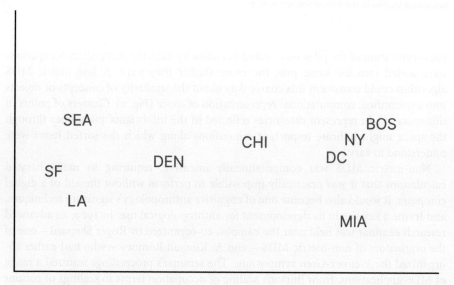

Figure 3. Two-dimensional scaling of cities, according to geographical distance. (Redrawn by author.)

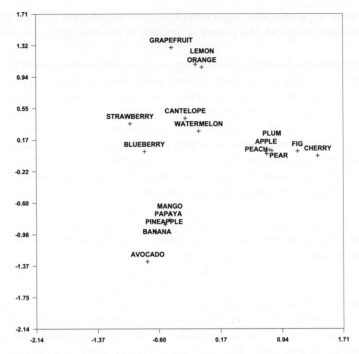

Figure 4. Two-dimensional scaling of fruit, according to one subject's similarity evaluations. (Bernard 2006: 687; courtesy of AltaMira Press.)

Having thus confirmed that the technique works, textbooks move from physical distances to conceptual ones. Bernard introduces what he calls a 'cognitive world example' (2006: 684), where the input is an unnamed informant's pile sorting of various fruit. The resulting plot (Fig. 4) reflects this particular person's subjective sense of the 'fruit space'. As we might expect from examples used for teaching, these results appear very straightforward. The MDS plot of inter-city distances looks like a map. The arrangement of fruits presents readily interpretable clusters, with citrus at the top, melons in the middle, and tropical fruit at the bottom.

While the city map appears self-evident, MDS textbooks typically emphasize the role of intuition in making sense of the conceptual map, enjoining the reader to search for patterns. One text, written by the technique's originators, reads: 'Take as much time as needed, and look for something systematic. Your attempt to find this is an important step!' (Kruskal & Wish 1978: 14). Bernard writes: 'This is the fun part. Look at figure 21.6. Keep looking at it. Think about the distribution of those items … Do you see any pattern?' (2006: 688). The student is instructed to see for themselves, to rely on their own intuition as they develop an interpretation of the spatial configuration.

This is instruction in what Catelijne Coopmans (2014) has called 'artful revelation' – the use of visualization to reveal 'hidden' patterns in data – and it embodies the contradictions of MDS in anthropological use. The last step of what has been a rather technical computational process is an explicitly intuitive and interpretative moment of sense-making, what Bernard describes as 'a brazen, flat-out qualitative exercise, a Rorschach test for social scientists – which is why I like it so much' (2006: 689). To make MDS 'work', anthropologists had to rely on their own prior cultural knowledge to make sense of patterns that might otherwise seem inexplicable: what do pineapples have to do with mangoes? The pattern is not only in the data, but in the researcher's head.

In actual research, however, the satisfying resonance that textbooks seek to engender in students who recognize a latent cultural order does not always appear. As one reviewer of the Irvine MDS seminar's proceedings put it in *American Anthropologist*: '[W]hat may represent an interpretable pattern to one researcher may be chaos or a Euclidean fantasy to another' (Sanday 1975: 106). Given the basic axioms of geometry and the fact that the United States is roughly two-dimensional, it is not surprising that MDS would produce something like a map. For similarity judgements, this is much less obvious. But the textbooks, having demonstrated that MDS works with spatial data, then use it to figure other data as though it were already spatial. MDS transforms rough, qualitative similarity judgements into measurable, quantifiable structures of difference.

Psychology has a long history of using scaling methods to grant reality to mental phenomena that seem otherwise elusive (Stark 2018). MDS offered a link between anthropology and psychology, filling the mind with cultural content, understood spatially. 'If the model of man in behavioral psychology is characterized as a black box with nothing inside', one contributor to the Irvine MDS seminar wrote, 'then the scaling model can be seen as a black box with space inside' (Boyd 1972: 214). But for the psychologists who first developed MDS, the question of what 'psychological distance' meant and whether it behaved like geometrical distance remained an open question; experimental tests gave ambivalent results (e.g. Tversky 1977). In a 1983 textbook on MDS, the author notes that of the four geometrical axioms defining Euclidean distance, only three could be said to reasonably hold for subjective assessments of similarity: 'In the social and behavioral sciences, however, three axioms out of four is not bad, so the analogy caught on' (Davison 1983: 3).

In other words, MDS (and related techniques) provided models that often failed experimental tests and lacked rigorous theoretical grounding in many of the domains where they were applied. For the early anthropological developers of the technique, the status of these models was not always clear. What was an MDS plot a map *of*? Did people actually rely on these internal spaces as they went about their lives? When cognitive cultural sociologists adopted these techniques in the 1990s, one claimed that the models generated by MDS were 'iconic': 'They look like what they represent' (Mohr 1998: 364). But this is not literally true: the referent of an MDS plot is not easy to pin down. Bernard even suggests that 'No one claims that MDS graphs are one-for-one maps of what's happening inside people's heads' (2006: 687). Yet these plots circulate with the power of iconicity, as though they map actually existing, albeit conceptual, spaces.

Collecting data about more cultural domains from more people provided an agenda for what we might now call a 'data-driven' anthropology – one defined by the computationally aided production of analytic spaces. But it was not to be – at least not within mainstream cultural anthropology. Despite efforts to frame MDS as 'humanistic' by figures like Hymes, critics like Hortense Powdermaker saw the rise of computational methods as reducing anthropology to 'the work of technicians' (1966: 300). Clifford Geertz defined interpretative anthropology precisely against cognitive anthropology and its formal methods, which he described as 'dark sciences' and 'cabbalism' (1973: 30). This computer-friendly subfield, which had once presumed to call itself 'the new ethnography' (Keesing 1972), raising fieldwork to a scientific status that might 'relegate all previous ethnographies to the status of "preethnographies"' (Colby, Fernandez &

Kronenfeld 1981: 426), is today only a ghostly presence in much graduate training, a foil to the humanistic turn the field would soon take. One leading cognitive anthropologist wrote at the turn of the century of 'the sad story of anthropology 1950-1999' (D'Andrade 2000); if cognitive science once seemed potentially central to anthropology, today 'cognitive challenges' (Bloch 2004) are mounted from its margins.

The magic of matrix factorization

Across campus from the Irvine School of Social Sciences, forty years later, I sat in on an undergraduate course in recommender systems design, meant to introduce students to the basics of machine learning. Recommender systems are common topics in introductory machine learning classes – they demonstrate a popular, familiar application of the technology, and they provide outputs that are easy to interpret and evaluate. I discovered that computer science students are introduced to the mechanics of recommendation in much the same way that anthropologists were once introduced to MDS.

We are learning about a technique called 'collaborative filtering' – one of the first methods for algorithmic recommendation, by most accounts, which was invented in the mid-1990s. Even today, collaborative filters remain one of the most popular techniques for recommendation in commercial use, and in their simplest form, they are common toy projects for students.

We begin with a data set that would be readily recognizable to a cognitive anthropologist working in the 1970s: a table of preference data, containing the ratings a set of hypothetical users have assigned to a set of real movies. Most of the table is empty, reflecting movies that have not been rated. The goal of the recommender is to guess what ratings will appear in those blank spaces, using the existing ratings as a guide. Items with high predicted ratings can then be recommended to the user.

The instructor guides us through a method for parsing the data called matrix factorization. Like the students learning to use MDS, we don't know how it works: we load the data into a computer program and pick 'Matrix Factorization' from a drop-down menu. The output that we are interested in is a pair of tables, one containing users and the other movies. Every user and movie has been assigned two numbers, labelled 'Dimension 1' and 'Dimension 2'. These numbers reflect statistical patterns in our data, 'summarizing' the set of ratings.

The instructor points at the first user and says, 'We've represented Alice with two numbers, so I can make a two-dimensional plot, and I can locate Alice'. Numbers are taken to be intrinsically spatial: if we have pairs of numbers, we have co-ordinates. Moving through all the users and items, we fill a space with people and movies (Fig. 5).

This is a similarity space – the computational equivalent of the space Jason gestured into existence in the bar. Proximity means similarity, but also affinity: Mary is more like Alice than Bob, and she will probably like *Eat Pray Love* more than *Die Hard*. In a space like this, we can identify 'neighbourhoods' of users and movies or interpret their distribution as reflecting 'latent factors' in the data.

Like the students of MDS, we look for patterns in the space, and we find one: the movies seem to have separated by genre, with romances to one side and action films to the other. A student asks how the algorithm can know about the movies' genres, when the only data it had to work from was the set of ratings. 'It seems like magic, I know', the instructor replies. Genre was a 'secret thing', latent in the data, artfully revealed by locating it in a space.

Journal of the Royal Anthropological Institute (N.S.) **27**, 43-61
© Royal Anthropological Institute 2021

Figure 5. A space of users and movies derived from matrix factorization. (Redrawn by author.)

Our recognition of genre confirms that the technique has worked. The 'magic' of matrix factorization is in our heads as much as it is in the computer, depending on our prior cultural knowledge. If the plot did not resonate with our preconceptions about the structure of the cultural world, we might worry that we had made a mistake. As with MDS, the examples have been chosen because of their presumed interpretability. When I attended a popular online course on machine learning, I found the action/romance dimension there as well.

Our classroom exercise has been designed to replicate a famous figure from the recommender systems literature (Fig. 6), produced by the winners of the Netflix Prize – a contest that ran from 2006 to 2009 and is often credited with popularizing the field. That figure similarly casts movies and people around a two-dimensional space, with axes labelled from 'serious' to 'escapist' and from 'geared toward males' to 'geared toward females'. As in MDS, these labels are the result of the researchers' own interpretation, and they offer a window into the cultural understanding of the people behind the system. Gender and genre are collapsed, presenting a vision of gender that is not rooted in human essences, but defined by choices and tendencies, spread across a spectrum that is nonetheless defined by the gender binary. Looking more closely at the figure, which is not a data visualization, but rather an illustration, we can see that users who appear to be male and female have been distributed across the space so that they do not neatly separate by gender.

What could, but does not yet, exist

'Box products, not people', wrote John Riedl and Joseph Konstan in *Word of mouse: the marketing power of collaborative filtering* (2002).[4] Riedl and Konstan were founding figures in the field of algorithmic recommendation, responsible for some of the earliest collaborative filters. Since their beginning, collaborative filters have been presented as tools to help people broaden their tastes, breaking free from the rough categories of conventional demographic profiling through data about individuals' actual behaviour. 'Think about how much more people would step outside their demographic groups if they were not only permitted to, but *encouraged* to', Riedl and Konstan wrote (2002: 113, emphasis in original).

Journal of the Royal Anthropological Institute (N.S.) **27**, 43-61
© Royal Anthropological Institute 2021

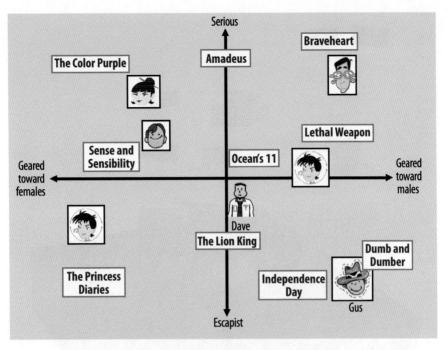

Figure 6. Movies and users distributed across a latent factor space. (Koren, Bell & Volinsky 2009: 44; courtesy of IEEE.)

On the cover of *Word of mouse* was a conspicuously diverse crowd, waving from inside a computer screen. However, this crowd's real diversity, the book suggested, was found not in their demographic qualities, but in their preferences, which collaborative filtering could finally recognize and cater to. As Marilyn Strathern wrote, around the time the first collaborative filters were being developed: 'Free-ranging access, such apparent freedom of choice, in the end turns the sense of plurality into an artefact of access or choice itself' (1992: 9). The ever-growing variety of material that people might choose to listen to, read, or watch was transforming from being understood as the *result* of human diversity to being its *source* – the cultural terrain across which people might spread.

Although they had not started as market researchers, the developers of collaborative filtering had ended up there, fitting neatly into a trajectory that was already underway in the world of advertising – away from coarse market segments and towards personalized targeting (Arvidsson 2002). Anthropologists had already experienced their own disciplinary encounter with marketing, much earlier. Writing in 1976, Marshall Sahlins suggested that anthropologists performed a task much like marketers, 'unflattering as the comparison may be': 'In the nervous system of the American economy, theirs is the synaptic function. It is their role to be sensitive to the latent correspondences in the cultural order whose conjunction in a product-symbol may spell mercantile success' (1976: 217). Anthropologists and market researchers alike were 'hucksters of the symbol' (1976: 217), Sahlins claimed, making their living by mapping out connections in an ambient cultural space.

Figure 7. One of Stefflre's three-dimensional 'market structure studies', showing a set of anonymized brands (in white) and associated adjectives (in black). (Stefflre 1971; courtesy of Market Structure Studies, Inc.)

MDS was taken up avidly in market research, and at least one of the Irvine anthropologists blended anthropological and marketing interests together. As portrayed in a 1969 *Orange County Illustrated* profile, Volney Stefflre was 'half anthropologist, half college professor, and half business executive. If this adds up to one-and-a-half, it is because Volney Stefflre is an oversized man, physically, intellectually, and enthusiastically' (Van Deusen 1969: 31). While his colleagues modelled kinship terms, occupational prestige, and ethnobotanical classification in societies around the world, Stefflre worked closer to home: studying the suburban residents of Orange County.

Stefflre presented his subjects with fabricated advertisements, samples of toilet paper, and bottled drinks of different colours; he analysed the correlation between foods like pretzels or ham sandwiches and use cases like 'after a party' or 'for breakfast'. Using MDS, he generated what he called 'market structure analyses' (Fig. 7). These plots

Journal of the Royal Anthropological Institute (N.S.) **27**, 43-61
© Royal Anthropological Institute 2021

represented the latent structure of his data, revealing submerged correspondences in the cultural order of consumer products.

In his academic role, Stefflre (1965) published articles on 'people's behavior toward new objects and events'; from his market research consultancy, he advised companies to create a new kind of corporate division he called a 'New Products and New Enterprises Group'. Such a group, he wrote,

> can be seen as a greased hole in the institutional and psychological wall that separates *what exists* from *what could, but does not yet, exist*. The wall – which is built of customs, institutions and people – prohibits the appearance of technologically and economically attractive new product alternatives that consumers desire and are willing to pay money for (Stefflre 1971: 3-29, emphasis in original).

Already, in Stefflre's accounting, we see that these spaces do not only provide meaning for the data points located within them; even unoccupied parts of the space could be interpreted, suggesting configurations of qualities that had not yet been tried, areas into which companies might 'move'. Stefflre vividly described this task as 'a suicide mission – Kamikaze pilots – trying to bring into existence something that was not before – at a cost to themselves of years of their life and the tortures of the damned' (1971: 43-5). To this end, he started a series of businesses and reportedly bought a local supermarket in which to conduct ethnographic experiments *in vivo*.

Within anthropology, the apparently stable complexes of meaning represented by techniques like MDS would be critiqued as overly synchronic, unable to capture novelty and change. Yet for Stefflre, the point was change: to anticipate what might happen, mapping out possible trajectories in cultural space. Along similar lines, critics of recommender systems often suggest that the problem with these models is that they are static, profiling users and locking them into classifications based on old, limited data (e.g. Galloway 2006). What Riedl and Konstan saw as liberating, relative to the boxes of demography, their critics see as stultifying, pinning users to a map. To think through this tension, we need to delve deeper into these competing visions of social space.

Post-demographic hyperspace

Collaborative filtering, like MDS, transformed a sparse collection of discrete data points into an apparently continuous cultural manifold, offering countless locations to reside in and travel through. This transformation made even 'empty' space meaningful, turning the momentary events of ratings into a terrain that could then be navigated over time. This navigability represented a kind of freedom: people could move out of boxes and into spaces, along any dimension they might imagine. Where MDS plots were typically limited to the two or three dimensions that humans can readily see as space, machine learning has no such limits, and its dimensions can proliferate without end, responding to whatever patterns may appear in the data.

This vision of freedom matched that of early internet advocates, who imagined that 'cyberspace' offered a new, unlimited frontier, liberating individuals to travel wherever in the cultural milieu they wished (e.g. Barlow 1996). The flexibility of these spaces was presented as not only liberating but also empirical: a collaborative filter did not impose pre-ordained categories, but rather recognized tendencies in data. If a dimension like the gendered axis in Figure 6 appeared to reflect a demographic category, that was because it was latent in the data. Under this paradigm, a dimension that appears to correspond to gender enacts gender in a new and unusual way, as the statistical aggregate of choices that a human interpreter might ascribe to gender

Journal of the Royal Anthropological Institute (N.S.) **27**, 43-61
© Royal Anthropological Institute 2021

(cf. Cheney-Lippold 2011). These models' dependence on data means that they can shift over time, and a pattern that once looked like 'gender' might evolve in unexpected directions, loosened as it is from what had been gender's putative stability.

I've described how the recognition of expected cultural patterns is central to the verification of these systems; but what distinguishes the spaces of algorithmic recommendation in use is that no one needs to interpret them. Algorithmic recommenders will identify clusters or dimensions and produce recommendations accordingly, without any intervening moment of human classification. So, within the recommender, it does not matter if a label turns out to be 'wrong', or if a dimension drifts away from its initial apparent meaning – the basic calculations of proximity and similarity are unaffected by the labels people use to interpret them.

Thus, the dimensions along which a collaborative filter might encourage users to explore could depart from the conventional categories of demographic targeting. However, as indicated by the gendered axes in Figure 6, the space open for exploration has already been shaped by demographic patterns of cultural production and consumption. Here, too, we can find antecedents in critical writing about the web, where visions of the unstructured electronic frontier were met by scholars in the humanities and social sciences who documented the persistence of connections to previously existing systems of power and geography (e.g. Chan 2014; Markham 1998; Nakamura 2000). Critics of recommender systems in particular have noted how, in spite of visions of omnivorous diversity, personalization may actually intensify vicious identifications of difference, helping white supremacists, for instance, find each other and ever more extreme racist material online (Chun 2018; Tufekci 2018).

While recommender systems are framed as post-demographic, since they do not require any explicitly demographic data to function, they encounter the evidence of gender, race, and countless other social categories in the data they do analyse. Recent critical work on machine learning identifies this as a 'proxy problem': in domains shaped by race, like predictive policing, one will find racial patterns in the data, even if explicit race data is absent (cf. Barocas & Selbst 2016). Thus, in domains shaped by social identity, claims to be 'post-demographic' can serve to naturalize racial and gender difference, 'discovering' demographic variation latent in the data, where it is taken to be more real than when it is explicitly ascribed or claimed (Cohn 2019; and see, e.g., McRobbie 2004 on 'post-feminism' and James 2017 on 'post-identity'). The vision of freedom expressed in texts like *Word of mouse* carries with it a particular view of what it means to be a person, figuring race and gender, among other social categories, as burdens to be relieved, rather than salient parts of a person's identity (cf. Nelson 2002).

In the vernacular social theory embedded in the spaces of algorithmic recommendation, we can hear another anthropological echo – this time from late twentieth-century efforts to theorize space and cultural difference. Describing anthropology's own tendency to spatialize difference, Akhil Gupta and James Ferguson wrote: 'Representations of space in the social sciences are remarkably dependent on images of break, rupture, and disjunction. The distinctiveness of societies, nations, and cultures is based upon a seemingly unproblematic division of space, on the fact that they occupy "naturally" discontinuous spaces' (1992: 6). The analogy between proximity and similarity that animates machine learning's latent spaces was there in anthropology too, in the conflation of distance and difference that has been the long-standing core of the field's disciplinary identity.

Journal of the Royal Anthropological Institute (N.S.) **27**, 43-61
© Royal Anthropological Institute 2021

Gupta and Ferguson, not unlike Riedl and Konstan, mounted a critique of the coarse categories of their predecessors, calling for attention to 'connection and contiguity' – to fluid and multiplex social orders that needed to be rendered as 'multiple grids' (1992: 20; cf. Narayan 1993). But where utopian online spaces were imagined as smooth and limitless, Gupta and Ferguson warned against thinking of subjects as 'free-floating monads' (1992: 19), liberated to play in a field of free choice. Instead, they wrote, connection and contiguity 'vary considerably by factors such as class, gender, race, and sexuality, and are differentially available to those in different locations in the field of power' (1992: 20).

This critique did not reject the analogy between proximity and similarity. Rather, it insisted on other forms of proximity beyond the physical. Fields of power are still spaces, and it is telling that we move to them from geography via the mathematical figure of the 'grid'. Even among critics of what Fredric Jameson (1991) called 'postmodern hyperspace', mathematics provides a common currency for trading among various sorts of difference. Mathematical imaginaries persist, as Kath Weston has argued, in 'avant-garde social science metaphors: borders, lines, intersections, levels, scales, points, grids' (2008: 133). While the political visions may seem quite different, the spatial understandings are not.

Everything lies in a space

These spatializing techniques, as I've described them, draw together ordinary intuitions about space and mathematical methods that figure space as an essential quality of quantification. Such pairings are not unique to computer science, but can also be found in the social sciences. More famous than anthropological dalliances with MDS is the field theory of Pierre Bourdieu, who defined the 'social field' as 'a multi-dimensional space of positions such that every actual position can be defined in terms of a multi-dimensional system of coordinates' (1985: 724). Bourdieu's work depended on data spatializing techniques like correspondence analysis, a close relative of MDS (see Desrosières 2012). His famous forms of capital emerged from his own interpretation of dimensions: latent factors in the organization of social space.

In a 1995 review, the sociologist Ilana Silber argued that spatial metaphors like Bourdieu's provided 'a specific combination of concreteness and abstraction' (1995: 348) that appealed to theorists looking to make theory that felt both rigorous and realistic:

> Situated somewhere between models imported from the scientific disciplines and everyday life and language, spatial metaphors appear to displace constructs and metaphors emblematic of positivist or systemic theoretical trends now considered obsolete, while also reflecting the prevalent distrust of any kind of encompassing, totalistic image or paradigm (Silber 1995: 348).

The apparent givenness of space offered a way to escape prior theoretical frameworks through simultaneous recourse to the pragmatics of social action (the idea that people do things within the ordinary envelope of a vernacular 'space') and to the mathematical language of the natural sciences. Because they depend so much on common-sense understandings of what space is and how it relates to similarity, they appear theoretically unburdened; because they are mathematized, they appear scientific.

As Michael Lynch has written of other scientific representations, 'mathematical analysis and natural phenomena do not so much *correspond* as do they *merge* indistinguishably on the ground' of such figures (1988: 229, emphasis in original; cf. Morgan 2020). The sense of reality engendered by these spaces is so strong that they

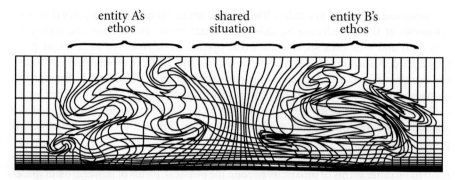

Figure 8. A taste fabric, deformed by the 'ethos', or taste, of two entities. (Liu, Davenport & Maes 2006; courtesy of Hugo Liu.)

enable their wielders to sidestep significant dichotomies: between representation and reality, the formal and the informal, or the subjective and the objective. Bourdieu can speak of the social field as though it is an actual environment and not an algorithmic output; cognitive anthropologists could imagine cultural space as filling up the mind; recommender systems researchers can move easily between mathematical manipulations of abstract space and embodied imaginations of travel through it (cf. Myers & Dumit 2011).

At a conference on machine learning and music, I remarked on the ubiquity of spatial metaphors to a graduate student, who was himself working on similarity measurement. But he corrected me: space was no mere metaphor imposed by human interpreters – it was a basic fact of existence. 'Everything lies in a space, whether or not we're there', he said. Everything – sound, culture, data – was already spatial. 'Our perception, because of our enculturation, is a deformation of that space', he explained; while the objective qualities of music might locate songs in one space, our subjective preferences and perceptions transformed that space into another. Taste, as one recommender systems research group had begun to theorize it, was like the gravitational deformation of an ambient cultural spacetime (Fig. 8).

Silber's analysis captures the ubiquity and unremarkability of space in machine learning. Of course everything lies in a space; where else could it be? Spatialization is a powerful generic operation that is almost maximally abstract, and thus hard to bring into focus; this makes it an appropriate companion for 'data' itself, which is also conceptually slippery while appearing to be essentially self-evident.

Similarity spaces are ambivalent objects. Although they borrow from physical distance a sense of concreteness and objectivity, they depend on subjective interpretation and intuition in the last instance. Although they present the rigour of mathematical theorizing and algorithmic processing, they rarely meet standards of mathematical proof or experimental verification. Their appeal, then, is not just that they are mathematical, bringing rigour and science to hazy interpretative domains, but rather that they embody a powerfully intuitive sense of resembling cultural or cognitive reality. They somewhat awkwardly bridge interpretative and positivist methodological tendencies. When it comes to 'cultural' phenomena, spatialization produces a kind of reality effect, rescuing them from potential unreality by charting them out. If everything lies in a space, then spatializing culture makes it something, rather than nothing.

NOTES

Thanks to my co-editors, fellow contributors to this special issue, and the anonymous reviewers. Bill Maurer, Marilyn Strathern, and Michael Barany provided comments that expanded my conceptual horizons. This research was funded by the Wenner-Gren Foundation (DFG 8797) and the National Science Foundation (DDRIG 1323834).

[1] This 'music space' is thus not the same as the space businesspeople refer to when they say they work in 'the music space' as opposed to, say, 'the pharmaceutical space'.

[2] Following my interlocutors, I use the terms 'data science' and 'machine learning' interchangeably.

[3] See also Haraway's (1997) writing on figuration and Strathern's (1992) on metaphor in technoscience.

[4] I have written about some of the material in this and the following section previously (Seaver 2012; in press).

REFERENCES

ARVIDSSON, A. 2002. On the 'pre-history of the panoptic sort': mobility in market research. *Surveillance & Society* **1**, 456-74.

BARLOW, J.P. 1996. A declaration of the independence of cyberspace. Electronic Frontier Foundation, 8 February (available online: *https://projects.eff.org/~barlow/Declaration-Final.html*, accessed 14 January 2021).

BAROCAS, S. & A. SELBST 2016. Big data's disparate impact. *California Law Review* **104**, 671-732.

BERNARD, H.R. 2006. *Research methods in anthropology: qualitative and quantitative approaches* (Fourth edition). New York: AltaMira Press.

BLOCH, M. 2004. *Anthropology and the cognitive challenge*. Cambridge: University Press.

BOURDIEU, P. 1985. The social space and the genesis of groups. *Theory and Society* **1**, 723-44.

BOYD, J.P. 1972. Information distance for discrete structures. In *Multidimensional scaling: theory and applications in the behavioral sciences*, vol. **1** (eds) R.N. Shepard, A.K. Romney & S.B. Nerlove, 213-23. New York: Seminar Press.

BURTON, M. 1972. Semantic dimensions of occupation names. In *Multidimensional scaling: theory and applications in the behavioral sciences*, vol. **2** (eds) R.N. Shepard, A.K. Romney & S.B. Nerlove, 55-71. New York: Seminar Press.

——— 1970. Computer applications in cultural anthropology. *Computers and the Humanities* **5**, 37-45.

CHAN, A.S. 2014. *Networking peripheries: technological futures and the myth of digital universalism*. Cambridge, Mass.: MIT Press.

CHENEY-LIPPOLD, J. 2011. A new algorithmic identity: soft biopolitics and the modulation of control. *Theory, Culture & Society* **28**, 164-81.

CHUN, W.H.K. 2018. Queerying homophily. In *Pattern discrimination*, C. Apprich, W.H.K. Chun, F. Cramer & H. Steyerl, 59-98. Lüneberg: Meson Press.

COHN, J. 2019. *The burden of choice: recommendations, subversion, and algorithmic culture*. New Brunswick, N.J.: Rutgers University Press.

COLBY, B.N., J.W. FERNANDEZ & D.B. KRONENFELD 1981. Toward a convergence of cognitive and symbolic anthropology. *American Ethnologist* **8**, 422-50.

COOPMANS, C. 2014. Visual analytics as artful revelation. In *Representation in scientific practice revisited* (eds) C. Coopmans, J. Vertesi & M. Lynch, 37-60. Cambridge, Mass.: MIT Press.

D'ANDRADE, R. 1995. *The development of cognitive anthropology*. Cambridge: University Press.

——— 2000. The sad story of anthropology 1950-1999. *Cross-Cultural Research* **34**, 219-32.

DAVISON, M.L. 1983. *Multidimensional scaling*. Malabar, Fla: Krieger Publishing Company.

DESROSIÈRES, A. 2012. Mapping the social world: from aggregates to individuals. *Limn* **2**, 59-62.

DOUGLAS, M. 1986. *How institutions think*. Syracuse: University Press.

GALLOWAY, A. 2006. *Protocol: how control exists after decentralization*. Cambridge, Mass.: MIT Press.

GEERTZ, C. 1973. Thick description: toward an interpretive theory of culture. In *The interpretation of cultures*. New York: Basic Books.

GUPTA, A. & J. FERGUSON 1992. Beyond 'culture': space, identity, and the politics of difference. *Cultural Anthropology* **7**, 6-23.

HARAWAY, D. 1997. *Modest_Witness@Second_Millennium. FemaleMan_Meets_OncoMouse*. New York: Routledge.

HELMREICH, S. 2016. Gravity's reverb: listening to space-time, or articulating the sounds of gravitational-wave detection. *Cultural Anthropology* **31**, 464-92.

HYMES, D. 1965. Introduction. In *The use of computers in anthropology* (ed.) D. Hymes, 15-32. London: Mouton & Co.

JAMES, R. 2017. Is the post- in post-identity the post- in post-genre? *Popular Music* **36**, 21-32.

JAMESON, F. 1991. *Postmodernism, or, the cultural logic of late capitalism*. Durham, N.C.: Duke University Press.

KAVANAGH, D. 2010. Reviewing March's vision. 28th Standing Conference on Organizational Symbolism, Lille, France (available online: *https://researchrepository.ucd.ie/handle/10197/5805*, accessed 14 January 2021).

KEESING, R.M. 1972. Paradigms lost: the new ethnography and the new linguistics. *Southwestern Journal of Anthropology* **28**, 299-332.

KOREN, Y., R. BELL & C. VOLINSKY 2009. Matrix factorization techniques for recommender systems. *Computer*, August, 42-9.

KRUSKAL, J.B. 1964. Multidimensional scaling by optimizing goodness of fit to a nonmetric hypothesis. *Psychometrika* **29**, 1-27.

——— & M. WISH 1978. *Multidimensional scaling*. London: Sage.

LEFEBVRE, H. 1991. *The production of space* (trans. D. Nicholson-Smith). Oxford: Basil Blackwell.

LIU, H., G. DAVENPORT & P. MAES 2006. Taste fabrics and the beauty of homogeneity. SIGSEMIS (available online: *http://web.media.mit.edu/~hugo/publications/drafts/SIGSEMIS-homogeneity.doc*, accessed 14 January 2021).

LYNCH, M. 1988. The externalized retina: selection and mathematization in the visual documentation of objects in the life sciences. *Human Studies* **11**, 201-34.

McROBBIE, A. 2004. Post-feminism and popular culture. *Feminist Media Studies* **4**, 255-64.

MARKHAM, A. 1998. *Life online: researching real experiences in virtual space*. Walnut Creek, Calif.: AltaMira Press.

MOHR, J.W. 1998. Measuring meaning structures. *Annual Review of Sociology* **24**, 345-70.

MORGAN, M. 2020. Inducing visibility and visual deduction. *East Asian Science, Technology and Society* **14**, 225-52.

MYERS, N. & J. DUMIT 2011. Haptic creativity and the mid-embodiments of experimental life. In *A companion to the anthropology of the body and embodiment* (ed.) F.E. Mascia-Lees, 239-61. Oxford: Blackwell.

NAKAMURA, L. 2000. 'Where do you want to go today?': Cybernetic tourism, the internet, and transnationality. In *Race in cyberspace* (eds) B.E. Kolko, L. Nakamura & G.B. Rodman, 15-26. New York: Routledge.

NARAYAN, K. 1993. How native is a 'native' anthropologist? *American Anthropologist* **95**, 671-86.

NELSON, A. 2002. Introduction: Future texts. *Social Text* **20**: **2**, 1-15.

POWDERMAKER, H. 1966. *Stranger and friend: the way of an anthropologist*. New York: Norton.

PREY, R. 2015. Henri Lefebvre and the production of music streaming spaces. *Sociologica* **9**, 1-22.

RIEDL, J. & J. KONSTAN 2002. *Word of mouse: the marketing power of collaborative filtering*. New York: Warner Books.

SAHLINS, M. 1976. *Culture and practical reason*. Chicago: University Press.

SANDAY, P.R. 1975. Review of *Multidimensional scaling: theory and applications in the behavioral sciences*, vol. I: *Theory* (eds) R.N. Shepard, A.K. Romney & S.B. Nerlove. *American Anthropologist* **77**, 106-7.

SAVAGE, M. & R. BURROWS 2007. The coming crisis of empirical sociology. *Sociology* **41**, 885-99.

SCHIFFMAN, S., M.L. REYNOLDS & F.W. YOUNG 1981. *Introduction to multidimensional scaling: theory, methods, and applications*. New York: Emerald Group Publishing.

SEAVER, N. 2012. Algorithmic recommendations and synaptic functions. *Limn* **2**, 46-9.

——— in press. Seeing like an infrastructure: avidity and difference in algorithmic recommendation. *Cultural Studies*.

SHEPARD, R.N. 1962. The analysis of proximities: multidimensional scaling with an unknown distance function. *Psychometrika* **27**, 125-40.

SILBER, I.F. 1995. Space, fields, boundaries: the rise of spatial metaphors in contemporary sociological theory. *Social Research* **62**, 323-55.

STARK, L. 2018. Algorithmic psychometrics and the scalable subject. *Social Studies of Science* **48**, 204-31.

STEFFLRE, V. 1965. Simulation of people's behavior toward new objects and events. *American Behavioral Scientist* **8**: **9**, 12-15.

——— 1971. New products and new enterprises: a report on an experiment in applied social science. Unpublished manuscript, University of California, Irvine.

STRATHERN, M. 1992. *After nature: English kinship in the late twentieth century*. Cambridge: University Press.

——— 2020. *Relations*. Durham, N.C.: Duke University Press.

STRIPHAS, T. 2015. Algorithmic culture. *European Journal of Cultural Studies* **18**, 395-412.

TUFEKCI, Z. 2018. Opinion: YouTube, the great radicalizer. *The New York Times*, 8 June (available online: *https: //www.nytimes.com/2018/03/10/opinion/sunday/youtube-politics-radical.html*, accessed 14 January 2021).

TVERSKY, A. 1977. Features of similarity. *Psychological Review* **84**, 327-52.

VAN DEUSEN, E. 1969. Volney Stefflre: his bag is people. *Orange County Illustrated* **7**: **8**, 30-3.

WALFORD, A. 2017. Raw data: making relations matter. *Social Analysis* **61**: **2**, 65-80.

WESTON, K. 2008. 'Real anthropology' and other nostalgias. In *Ethnographica moralia: experiments in interpretive anthropology* (ed.) N. Panourgiá & G. Marcus, 126-37. New York: Fordham University Press.

WILSON, J. 2013. 'The devastating conquest of the lived by the conceived': the concept of abstract space in the work of Henri Lefebvre. *Space and Culture* **16**, 364-80.

Tout n'est qu'espace : données culturelles et réalité spatiale

Résumé

En s'appuyant sur un travail de terrain réalisé aux États-Unis auprès de développeurs de systèmes de recommandation musicale, cet article s'intéresse à l'utilisation de techniques de spatialisation dans l'analyse de données culturelles. En comparant ces pratiques avec des techniques analytiques similaires développées par l'anthropologie cognitive d'après-guerre, l'auteur explore trois grandes questions : comment ces techniques créent l'impression d'un milieu continu et enveloppant à partir de données distinctes et souvent rares ; comment la spatialisation est employée afin de conférer à la culture une sorte de réalité enracinée dans l'action pragmatique et la quantification scientifique ; et comment les représentations spatiales de la culture s'avèrent fondamentalement anticipatives pour les personnes qui les construisent, permettant une géolocalisation de l'avenir proche.

3

The datafication of nature: data formations and new scales in natural history

TAHANI NADIM *Museum für Naturkunde Berlin/Humboldt-Universität zu Berlin*

In this essay, I consider the scales and connections lost and gained as natural history adopts digital data infrastructures. On the basis of ongoing work in the Museum für Naturkunde Berlin, I track the relations between insect specimens and their material and digital informational ecologies. Using Latour's notion of the 'circulating reference', I follow the insect specimens as they make their way into taxonomies, databases, and digitization apparatuses. In focusing on human-data mediations in museum practices of ordering, describing, and distributing specimens, I show how the datafication of nature makes present conventionally dissociated contexts, including German colonialism. Proposing the concept of a data formation, I suggest that ethnographers have much to contribute in bringing forward the sociocultural and historical specificities and contingencies within data.

I'm sitting in the office of the head curator for the Lepidoptera (butterflies and moths) collection at the Museum für Naturkunde Berlin, one of the world's oldest and largest natural history museums, to talk about the relation between global data infrastructures and museum collections. Perched between us atop the table is an insect drawer, a wooden rectangular box with a glass lid that is filled with dozens of tiny moths neatly pinned in tight rows. An A4 sheet of paper lies on top of the drawer. It shows a phylogenetic tree diagram, consisting of branches, nodes, and leaves arranged in a circle that represent the evolutionary relationships between the moth species assembled in the drawer underneath. The moths' genetic data, derived from their legs, had just been received from a Dutch-based biotechnology company specializing in DNA sequencing services. Based on similarity analysis, the sequences were grouped and subsequently translated into the diagram, where the lengths of the tree's branches are proportional to the amount of character change, thus indicating the relationship level between the moth species.

We are talking about the speed of taxonomic research, which, together with the care and management of collections, constitutes the curator's main work. Taxonomic research is concerned with the description, identification, and naming of species, and

Journal of the Royal Anthropological Institute (N.S.) **27**, 62-75

natural history museums form a central site for this pursuit in providing a home for experts and materials, most importantly specimens. Nowadays also referred to as biodiversity discovery, taxonomic work has a long history, usually said to originate with Carl Linnaeus (1707-78), whose system for naming organisms remains in place to this day. The artefacts furnishing the curator's office bear witness to the ongoing traditions still directing much of this work: a microscope; system trays (small cardboard boxes containing specimens); pincers and pens; more wooden drawers filled with pinned butterflies; a desktop computer; boxes overflowing with spare pins and labels. Book shelves line two walls, crammed with aged leather-bound volumes, papers, and journals. At the same time, the piece of paper bearing the tree diagram is indicative of how novel data-based technologies, including DNA sequencing, are changing species discovery, the material practices of taxonomic work, and its infrastructures and institutions. The curator tells me that the real bottleneck in scaling up taxonomy and fully realizing a data-driven biodiversity discovery is the tenuous, often non-existent connection between molecular (genetic) data and the published species names. 'We have', he emphasizes, '250 year's worth of species names' derived from identifications based on morphological traits such as colour, size, and shape. Now these need to be matched to the unique genetic signatures for each species, so-called barcodes, that became attainable through genetic sequencing at the end of the twentieth century. And, indeed, the diagram bears no species for the moths, just so-called Barcode Index Numbers (BINs), denoting algorithmically derived clusters of barcode sequences assumed to represent distinct species.

What interests me in this essay are the scales and connections lost and gained as natural history becomes populated by BINs, barcodes, and digital data infrastructures. In the following, I explore the meeting of what the editors have called the 'data moment' and practices of natural history, including discovering, naming, and digitizing, in the Museum für Naturkunde Berlin. My aim is to track this conjuncture through the connections and disconnections between the specimen and its emergent informational ecology. In doing so, I advance the concept of 'data formation' to gather the heterogeneous, contingent, and not always explicit processes that make and remake data in the context of natural history collections as they seek to transform themselves into global data infrastructures. Guided by Stoler's use of the term 'imperial formations' (2008: 192), data formations refer to human-data mediations adjacent to and exceeding the formal processes of computerized programming and coding. I argue that thinking and handling data as data formation complicates expectations and assumptions associated with data (Kitchin 2014), including the abstraction and standardization of phenomena, while also prompting a rethink of the categorical differences between big and small, digital and physical, past and present. Specifically, I demonstrate how the decontextualization of museum specimens in the course of databasing, classifying, and digitizing always entails a recontextualization that does not so much dispel as distribute complexity. My concern here is also to make evident how data formations point to a datafication of nature that is characterized by novel scales for natural history.

With this text, I want to bring into conversation two sets of literature: the body of work generally concerned with what has become called datafication (boyd & Crawford 2012; Ruckenstein & Schüll 2017; van Dijck 2014) and its sociopolitical effects; and social and cultural studies of science, more specifically, studies examining the lives of the objects and materials that go into the making of science and its claims (Franklin 2003; Knorr Cetina 1999; Latour 1999; Latour & Woolgar 1986). A specific analytical category to emerge from the latter is the 'inscription', which describes the transformation of entities and phenomena into mobile traces such as diagrams, documents, or signals (Latour & Woolgar 1986). It is in the form of inscriptions that claims about the world can move beyond the field and the laboratory, get tested against and combined with other inscriptions, thus allowing the construction and manipulation of entities, from planetary boundaries to genetic barcodes. Inscriptions are not representations of the world but specifically materialized representations in the world that possess obduracy and agency and thus shape the world. For ethnographies of laboratories and scientific knowledge production, inscriptions and 'circulating references', which describe the contiguous translations of entities into signs, have served as central objects to follow and observe in action (Latour 1999). With expanding datafication, not only do these objects multiply, but their trajectories are ever harder to trace across machines, databases, software, and formats. Studies examining the proliferating incursions of data-driven quantification and governance into most domains of life afford data similar capacities to intervene in the world (Turnhout, De Lijster & Neves 2014). Here, too, entities and phenomena such as pollution (see Blacker, this volume) are transformed into inscriptions that can circulate, be aggregated, and become the target of policy interventions. Both sets of literatures are thus concerned with the power of data (and of inscriptions as data) to materialize and scale the world, and, furthermore, with the methodological challenges posed by the scale of data.

In the context of the data moment, the problem of scale is conventionally imagined through the tensions and trade-offs between big data and small data (boyd & Crawford 2012). As the editors of this special issue point out, this is usually where anthropology comes in, since 'small' here means empirically constructed thick data derived from local and situated engagements. Small data is regarded as close to bodies and the ground and steeped in context that can be neither vanquished nor abstracted without considerable information loss. And so the tension between big and small data reproduces a scalar problem common to both anthropology and natural history, namely the incongruity between 'taxonomic' and 'relational' precision (Wagner quoted in Strathern 2004: 121 n. 3). One could either hone in on the individual butterfly and describe it in all its details (taxonomic precision), or take in the entire drawer, consider the entire collection and all of the species' ecological encounters to describe its evolutionary development, environmental function, or similar relational complexes (relational precision). By proposing the figure of data formation for imagining and tracing data-human mediations in natural history, I want to move away from this dichotomy and suggest instead that data formations gain detailed shape as they also gain relationality. This is an urgent question as natural history collections are moving to comprehensively digitize and make their specimens available in global data infrastructures. In the course of this, decisions need to be taken as to what information to retain and at which level of detail, thus structuring access and inquiry in particular ways.

Taking my cues from anthropological and, more recently, science and technology studies engagements with scale and scaling, I want to examine scale as an empirical question and by doing so move away from the convention that sees big and small, the general and the specific, as mutually exclusive domains (Asdal 2020; Strathern 1995). The essay specifically attends to how data is imagined in natural history, past and present, by tracing and describing different yet connected moments of data formations: a database record and its specimen; the naming of a wasp; and the mass digitization of insects. Guided by actor-network theory's methodological proposition to 'follow the

Journal of the Royal Anthropological Institute (N.S.) **27**, 62-75
© 2021 The Authors. *Journal of the Royal Anthropological Institute* published by John Wiley & Sons Ltd on behalf of Royal Anthropological Institute

actors' (Latour 1987), both human and nonhuman, I track inscriptions, references, and specimens through practices in the Museum für Naturkunde Berlin, which has been my institutional home and fieldsite since 2013. This following is based on participant observation, ongoing dialogues with colleagues, and an engagement with data-related developments through literature and observation.

Retracing references, returning complexities

At one point in my conversation with the Lepidoptera curator, we move to his computer so that he can show me the barcode sequences which have been derived from the moths and form the basis for the phylogenetic tree diagram. He opens the barcodes as a text file, revealing a set of sequences of As, Cs, Gs, and Ts, copies one of the sequences, and pastes it into the search function of the Barcode of Life Data System (BOLD) which he has called up in his browser. BOLD provides, among other things, a public database of reference sequences from vouchered specimens: that is, animals or plants preserved in institutional collections that serve as a verifiable and permanent record for the species. At first, no match is found, but a second sequence matches an Australian moth in the Australian National Insect Collection by over 90 per cent, allowing the curator to establish an informed connection between the moths in his office, the barcode, the valid species name, and the voucher specimen. According to Latour (1999), this traceability is a key condition for the efficacy of references to serve as both representative (of a species, environments, collections) and guarantor for downstream inscriptions such as publications. Given the plethora of historical and ongoing natural history collections, the proliferation of data portals like BOLD and data-based biodiversity discoveries like barcoding make these 'chains of transformation' (Latour 1999: 70) – that is, retraceable connections between specimens and references – more imperative since they multiply the specimen and its data. Retracing, however, might also proliferate relations.

I was searching through the Global Biodiversity Information Facility (GBIF), the largest online public database of biodiversity information, when I arrived at a small set of butterflies from the Museum für Naturkunde collected in Cameroon.[1] The thirty-nine database records appeared on my screen listed alphabetically by species name: *Anapisa aurantiaca*, *Automolis invaria*, *Balacra daphaena*, and so on. The entries shared geographical co-ordinates (4.3N, 9.1E), a date (1991 December), and the 'basis for the record' (Preserved specimen). They also comprised full taxonomic lineages, from Kingdom (Animalia) all the way to the species level. Clicking on the record for *Graphium fulleri*, the full database entry is called up. It is titled 'Graphium fulleri (Grose-Smith 1883)', indicating that Henley Grose-Smith (1833-1911), a British entomologist, was the first to identify the species and publish the name in 1883. It further contains the butterfly's common name (Riley's graphium), a not very detailed map of present-day Cameroon, as well as three photographs. The first shows the specimen from the top, the second shows it from the bottom, and the third depicts all the specimen's labels neatly arranged side by side. Curiously, the labels state the species name as '*Papilio sanganoides*', but this escapes my initial perusal. The photographs are followed by a table holding data relating to the record, the occurrence, identification, taxon, and location and a set of rows providing 'Other' data, in this case information on the record licence (Creative Commons 4.0). The specimen is marked as a holotype, which describes the name-giving specimen for a species (thus counting among the most valuable holdings of the collection). Like most holotypes in the collection, this

Journal of the Royal Anthropological Institute (N.S.) **27**, 62-75
© 2021 The Authors. *Journal of the Royal Anthropological Institute* published by John Wiley & Sons Ltd on behalf of Royal Anthropological Institute

specimen, too, is accompanied by a tiny red label, captured in the photograph, bearing the word 'Type'.

In order to trace the reference of the database record back to the butterfly specimen, I meet the curator for the Lepidoptera collection. We make our way to the office of the collection care technicians, who are responsible for maintaining and preserving collection specimens. The collection rooms are cavernous, expansive yet dim, as cabinets and cupboards tower all the way to the ceiling, forming narrow alleys dotted with ladders and old-fashioned trolleys. Were it not for the odd piece of modern equipment, such as a vacuum cleaner or a freezer, a cursory view of the space would cast the observer back into the time when the building first opened in 1889. In addition to the species name, I had gleaned from GBIF the specimen's 'catalogue number' in the hope that the collection's catalogue might contain some contextual information which had not been integrated into the database record and which could tell me more about the circulation of the reference. Stacked in the technician's office, the collection catalogues are oversized leather-bound volumes of mildly yellowed pages bearing a double-spread grid that contains, in extremely neat handwriting, catalogue number, species name, location, collector, and, in rare cases, additional information such as details concerning acquisition. Unfortunately, as the technician remarks, the catalogue entries do not include dates, making it difficult to cross-reference with specimen labels and other documentation (such as accession books, inventories, auction catalogues, or annual reports). The number I had noted down for the specimen did not correspond to the specimen listed under the same number in the collection catalogue, prompting the technician to surmise that it probably matches the 'main catalogue', which is kept in the historical archives of the museum. This mismatch points to the specific history of the collection, which had initially begun as part of the zoological collection before this was divided into sub-collections corresponding to taxonomic groups (Mammals, Birds, Reptiles and Amphibians, Fishes, etc.). The technician grabs a slim brochure from behind her desk, the *Mitteilungen aus dem Zoologischen Museum in Berlin* (Notes from the Zoological Museum in Berlin) from 1904, which documents collection development. For the Lepidoptera collection, the report notes that most work consisted of preparing butterflies from the African colonies and that work on a general systematic catalogue for butterflies had started.

The curator and I continue on our search for the GBIF specimen, which takes us to the second floor of the building, where another part of the Lepidoptera collection is stored. Once more, we find ourselves between towering cabinets, each of which holds hundreds of specimens carefully pinned in insect drawers. At the back of one of the alleyways, we meet a volunteer, an elderly woman, carefully moving butterflies from old drawers into new ones. Volunteers are a common sight in the museum, providing indispensable help in caring for collections. In addition, by transferring specimens into new drawers and updating labels, they assist in the transformation of collections into modern information infrastructures. We move further down into the collection and finally arrive at a cabinet containing specimens collected on the African continent meant to hold the taxon *Graphium fulleri*. The curator slides out drawers, searching for the species while I call up the GBIF record on my smartphone to provide him with a visual for the butterfly. He pulls out a drawer, places it on a nearby table, opens it, and delicately removes a promising-looking butterfly. In order to check its identity, he removes the stack of labels pinned underneath it piece by piece. Despite the similarity, the information on the labels reveals this to be the wrong specimen and we return to the

Journal of the Royal Anthropological Institute (N.S.) **27**, 62-75
© 2021 The Authors. *Journal of the Royal Anthropological Institute* published by John Wiley & Sons Ltd on behalf of Royal Anthropological Institute

cabinet, where another butterfly catches the curator's attention. Once more, however, we encounter a mismatch. While this certainly is the specimen in the photograph on GBIF – the markings are identical, as are the tiny oddities (missing antenna, crooked leg) – the taxonomic name on the label appears as '*Papilio foersterius*'. The curator looks again at the photographs provided on GBIF and inspects the labels there more closely, seeing, for the first time, the name given as *Papilio sanganoides*. This prompts him to speculate that while the database record lists the current valid name for the species (*Graphium fulleri*), all other names constitute synonyms, a product of multiple descriptions of the same species or of a change in classification or nomenclatural code.

One of the labels accompanying the museum specimen and featured on the photograph in GBIF bears the location of where the butterfly had been collected: 'S. Kamerun' (South Cameroon), 'Ngoko Sanga'. It also contains what presumably is the name of the collector ('Foerster'), who appears to have been honoured by having the species named after him (*Papilio foersterius*). It is likely that this refers to Oskar Foerster (1871-1910), a German colonial officer who had served in various expeditions in southern Cameroon while it was a colony of the German Empire (1884-1916) (Schnee 1920: 651). I had been told that the specimens from Cameroon listed in GBIF had most likely come to the museum in the late nineteenth or early twentieth century. This date range is consistent not only with the above-mentioned report from 1904, but also with the historical circumstances which saw German colonial troops engage in expeditions in southern Cameroon (Nghonda & Zacharie 2007). At the time, the region was the site of prolonged border negotiations and conflicts between German and French colonial powers. Expeditions combining military and scientific expertise were used to map territory and people, drawing boundaries and collecting specimens of local fauna and flora, which also served to naturalize colonized territories.[2]

Odd connections and disconnections accompany the database record once it is accessed not as a scientific reference but as a data formation. It makes evident that digital transformations inherit, and at times heighten, the problems that continue to haunt natural history, including its participation in imperial formations (Subramaniam 2014).

Names of transmission

When I joined the Museum für Naturkunde Berlin in 2013 on a post-doctoral fellowship as the museum's first social scientist, it was set to transform itself into a 'biodiversity discovery factory', as one key colleague put it. Laconically described by him as 'animals in, papers out', specimens would be delivered to and processed in the museum and turned into digital data about morphology and lineage, species abundance, distribution and trends, data about the state of ecosystems and biodiversity loss. This vision signals key aspirations undergirding the data moment, including automation and the seamless integration of disparate data, sites, and times, from historical specimens to genetic sequences, from museum collections to global databases. In retracing the database record, it has become evident that current digital data infrastructures remain deeply entwined with traditional taxonomic work and institutional histories. The vision of the biodiversity discovery factory imagined the transformation of natural history into a data-driven science and natural history museums as the centre of calculation and datafication. In fact, as colonial collections demonstrate, natural history museums have long been key to rendering worlds and their inhabitants into (digital) data. Not only does natural history constitute a vast archive of data, but also its technologies for sorting, storing, relating, and distributing data persist in current data efforts that go beyond the 'traditional' remit of natural history (although, of course, this remit has never been strictly domained, as feminist and postcolonial scholars have demonstrated repeatedly). Despite the data diversity and unstable taxonomies, it is important to note that these remain hegemonic descriptions of the world. The datafication of nature, and, by extension, the data moment with which the essays in this volume grapple, are outcomes and continuations of specific histories that endure, even when technologies, economies, and routines change. The datafication of nature thus compels a reckoning with the tenacity of natural history's modes of ordering, especially its naming practices. Names are scalar devices in that they allow a species to emerge from a specimen, thus affording a switch of perspective from the taxonomic to the relational. In the following, I retrace the naming of a wasp to further contour the ongoing nature of data formations in natural history.

Shortly after arriving at the museum, I joined the Hymenoptera (ants, bees, wasps, and sawflies) department of the museum to learn more about how 'biodiversity' is constructed and negotiated in collections and in the practices of scientists working there. It is the largest of the collections in the museum, comprising an estimated 2.2 million specimens. Like the Lepidoptera collection, it is spread across two floors and held in some of the most spectacular, custom-built wooden cabinets. A musty and slightly sweet smell pervades the space. Clusters of modern metal collection storage and the distribution of small QR (quick response) codes on labels, drawers, and cabinets, however, signal a transitional moment. It is here that the first batch of mass digitization of specimens has occurred (more on this below). At the time, I found myself examining a set of shiny wasps, each no bigger than about one centimetre. Thin metal pins had been driven through their bodies, which were stuck to the foam lining of a small white box, a so-called system box or unit pinning tray. Such boxes populate collections in many different sizes and function as a key device for moving, ordering, and protecting specimens (Nadim 2020). Stacks of empty boxes wait in different corners of the collection to be filled, signalling the expected arrival of more specimens. The wasps had recently arrived from northern Thailand, where they had been collected as part of a biodiversity survey carried out by the University of Kentucky. This is not an unusual arrangement, I soon learned. Biodiversity surveys continue the traditional expedition in seeking to establish knowledge of species occurrence in specific areas, mobilizing actors and institutions world-wide while continually filling the empty boxes and jars in museum collections.

Once killed and collected, the animals are roughly sorted in the field before being sent on to respective taxonomic experts in institutions such as natural history museums or universities for further identification. The curator of the Hymenoptera collection invited me to participate in the taxonomic work describing, identifying, and, possibly, naming the wasp, should it turn out to be new to science. A Ph.D. student with whom I was to collaborate had worked on a preliminary survey of the regional wasp diversity and had already narrowed their taxonomic rank to the genus of Alysson, part of the Bembicinae tribe, a group of solitary and predatory wasps that excavate their nests in soil, digging shallow tunnels in which to lay their eggs. The question for us now was whether our wasps constituted new species within this genus, and so we began gathering published descriptions for all known Alysson wasps based on the ultimate reference list, the *Catalogue of Sphecidae*. This was created and is still maintained by Dr Wojciech J. Pulawski, emeritus curator of entomology at the California Academy

Journal of the Royal Anthropological Institute (N.S.) 27, 62-75
© 2021 The Authors. *Journal of the Royal Anthropological Institute* published by John Wiley & Sons Ltd on behalf of Royal Anthropological Institute

of Sciences (the natural history museum in San Francisco). Available online as a pdf document since September 2003, the list remains updated to this day, representing a catalogue of all known Sphecidae wasps and an indispensable instrument for knowing wasps. The oldest description we worked with dated back to 1852 and was published in Latin in *Analecta ad Entomographiam*, a 200-plus-page compilation of entomological descriptions covering the insects of the Russian Empire. In contrast, the most recent description was a 1987 paper from the journal *Acta Entomologica Sinica* written in Chinese. Parsing the materials required interpretation and conjecture – often in discussions with the Ph.D. student and the curator – in order to make them congruent and serviceable for comparisons with the wasps from Northern Thailand. But published descriptions lack comparability: there are no enduring standards for describing morphological characteristics, and there is no agreement on the selection of characteristics to be described in more detail. We therefore embarked on a second-order collection, obtaining the physical specimens behind the descriptions from museum collections in Thailand, the United States, Austria, and the Netherlands. Our wasps were soon joined with more wasps, and I found myself zooming in on and out of many tiny bodies in order to compare veins on wings, abdominal contours, and their published descriptions. Taxonomic work can be a slow process, taking many years to complete.

Historian of science Lorraine Daston has described nomenclature in natural history as an 'art of transmission' (2004: 157), thus shifting the focus from the stability of names as references to the material and semiotic means by which naming is done in practice. The notion of transmission emphasizes the logistical nature of natural history, which has always been concerned with managing the circulation of specimens and names through territories, collections, and inscriptions such as catalogues. This is a slow process which the biodiversity discovery factory intends to speed up. But given the endurance of names, inscribed on museum labels and in catalogues and databases, the transmission might never be entirely unequivocal.

Digitization: testing connections

At the time that I was working on identifying the wasps, the museum embarked on its first large-scale digitization project as a test run for exploring the feasibility of and sociotechnical requirements for translating object-rich – insects comprise by far the largest collections – museum collections into the digital realm, including data releases to GBIF. The project, entitled *'Erschließung objektreicher Spezialsammlungen'* (Establishing an inventory of species-rich collections, EoS) sought to digitize insect drawers, provide virtual access through federated portals, and create efficient and innovative methods for mass digitization of collections, particularly of small, complex objects (Kroupa, Glöckler & Schurian 2015). This spectrum of concerns signals the complexity of digitization, which has become a core operational activity in museums but which remains, nevertheless, under-theorized (Geismar 2013; 2018). By the time I joined the EoS team, the digitization was in full flow. The work took place in a re-purposed office tucked away inside the butterfly collection. Like much of the museum's backstage area, the space is an assemblage of cupboards, shelving systems, and other storage and work furniture spanning three centuries. The central digitization device – a SatScan[3] scanner – rested atop an old wooden pedestal desk. I worked with two digitization assistants to retrieve insect drawers from collections and wheel them to the digitization room using a small trolley. After having moved one of the drawers to my workstation, I carefully opened it by removing the lid. Next, using pinning forceps,

I made sure that all labels were uniformly arranged, orderly pointing in the same direction, because the digital image would capture the entire drawer and its contents, the animal bodies, pins, and labels. Each drawer, species group within the drawer, and type specimen was issued with a QR code that pointed to a unique resource identifier (an alphanumerical code) to retain a connection between specimens, drawers, and digitized objects (more on this below). I then moved the drawer into the scanner and, via a desktop computer attached to it, initiated the scan. A computer screen would gradually reveal the digitized insects as the camera took picture after picture. While I watched the animals appear on the screen, I could see the piles of insect drawers mounting as my colleagues brought in more and more from the museum's collections. That it should be insects that were the first to be subjected to mass digitization betrays a central aspect of the logic of datafication. Insects are, as Raffles writes, 'without number and without end' (2010: 201), signalling the scope of data to be endlessly generated, combined, and multiplied. Like insects, data is conventionally imagined en masse – little is said about an individual insect outside taxonomic work proper as there is little concern over one singular data point in debates around the effects of datafication. In using insects, digitization 'means to ensure their number for [itself]', to appropriate Elias Canetti's (1981 [1960]: 110) reflection on human-insect relations (see Hayden, this volume). Digitizing insects thus spectacularly performs the power of data to go big.

I re-encountered the workflows and the SatScan six years later when the digitization ensemble had indeed been scaled up and moved into the public exhibition area of the museum. The workflows that had been carefully prototyped and tested in the insect digitization now serve as the baseline for the next step in the digitization process, which aims to comprehensively digitize all of the museum's collection in full view of museum visitors. For this, large parts of the Hymenoptera collection were moved into the public exhibition right next to the central dinosaur hall. Beautiful old wooden cabinets filled with bees, wasps, ants, and sawflies bracket one end of the public digitization hall. The other end is furnished with new uniform metal cabinets that await the insects once they have been digitized.

Digitization here is performed as a multidimensional modernizing process. Between past and future, a number of digitizing workstations form an ensemble of humans and machines, surrounded by specimens, labels, pins, papers, and tools. While some stations are dedicated to macroscopic digitization of individual specimens, the mass digitization of insect drawers remains the core process. Once a drawer has been scanned using the SatScan, it is moved to a new station which consists of a custom-built 'digitization street', an ensemble of equipment wound along a small, semi-circular conveyor belt. A digitization assistant removes specimens from the drawer and carefully detaches the labels from the pins. Stacks of QR codes sit on the desk integrated into the station as well as on almost every desk in the digitization hall. They are printed on small strips of rectangular paper and feature a machine-readable label in the form of black squares arranged in a quadratic grid on a white background, the name of the museum, and a unique identifier in the form of a URL (which can be accessed when the label is scanned with a camera or other imaging device). The assistant pins the now label-less insect onto a Styrofoam tray, places a QR code next to it, and neatly arranges the labels. Once the tray is placed on the conveyor belt, it is taken on a quarter-revolution around the semi-circular tracks into a set-up featuring a camera. There it stops for the camera to take three or four images of the specimen and its label(s). Once this is completed, the conveyor belt resumes, taking with it the tray bearing insect, labels, and QR code. At the

Journal of the Royal Anthropological Institute (N.S.) **27**, 62-75

end of the conveyor belt, new unit pinning boxes await the objects. Again, QR codes are issued for each box before it is moved into a new drawer that, once more, is issued with a QR code. Finally, these drawers are placed in one of the new collection cupboards.

A key practical and conceptual problem amidst the proliferations of digitization pertains to relations and the question of how things are connected and, importantly, stay connected. The final EoS report stresses the importance of the QR code for the 'provenance of the connection between the physical specimens and the digital representations' (Kroupa *et al.* 2015: 9). The challenge here is not only to connect physical specimens with their paper records but also to trace object references across historical documents and documentation such as catalogues, inventories, and accession books, which are mostly kept in the museum's historical archive and thus do not mirror the taxonomic order of the collections. MacKinney (2019) notes a veritable breakdown in record-keeping beginning in the 1820s-1830s when imperial networks brought in more and more specimens. Rather than noting each incoming individual specimen, museum staff had switched to note shipment numbers instead, thus moving to a transactional order that made numbers and counts the central data element. The digitization compels the museum to revisit, perhaps even confront, these histories (e.g. Heumann, Stöcker, Tamborini & Vennen 2018) as it looks to reconstruct the trajectories of specimens in order to ensure their function as reference.

Next to the QR code, another type of connection is mobilized in the digitization. In a system tray sitting next to the operator of the 'digitization street' rests a single bee. It remains untouched as I watch the operator run the machine, and after encountering it once more as I return to the digitization hall, I enquire about its fate. It is, I learn, the 'test bee', an orphaned specimen from the collection whose place and origin have been lost. It now serves to calibrate the machine when this is switched on. The test bee thus acts as the sole vanguard for the entire class of insects as it is transformed into millions of digital traces.

Conclusion

Data formations have always been a part of natural history (Müller-Wille 2017). Identifying, describing, and naming species and transforming specimens into inscriptions depend on human-data mediations that are often not readily discernible as such, including the careful handling of specimen labels or the painstaking comparison of descriptions and insect bodies. Data formations thus contour the contingent material-discursive constellation of sites, people, and materials that shape bodies and environments through data. Their labours endure beyond the moments and materials of inscription. The scaling up of efforts to discover species, which involve the use of novel molecular technologies, the digitization of museum collections, as well as the transformation of collections into globally accessible databases, adds new elements to these data formations and brings to the fore, with great force, the need for creating and maintaining connections between all elements, old and new. Specimens in the collection require valid and unambiguous names as well as resource identifiers so that they can be mobilized as sources for genetic material which can then circulate in the form of barcodes across databases. Species names on labels and photographs, in pdfs, databases, and descriptions, need to be disambiguated and made to refer to one localized type specimen. Collection objects, biotic and abiotic (drawers, cupboards), are issued with QR codes that need to point to unique resource identifiers, which in turn should connect related objects across ontological domains (wasp and drawer). The datafication of nature thus proliferates the specification of entities as well as patterns of relations. Asdal suggests that 'the size of nature is not simply there to begin with, but made by way of instruments and connections' (2020: 338). Following on from this, I would suggest that datafication extends the category of nature to encompass colonial histories, institutional cultures, logistics, and technologies, among many other things. So, while scientists might regard the biodiversity crisis also as an information crisis (e.g. Blagoderov, Kitching, Livermore, Simonsen & Smith 2012; Costello, May & Stork 2013) – not having enough data on the world's species occurrences and trends – it might more accurately be framed as a crisis of definition, as Escobar (1999) has argued. To him, the rise of the term 'biodiversity', which I would contend is not coincidental with the datafication of nature, requires an understanding of nature that both is historicized and takes into consideration its economic, social, and political relations.

To conclude, I wish to suggest three ways in which anthropological engagements with scale might contribute to figuring more clearly the stakes in debates around data, big and small. My first point concerns the observation that it is not just that the big contains the small but that the small contains the big (Strathern 1995). Where agency is distributed across human and nonhuman actors, scale becomes an empirical question tied to specific contexts: a butterfly becomes 'large' once folded into a global biodiversity data infrastructure where it can multiply across screens everywhere, while species, the hegemonic ordering logic of life on earth, become a matter of localized documentary traces. Similarly, the world-wide digitization of natural history collections is done through local, often prototypical, human-data mediations embedded in historically specific contexts, guided by idiosyncratic workflows. Importantly, the domaining and magnifying that occur through scaling resist any easy equation of local/diverse/concrete and global/homogeneous/abstract. This does not, of course, mean that such workflows and digitizations are fundamentally tainted or unserviceable. Instead, recognition of the conservation or displacement of heterogeneity as it travels from situated practice to globally accessible data infrastructures (and back) draws attention to the politics of scale. Much consideration has gone into the conventions of taxonomic nomenclature, and debates about biodiversity data integration have given rise to efforts seeking to formalize and standardize data practices. Yet the 'values, norms, interests, and working conditions' (Simons, Lis & Lippert 2014: 636) that are guiding scale production and mobilization, while immanent in, for example, the choice of 'relevant' data points, remain bracketed out of these debates.

My second point considers the issue of context. Scale is a product of contexts, or, as Woolgar and Neyland put it, context has a 'scalar quality' in always being bigger than that which it is said to contain (2013: 108). As a central sense-making device, it has come to dominate much critical engagement with the datafication of life (and lives), also because it facilitates an easy enculturation and socialization of data. The presumed separation of object and background, text and context also plays a role in the construction of biodiversity data and its processes of decontextualization and recontextualization (Leonelli 2016). Here debates as to the proper level of metadata, data about data, for the specimen, its digital representation, and its digitized version are guided not just by arguments of efficiency (in the form of, for example, minimum data requirements) but also by the organisms themselves, the epistemic communities that have formed around them, and the communities of expected and unexpected data users (Kirksey 2015). Some traces of the context of production are retained through the metadata that accompanies data, such as location, collection method, or date;

others are shed – or 'purified' – in order to allow data mobilization and application across many different contexts. Yet the notion of data formation makes evident that any a priori distancing of data and context is anything but self-evident. Data in the context of data formations appears as an 'uncooperative figure' (Ballestero 2019: 20) as it does not easily separate from its background. The taxonomic work of making species (data) shows the difficulty of rendering object-environment distinctions and of drawing boundaries. Similarly, digitization and, more generally, the datafication of nature are enacted in multiple contexts (natural history, museums, global data infrastructures), which make them never only ever part of just one programme, logic, or culture. Again, as with scale, the continual figure-ground reversals compel a sensibility towards the politics of what we might call 'multimodal contexting': the enrolment of materials, actors, networks, and histories in making and appealing to certain contexts and not others.

Lastly, I want to suggest that multisited, interdisciplinary ethnographic engagements can not only furnish more precise understandings of the nature and politics of data and digitization but also offer instructive insights for designing data models, workflows, and data infrastructures. Scholars of infrastructure studies have already proposed ways of collaborating with scientists on ensuring sustainable and usable systems (Edwards, Bowker, Jackson & Williams 2009). At the same time, anthropologists are building their own data infrastructures and inform the development of metadata standards for cultural and social science research (Crowder, Fortun, Besara & Poirie 2020). But there remains more and ongoing work to be done on developing analytical tools to think about the nature, function, and effects of data and digitization. While the dichotomy analogue/digital might suggest digitization to be a straightforward process from one to the other, attention to situated practices of human-data mediations betrays the complexity of digitization as well as the instability of the dichotomy. The material and the digital are intertwined aspects of complex processes and phenomena and not binary opposites (Sumartojo, Pink, Lupton & Heyes le Bond 2016). Similarly, data contains and is contained by manifold sociocultural practices. With the notion of 'data formation', I have tried to convey the sociocultural and historical specificities and contingencies within data.

NOTES

I would like to thank my colleagues at the Museum für Naturkunde Berlin for sharing their insights and curiosity. I would also like to thank Hagit Keysar, Felipe Mammoli, Sarah Blacker, Ingmar Lippert, and Filippo Bertoni for inventive discussions of parts of this essay. Lastly, a special thanks to the fabulous Editors of this special issue for their kind exactitude and exceptional support.

Open Access funding enabled and organized by Projekt DEAL.

[1] GBIF is an expansive resource providing over 1.6 billion species occurrence records: that is, data about the presence of species in specific locations across the globe. Many funding streams stipulate a default data release to GBIF and their datasets feed into high-level policy documents such as Intergovernmental Panel on Climate Change (IPCC) reports (e.g. Warren, Price, Graham, Forstenhaeusler & VanDerWal 2018). It is freely available online through a web browser (at gbif.org) and offers a prominent search bar where users can input a taxon name and retrieve a list (and map) of locations for the species. GBIF data is provided by collections and institutions worldwide, including the Museum für Naturkunde Berlin.

[2] All natural specimens taken from the German colonies were initially sent to the Museum für Naturkunde Berlin, which had been designated the central collection point through a resolution of the Reichstag.

[3] The SatScan was developed by the (now defunct) UK-based company Smartdrive Limited. It resembles a black box measuring about 120 × 70 × 70 cm fitted with a camera suspended from the inside ceiling and running on precision rails allowing it to move in two dimensions to capture images of the object placed

underneath it. The camera takes 256 slightly overlapping images that, in a second step, are stitched together to form a contiguous high-resolution image of the object placed underneath it, in this case insect drawers.

REFERENCES

Asdal, K. 2020. Is ANT equally good in dealing with local, national and global natures? In *The Routledge companion to actor-network theory* (eds) I. Farias, C. Roberts & A. Blok, 337-44. London: Routledge.

Ballestero, A. 2019. The underground as infrastructure? Water, figure/ground reversals, and dissolution in Sardinal. In *Infrastructure, environment, and life in the Anthropocene* (ed) K. Hetherington, 17-44. Durham, N.C.: Duke University Press.

Blagoderov, V., I. Kitching, L. Livermore, T. Simonsen & V. Smith 2012. No specimen left behind: industrial scale digitization of natural history collections. *ZooKeys* **209**, 133-46.

boyd, d. & K. Crawford 2012. Critical questions for big data. *Information, Communication & Society* **15**, 662-79.

Canetti, E. 1981 [1960]. *Crowds and power* (trans. C. Stewart). New York: Continuum.

Costello, M.J., R.M. May & N.E. Stork 2013. Can we name earth's species before they go extinct? *Science* **339**, 413-16.

Crowder, J.W., M. Fortun, R. Besara & L. Poirie (eds) 2020. *Anthropological data in the digital age: new possibilities – new challenges*. Cham: Springer.

Daston, L. 2004. Type specimens and scientific memory. *Critical Inquiry* **31**, 153-82.

Edwards, P., G. Bowker, S. Jackson & R. Williams 2009. Introduction: An agenda for infrastructure studies. *Journal of the Association for Information Systems* **10**, 364-74.

Escobar, A. 1999. After nature: steps to an antiessentialist political ecology. *Current Anthropology* **40**, 1-30.

Franklin, S. 2003. Re-thinking nature-culture: anthropology and the new genetics. *Anthropological Theory* **3**, 65-85.

Geismar, H. 2013. Defining the digital. *Museum Anthropology Review* **7**, 254-63.

——— 2018. *Museum Object Lessons for the Digital Age*. London: UCL Press.

Heumann, I., H. Stöcker, M. Tamborini & M. Vennen (eds) 2018. *Dinosaurierfragmente: Zur Geschichte der Tendaguru-Expedition und Ihrer Objekte, 1906-2018*. Göttingen: Wallstein.

Kirksey, E. 2015. Species: a praxiographic study. *Journal of the Royal Anthropological Institute* (N.S.) **21**, 758-80.

Kitchin, R. 2014. Big data, new epistemologies and paradigm shifts. *Big Data & Society* **1**: 1 (available online: *http://journals.sagepub.com/doi/abs/10.1177/2053951714528481*, accessed 15 January 2021).

Knorr Cetina, K. 1999. *Epistemic cultures: how the sciences make knowledge*. Cambridge, Mass.: Harvard University Press.

Kroupa, A., F. Glöckler & B. Schurian 2015. Effiziente Arbeitsabläufe und innovative Methoden zur Erschließung und dauerhaften Verfügbarmachung objektreicher Spezialsammlungen am Beispiel der entomologischen Sammlung des Museum für Naturkunde Berlin. Abschlussbericht. Berlin: Museum für Naturkunde Berlin (available online: *https://www.museumfuernaturkunde.berlin/sites/default/files/abschlussbericht_eos_mfn.pdf*, accessed 15 January 2021).

Latour, B. 1987. *Science in action: how to follow scientists and engineers through society*. Cambridge, Mass.: Harvard University Press.

——— 1999. *Pandora's hope: essays on the reality of science studies*. Cambridge, Mass.: Harvard University Press.

——— & S. Woolgar 1986. *Laboratory life: the construction of scientific facts*. Princeton: University Press.

Leonelli, S. 2016. *Data-centric biology: a philosophical study*. Chicago: University Press.

MacKinney, A.G. 2019. Nature's registry: documenting natural historical collection and trade in Prussia, 1770-1850. Ph.D. thesis, Humboldt-Universität zu Berlin.

Müller-Wille, S. 2017. Names and numbers: 'data' in classical natural history, 1758-1859. *Osiris* **32**, 109-28.

Nadim, T. 2020. System box (tray) with wasp. In *Boxes: a field guide* (eds) S. Bauer, M. Schlünder & M. Rentetzi, 109-23. Manchester: Mattering Press.

Nghonda, J. & S. Zacharie 2007. Colonial cartography as the diplomatic tool in the territorial formation of Kamerun (1884-1916). In *Proceedings of the 23th International Cartographic Conference*, 4-10. Moscow.

Raffles, H. 2010. *Insectopedia*. New York: Pantheon.

Ruckenstein, M. & N.D. Schüll 2017. The datafication of health. *Annual Review of Anthropology* **46**, 261-78.

Schnee, H. (ed.) 1920. *Deutsches Kolonial-Lexikon*, vol. **1**. Leipzig: Quelle & Meyer.

Journal of the Royal Anthropological Institute (N.S.) **27**, 62-75

SIMONS, A., A. LIS & I. LIPPERT 2014. The political duality of scale-making in environmental markets. *Environmental Politics* **23**, 632-49.

STOLER, A.L. 2008. Imperial debris: reflections on ruins and ruination. *Cultural Anthropology* **23**, 191-219.

STRATHERN, M. 1995. *The relation: issues in complexity and scale*. Cambridge: Prickly Pear Press.

——— 2004. *Partial connections*. Walnut Creek, Calif.: AltaMira Press.

SUBRAMANIAM, B. 2014. *Ghost stories for Darwin: the science of variation and the politics of diversity*. Urbana: University of Illinois Press.

SUMARTOJO, S., S. PINK, D. LUPTON & C. HEYES LE BOND 2016. The affective intensities of datafied space. *Emotion, Space and Society* **21**: November, 33-40.

TURNHOUT, E., E. DE LIJSTER & K. NEVES 2014. Measurementality in biodiversity governance: knowledge, transparency, and the Intergovernmental Science-Policy Platform on Biodiversity and Ecosystem Services (IPBES). *Environment and Planning A* **46**, 581-97.

VAN DIJCK, J. 2014. Datafication, dataism and dataveillance: Big Data between scientific paradigm and ideology. *Surveillance & Society* **12**, 197-208.

WARREN, R., J. PRICE, E. GRAHAM, N. FORSTENHAEUSLER & J. VANDERWAL 2018. The projected effect on insects, vertebrates, and plants of limiting global warming to 1.5°C rather than 2°C. *Science* **360**, 791-5.

WOOLGAR, S. & D. NEYLAND 2013. *Mundane governance: ontology and accountability*. Oxford: University Press.

La donnéification de la nature : formations de données et nouvelles échelles en histoire naturelle

Résumé

Cet article s'intéresse à la disparition de certaines échelles et connexions tandis que d'autres font leur apparition, dans un contexte où l'histoire naturelle adopte des infrastructures de données digitales. Sur la base de travaux en cours au Musée d'histoire naturelle de Berlin, l'autrice suit la piste des relations entre les spécimens d'insectes et leurs informations écologiques matérielles et numériques. L'autrice applique la notion de « référence circulante » de Latour pour suivre les spécimens d'insectes au fil des taxonomies, des bases de données et des dispositifs de numérisation. En se concentrant sur les médiations humain-données dans les pratiques du musée en matière de commande, de description et de distribution des spécimens, l'article montre comment la « donnéification » de la nature rend présents des contextes conventionnellement dissociés, parmi lesquels le colonialisme allemand. En proposant le concept de formation de données, il suggère que les ethnographes ont une contribution forte à apporter en abordant les aléas et spécificités socioculturelles et historiques que renferment les données.

4
Future-proof: bunkered data centres and the selling of ultra-secure cloud storage

A.R.E. TAYLOR *University of Cambridge*

Abandoned after the Cold War, nuclear bunkers around the world have found afterlives as ultra-secure data storage sites for cloud computing providers. The operators of these bunkered data centres capitalize on the spatial, temporal, and material security affordances of their subterranean fortresses, promoting them as 'future-proof' cloud storage solutions. Taking the concept of 'future-proofing' as its entry-point, this essay explores how data centre professionals work with the imaginative properties of the bunker to configure data as an object to be securitized. The essay takes the form of an ethnographic tour through a UK-based data bunker. During this tour, threatening data futures and fragile data materialities are conjured in order to secure the conditions of possibility for the bunkered data centre's commercial continuity. Future-proofing, it is argued, provides a conceptual opening onto the entangled imperatives of security and marketing that drive the commercial data storage industry.

Underground clouds

Since the late 1990s, the material remnants of Cold War bunkers around the world have been progressively repurposed as digital data storage facilities for cloud computing companies. Civil defence shelters in Sweden and China, derelict Soviet command and control centres in Latvia and Lithuania, and abandoned Department of Defence bunkers in the United States have all been repackaged as commercial data centres to service the needs of information capitalism. Engineered to withstand the blast and radiation effects of megaton-level thermonuclear detonations, the bunkered data centre promises to provide the data it houses with a level of security unsurpassed by any other built structure. If, as historian Luke Bennett has observed, bunkers 'are a material testimony to the anxieties of their creators' (2011: 157), then the bunkered data centre is a site where anxieties surrounding digital data security take architectural form. While anthropologists have begun to explore the role that the accumulation of large volumes of digital data ('Big Data') now plays in security regimes, ranging from predictive policing to pandemic preparedness to the climate crisis, anthropological attention has yet fully to turn to the ways in which data itself is arising as an object to be securitized.

Journal of the Royal Anthropological Institute (N.S.) **27**, 76-94
© 2021 The Authors. *Journal of the Royal Anthropological Institute* published by John Wiley & Sons Ltd on behalf of Royal Anthropological Institute

Through an ethnographic tour of a bunkered data centre in Northern England, in this essay I trace the ways that data centre professionals work with the material-imaginative affordances of the bunker to market and sell what they call 'future-proof' data security. The term 'future-proof' was regularly invoked by employees of the bunkered data centre to describe and promote the security that the site offers. A focus on future-proofing provides an entry-point for exploring the ways that data centre security and marketing discourses, practices, and imaginaries strategically situate digital data storage in time. Such a focus also adds to understandings of the diverse temporal relationships that human beings imaginatively construct with bunkers. These haunting architectural objects have long proven to be complex sites of temporality and security, their concrete materiality generating imaginaries of protection from future threats and durability through time. Nuclear bunkers, in particular, are architectures through which humans have sought to manage time, generating alternative futures in the face of existential risk. As Joseph Masco has observed in his analysis of bunker-building projects during the Cold War: '[V]ia the promise of the bunker, the logical outcome of nuclear war – the destruction of the nation state in a radioactive firestorm – was denied and a different future horizon opened' (2009: 16). Today, with bunkers being rebranded as 'future-proof' cloud storage sites, their material, affective, and temporal intensities are being directed towards securing the future of digital data.

The empirical material presented here is drawn from fieldwork that was conducted in a bunkered data centre that is owned and operated by the cloud computing provider Fort Data Centres (hereafter referred to as 'Fort').[1] The following tour of Fort's data bunker is divided into four sections. The first section sets the scene for the tour. The second section explores how data centre professionals conjure threatening futures from which the bunker promises protection. The Fort team perform considerable work with the bunker to generate horizons of threat and insecurity that reaffirm the need for bunkered data storage. The third section traces the long-term futures of security that the material and temporal form of the bunker affords. The fourth section examines how the future-orientated durability of the bunker contrasts with the fragile materialities and temporalities of the data storage hardware it contains. Here I trace the ways that the Fort team foreground the vulnerable materiality of server hard drives in order to further certify the utility of the bunker. Through these four sections, I explore how the material properties of bunkered data centres, and the hardware they house, bring with them their own futures, fragilities, and durabilities that call forth different modalities of future-proofing. Following Andrew Shryock and Daniel Lord Smail's observation that, with any storage technology, 'the relationship between content and container is transformative' (2018: 49), this essay asks: how might a focus on data transform understandings of the bunker? And how might a focus on bunkers transform understandings of data?

In keeping with the dual mandate of this special issue, the aim of this essay is not only to demonstrate how anthropology, with its attentiveness to the socially generative qualities of materials, can help us better understand the temporal and material dimensions of cloud data storage, but also to expand anthropological explorations of future-orientated security practices and performances (Ghertner, McFann & Goldstein 2020; Holbraad & Pedersen 2013; Low & Maguire 2019; Maguire, Frois & Zurawski 2014). 'Future-proofing' adds a rich ethnographic concept to unfolding discussions within the discipline about the ways that futures are being acted upon within the current 'security moment' (Goldstein 2010: 487). The concept of future-proofing is

Journal of the Royal Anthropological Institute (N.S.) **27**, 76-94

increasingly finding purchase across a range of sectors and policy domains today, including cultural heritage and conservation, risk and resilience management, urban planning, and infrastructure engineering. Future-proofing typically defines a form of anticipative forward-planning that aims to ensure that the target object or asset – be it infrastructure, cities, businesses, valuable artworks, or digital data – will continue to operate, endure, or accrue value for a significant period of (linear) time 'into the future'. Future-proofing thus abuts with a number of future-orientated rationalities that have gained political traction over the last two decades, such as 'resilience' and 'preparedness' (Duffield 2011; 2013; Lakoff 2017). In line with these rationalities, the future is problematized as a timespace of uncertainty that can nevertheless be managed through strategic anticipatory action undertaken in the present (Anderson 2010). In the ethnographic context of the bunkered data centre, future-proofing is characterized by a temporal orientation that aims to protect data assets both *for* and *from* the future. Discourses, practices, and imaginaries of future-proof data storage place the emphasis on acting now to ensure the longevity of data whilst simultaneously protecting digital assets from a future that is figured as an unending field of imminent threat.

Beyond its role in data centre security discourses, future-proofing is a marketing term with which data centre professionals promote and position their facilities within a competitive cloud storage marketplace. A focus on future-proofing thus directs attention to the (often contradictory) entanglements of security and marketing in the commercial data centre. In the concluding section of this essay, I therefore reflect on the larger marketing logics of the future-proof data bunker. In doing so, this essay strengthens understandings of the visual politics and security performances of the data centre industry (Holt & Vonderau 2015; Jakobsson & Stiernstedt 2012; Taylor 2019; Veel 2018) and contributes to ongoing explorations of the relationship between digital data and the spaces and places in which it is stored (Johnson & Hogan 2018). Amidst growing interdisciplinary interest in the infrastructures that operate 'behind the screens' of cloud computing, data centres have surfaced as valuable infrastructural objects through which the materiality of the cloud, and its associated social and environmental costs, have been unpacked (Hogan 2015; Vonderau 2017). These buildings have provided an entry-point for investigating how cloud infrastructure has been grafted on top of previous industrial, military, colonial, and imperial legacies (Hu 2015; Jacobson & Hogan 2019; Johnson 2019; Pickren 2018; Rossiter 2016). Bunkered data centres have garnered considerable attention, with an array of news articles, magazine exposés, essays, and artworks exploring the striking dissonance between their excessive materiality and the image of immateriality conjured by the cloud metaphor (Charles 2016; Graham 2016; Jha 2009; Mingard 2014). These architectural curiosities have served not only as marked examples of the concrete materiality of cloud computing. With their history as spaces for the preservation and enactment of fractured state sovereignty in the aftermath of nuclear devastation, bunkered data centres have also proven to be valuable sites for thinking through the ways in which sovereign power hauntingly textures the cloud (Bratton 2015; Hu 2015).

While this burgeoning field of data centre studies has demonstrated that space and place continue to matter in globally distributed computing assemblages, considerably less attention has been paid to the security and marketing logics through which cloud providers themselves strive to make space and place matter to their clients. Contrary to the rhetoric that framed early discourses and imaginaries of the internet, which celebrated emancipation from the constraints of space, time, and materiality, the

Journal of the Royal Anthropological Institute (N.S.) **27**, 76-94
© 2021 The Authors. *Journal of the Royal Anthropological Institute* published by John Wiley & Sons Ltd on behalf of Royal Anthropological Institute

Figure 1. Barbed wire fencing surrounds the perimeter of the data bunker compound. (Image provided by DataGarrison.)

bunkered data centre presents an opportunity to further explore how these constraints are being rearticulated, reinforced, and attributed with security significance in relation to commercial data storage (DeNicola 2012). The tour that follows thus descends into the depths of subterranean cloud storage in order to examine the role that the bunker plays in the making and marketing of 'future-proof' data security.

A security safari
The first sign of Fort's data bunker, buried 100 feet beneath the countryside of Northern England, emerges in the form of a 11.5-foot-high chain-link fence, topped with barbed coils of razor wire (Fig. 1). The fence cuts through the surrounding farmland, aggressively demarcating the perimeter of the compound. Fort's main entrance area is complete with an assortment of security technologies: guardhouses, vehicle traps, galvanized steel security gates, rising arm barriers, hydraulic bollards, and CCTV cameras. Visitors are required to show two forms of ID at the security window of the guardhouse. The guard then checks their details against a visitor list and escorts them to the office complex, a flat-roofed, one-storey brick structure built above-ground within the compound. In the reception area, visitors must submit their ID documents to be scanned and logged. They are then issued with a visitor clearance pass.

One of the first things that visitors to the Fort data bunker encounter in the waiting room is a glass display cabinet that stands on the windowsill showcasing a 3-foot cylinder of concrete. The caption beneath reads: 'Diamond-drilled core showing the construction and depth of concrete between the upper and lower floors of the data centre'. Built from concrete as thick and durable as possible, the bunkered data centre has a 'brute materiality' (Dourish 2017: 140) that stands in stark contrast to the soft and fluffy 'cloud' conceit. Concrete walls themselves appear strangely at odds with the virtual 'walls' typically associated with data security: firewalls, anti-virus vaults, and spyware and spam filters. Similarly, the bunker's military logics of enclosure and defence seem somewhat outdated when faced with the transgressive digital 'flows' of networked data and the fibre-optic hyperconnectivity required of a data centre. Yet Cold War bunkers have always been paradoxical infrastructures, simultaneously connected and disconnected, open and closed. These sites were designed to ensure continuous communications with branches of government through secure cable corridors whilst also hermetically sealing themselves off from the outside world to function as self-contained 'security islands' (Duffield 2011: 766). More than an outmoded piece of security theatre, the reinforced concrete of the bunker is a key component in what Fort call their 'multi-layered' approach to security, which combines physical and digital security measures.

The symbolic properties of concrete as a construction material play a strategic role in the security capacities and aesthetics of Fort's facility, staging the solidity, strength, and durability of the bunker. Images of the concrete walls, along with reinforced steel doors, can be found throughout Fort's marketing materials, from the promotional leaflets in the waiting room to the image gallery on their website, where they brand their bunker as 'the UK's most resilient data centre'. These hardened materials also take centre stage during tours of the facility. Like most commercial data centres, Fort provide prospective clients with opportunities to visit the site. These site visits enable potential customers to experience the security of the data centre first-hand and to meet the data centre employees who will be looking after their precious digital assets. For the facility operators at Fort, these visits are valuable opportunities to showcase the security affordances of the site, promoting the bunker as the future-proof solution to the client's data storage needs. For this reason, at Fort, these site visits are referred to as 'security safaris'.

My security safari at the compound was arranged by Jonathan Applegate, Fort's Managing Director. Applegate met me in the waiting room and led me to his office. Proceeding through a security door with a biometric fingerprint lock, we entered a corridor with long rectangular windows on either side, presenting views onto employees typing at computers and talking on telephones: the service desk operators, systems administrators, and cybersecurity team. A wide range of customers store their data with Fort, including retailers, the NHS, IT disaster recovery vendors, district councils from around the United Kingdom, and some departments of the UK government. The vast majority of Fort's clients work in the payment card industry and banking. Fort offer a range of IT services, data storage options, and security and recovery solutions, promising to provide their clients with what Applegate called 'total data assurance'. In his office at the end of the corridor, he took a seat behind his desk in front of a bulletproof window facing the compound's car park. He talked me through the logic behind the bunkered data centre. In contrast to above-ground data centres, which are often constructed in what he referred to as 'flimsy-looking warehouses', he told me that 'the bunker addresses a need in the data centre marketplace for facilities that provide more robust and resilient physical security'. Applegate explained that data security is persistently dematerialized in popular imaginaries of computing: 'Most people tend to think of the cyber-side of data security: hackers, viruses, and cyberattacks', he told me, 'which dangerously overlooks the physical side'. The principal reasons behind this critical oversight, he suggested, were persistent media attention on

Journal of the Royal Anthropological Institute (N.S.) **27**, 76-94
© 2021 The Authors. *Journal of the Royal Anthropological Institute* published by John Wiley & Sons Ltd on behalf of Royal Anthropological Institute

cyberterrorism and the misleading metaphors that are commonly used to apprehend internet infrastructure, such as the 'cloud' and 'cyberspace'.

As many cultural commentators have noted, the metaphorical conceit of the 'cloud' presents online data storage as a transcendental, placeless operation, occurring 'everywhere and nowhere in particular' (Carruth 2014: 340). Applegate explained that this transcendental imaginary results in a narrow understanding of data security that can lead organizations to unknowingly compromise their 'digital assets'. He presented a scenario: while data is often duplicated across multiple storage facilities to reduce the likelihood of data loss, an organization's sensitive digital information could be compromised if an unauthorized actor breached one of those data centres and walked out with a server. 'It doesn't matter how backed-up your data is or how great your digital defences are', he elaborated, 'if you can't stop a brute force breach'. Over the last two decades, there have been a number of heists at high-profile data centres, where intruders have gained access and stolen servers containing customer databases, credit card information, and data related to criminal proceedings.[2] Applegate told me that Fort 'store a lot of sensitive and valuable information' and their clients need to know that their data isn't going to be stolen, whether physically or digitally. Fort's customers also need uninterruptible 24/7/365 access to their data. During our conversation, Applegate thus conjured a multitude of threats that could disrupt the operations of a standard data centre but from which the bunker promises protection, ranging from car bombs to hurricane-force winds to falling trees to microchip-melting electromagnetic pulses (EMPs). 'Every data centre can deal with cyberattacks', he told me, 'but the majority wouldn't stand a chance if there was a vehicle-ramming attack or a terrorist heist'. The security safari is a key tool through which possible threats to data are further conjured and concretized, providing Fort with an opportunity to foreground the role that materiality and location can play in 'proofing' data from these threatening futures.

Conjuring threatening futures

My tour of the Fort data bunker was led by Michael Bates, an ex-Royal Marine and the head of Fort's team of security guards. Most data centres source their guard labour from military or police backgrounds. At Fort, the uniform of the security team follows a military aesthetic, consisting of black 'army-tactical' combat boots, military-grade cargo trousers in black camo, and a black fleece with 'Fort: Ultra Secure' embroidered on the left chest. The security guards work in rotating shifts twenty-four hours a day throughout the year. They patrol the perimeter of the compound (often with their Ministry of Defence-trained guard dogs), operate various guard posts, and organize preparedness training exercises for Fort's staff. Alongside these activities, the security guards also double as 'tour guides', escorting clients during their site visits.

The bunker itself is a solid inclined mass of grass-covered concrete that surfaces in the centre of the compound (Fig. 2). As Bates and I left the office complex and made our way up the access road towards the bunker, we passed a derelict brick guardhouse and some large concrete radar plinths; the crumbling remains of the site's past life as a radar data centre. In their marketing, Fort capitalize on the military heritage of their facility, highlighting that 'the construction and security standards are what you might expect of such a purpose-built fortress'. A closer look at the site's past reveals a history of repurposing and technological obsolescence, while also providing a window onto Cold War military 'data histories' (Aronova, von Oertzen & Sepkoski 2017). The bunker was built in the early 1950s and formed part of a UK-wide network of radar sites for

Journal of the Royal Anthropological Institute (N.S.) **27**, 76-94
© 2021 The Authors. *Journal of the Royal Anthropological Institute* published by John Wiley & Sons Ltd on behalf of Royal Anthropological Institute

Figure 2. The exterior of Fort's bunkered data centre. (Image provided by Fort Data Centres.)

making and moving data in anticipation of nuclear warfare. The principal purpose of
the bunker was not to protect human beings, but to facilitate data processing. The radars
scanned the electromagnetic spectrum, monitoring the movement of potential nuclear
missile-carrying aircraft, providing personnel in the bunker below with a view onto an
electronic world of data feeds and illuminated blips mediated by console screens. This
data was then relayed to sector operations centres via teleprinter networks or in the
form of voice communications over dedicated telephone landlines.

Five years after opening, the facility was closed because the radar systems it used were
unable to accurately track the faster jet aircraft that had emerged. As David F. Bell has
observed, the length of time it took to build such fortifications often meant they were
'obsolete even before they could actually serve their imagined purpose' (2008: 216).
The bunker remained empty until the mid-1960s, when it was reopened as part of a
dual-purpose civil and military radar network. Signal data was stored on large magnetic
drums and transferred to command-and-control centres via narrow band data links. In
1974, the site was again closed, only to be reactivated six years later as a reserve Royal
Air Force (RAF) reporting centre, with radar data being transferred into the facility
from other stations and analysed by operators. The site continued to operate as a data
switching point until the dissolution of the Soviet Union in 1991. The bunker was left
largely abandoned, with Fort purchasing the freeholds to the site in 1998. The form of
the bunker has thus persistently outlasted its function.

As Bates and I neared the entrance to the bunker, he talked me through some
of the features that make the facility future-proof. He explained that the bunker's
strategic spatial location outside of high-risk city centre zones reduces its vulnerability
to terrorism. He pointed out a number of infrared CCTV cameras that monitor the
compound. Fort's surveillance practices extend beyond the perimeter of the site, with
members of the security team patrolling a two-mile radius around the facility, on

Figure 3. The armour-plated entrance doors to the data bunker. (Image provided by Fort Data Centres.)

foot and in vehicles. He directed my attention to two large EMP-resistant shipping containers above the bunker that contain diesel generators, enabling the facility to operate off-grid for up two months in the event of an extended power outage.

At the armour-plated entrance door to the bunker (Fig. 3), Bates tapped a passcode into the electronic lock and swiped his card through the access control system. The secure solidity and durability that the hardened materials of the bunker promise are sensorially foregrounded throughout the security safari in a well-rehearsed routine. Bates invited me to try to pull the door open, describing it as 'weighing several tons'. When I did so, the door moved only with great effort. Inside the facility, another security guard sat in a small room behind some bulletproof plexiglass. He buzzed us through a mantrap (Fig. 4), and we descended into the depths of the facility via a steel staircase, our footsteps echoing in the cavernous space.

The interior of the bunker is divided into three levels that form a nested series of securitized areas within a carapace of concrete, locked behind doors that run along dimly lit corridors. Bates explained that many of the rooms in the bunker remain empty. Empty space is vital to future-proofing Fort as a business. The ability to expand computing capacity in response to demand from future customers is essential to ensuring long-term growth. Unlike many above-ground data centres, which are modular in design, the square footage of the bunker is limited and must therefore be carefully managed. As we made our way through the facility, Bates conjured Cold War threats into the present. 'The Cold War might be over', he told me, 'but the nuclear threat has never gone away'. Patting his hand on the hardened ferrocement wall, he reassured me that, 'fortunately, this place has been designed to withstand the force of a 22-kiloton nuclear bomb'. Perpetuating the unending possibility of nuclear threat for visiting clients, Bates positioned the Fort bunker in a state of

Figure 4. The author entering the bunkered data centre through a full-height turnstile security gate. (Image provided by Fort Data Centres.)

active waiting for thermonuclear futures. The bunkered data centre stands in stark contrast to the Cold War bunkers that have been converted into heritage or museum sites. John Beck has suggested that musealized bunkers strive to distance visitors from the possibility of nuclear war, functioning as reassuring 'reminders of how things are no longer dangerous' (2011: 95). By contrast, the bunkered data centre strives to maintain the bunker's original threat-related uses and meanings (cf. Bennett 2020: 3). The Fort data bunker thus embeds cloud storage not only within the material remains of a military redoubt but also within its security logics, imaginaries, and futures.

Conjuring possible future threats against which the solid materiality of the bunker guarantees protection is central to the selling of bunkered data storage. Anna Tsing has used the term 'conjuring' to capture the imaginative work that investment companies engage in to entice speculators. 'In speculative enterprises', Tsing observes, 'profit must be imagined before it can be extracted; the possibility of economic performance must be conjured like a spirit to draw an audience of potential investors' (2001: 159). If financial speculation is based on conjuring utopian futures of profit, the selling of bunkered cloud storage is based on conjuring the spectre of disaster. The bunker plays an active role in the conjuring process, operationalizing certain imaginative horizons while closing down others. Applegate highlighted this during our conversation in his office when he exclaimed: 'You can't *not* think about the end of the world when you see a bunker!' The bunker is exemplary of the ways that certain infrastructures, landscapes or spaces afford 'particular imaginary scenarios' (Nielsen & Pedersen 2015: 250). As a building type born from the anticipation of catastrophe, bunkers are 'technologies' (Sneath, Holbraad & Pedersen 2009) through which imaginaries of threatening futures have long been generated.

At the same time, while the bunker may lend itself to end-of-the-world visions, Bates was careful to remind me that many of Fort's clients are concerned less with a global technological apocalypse and more with their own 'personal doomsdays'. He explained that, as organizational reliance on digital information continues to grow, data loss or disruption of service take on an increasingly existential quality, potentially putting an end to their clients' operations. During the tour, he thus conjured possible threats that could disrupt data centre service delivery, only to rhetorically dispel them with the 'future-proof' form of the bunker. 'Terrorists, nukes, floods: nothing is getting in here', he told me as he locked a 25-ton blast door behind us (Fig. 5), sealing us inside the 'closed world' (Edwards 1996) of Cold War concrete.

If the Cold War bunker primarily promised sanctuary (however illusory this may have been) from an irradiated nuclear future, in its repurposed form as a data centre, it now peddles protection for the ever-multiplying threats that vie for attention in contemporary securityscapes. As Bradley Garrett and Ian Klinke have observed, the bunkers that are being put to use today are 'no longer limited to a specific disaster imagination' (2018: 1075). Rather, they have been reimagined and rebranded as multi-disaster resistant structures for 'all-hazards' preparedness (Deville, Guggenheim & Hrdličková 2014). This is captured by the 'future-proofing' concept itself, which is orientated not towards a specific threat but towards an indeterminate future that is filled with catastrophic possibility (Horn 2018). Promising to provide their clients with uninterruptible access to data amidst an ever-expanding spectrum of threat scenarios, on their website Fort brand their bunker as 'ultra-secure' and, in reference to the continuous IT uptime it offers, 'ultra-available'.

Deep-time data storage

The bunker does not only promise to protect data *from* threatening futures but also strives to ensure that data can survive *into* the future. As we continued through the bunker, Bates foregrounded the security afforded by the durable form of the built

Figure 5. Steel blast-proof doors with hermetically sealed airlocks promise to ensure that the data stored in the bunker will survive any eventuality. (Image provided by DataGarrison.)

structure. He invited me to knock on the cold concrete walls to 'feel how solid they are', and confidently told me that 'bunkers are built to last, like the pyramids'.[3] The apparent timelessness of bunkers has previously invited comparisons to the enduring megastructures of ancient civilizations, with Paul Virilio famously comparing them to 'the Egyptian mastabas, the Etruscan tombs, the Aztec structures' (2009 [1975]: 11). Conjuring the durable monuments of the ancient Egyptians, Bates worked with the material-imaginative resonances of the bunker to promote the site as a structure that can withstand not only a nuclear blast, but time itself.[4] This material resistance to time is similarly evoked by the metaphor of 'future-proofing', which draws its rhetorical efficacy from other 'proofing' practices, such as waterproofing and soundproofing, to conjure the future as an almost-material entity against which the present can be shielded through the bunker's sheer materiality.

The material durability of the bunker has become a central aspect of Fort's marketing. Emerging regulatory frameworks increasingly require firms to retain and preserve data for decades after its use. Capitalizing on the temporal endurance that the materiality of the bunker affords, bunkered data centres have become key sites in which an emerging market for long-term data storage and preservation has taken root. Fort offer what they call a 'long-term deep archive solution' for clients who want to store 'cold' data that they don't need to access often. A number of subterranean data centres have begun to branch out from the provision of business continuity and move into the realm of cultural continuity, positioning themselves as deep-time media infrastructures (Mattern 2015; Zielinski 2006) for the long-term storage and preservation of digital cultural heritage.[5]

Continuing his narrative of eternal data storage, Bates informed me that 'when we're wiped out, the data down here will be all that's left of us'. In this scenario, the digital information stored on the subterranean servers becomes a 'new type of human remains'

Journal of the Royal Anthropological Institute (N.S.) **27**, 76-94
© 2021 The Authors. *Journal of the Royal Anthropological Institute* published by John Wiley & Sons Ltd on behalf of Royal Anthropological Institute

(Lupton 2018: 6) – a future fossil that will most likely be unreadable due to format obsolescence or data decay. Bunkers have long provided an eerie prism through which onlookers have envisioned artefacts of their own time as future ruins. W.G. Sebald famously reimagined the abandoned bunkers at Orford Ness in Suffolk as the 'remains of our own civilisation after its extinction in some future catastrophe' (1998: 237). In Bates's narrative, with the human race annihilated, the bunkered data centre becomes an accidental time capsule: a data tomb.

Scholarship on bunkers has often emphasized their 'womb- and tomb-like' properties (Beck 2011: 82; see also Bell 2008: 217; Virilio 2009 [1975]: 46). As Adam Fish and Bradley Garrett (2019) note, the bunker is 'a socially and culturally constituted womb from which objects, people, and information are meant to be recovered – and a tomb when recovery becomes impossible'. Fish and Garrett identify 'recovery' as a uniting logic of both bunkers and data centres. Recovery services are a key feature of cloud security packages. If a client should experience a disaster, data centres aim to quickly re-boot the IT systems that underpin their businesses. Yet a focus on recovery doesn't fully capture the everyday operating logic of the bunkered data centre, or the factors that drive clients to store their data with Fort. During my security safari with Bates, he suggested that 'resilience', rather than 'recovery', is the main selling point of the bunker. 'Recovery places the emphasis on cleaning up *after* an event', he told me, 'rather than operational continuance *during* an event'. I encountered a similar logic when I met with James Longley, the Marketing Director of DataGarrison, a London-based business continuity provider that use Fort's bunker as their primary data storage site. During our conversation, Longley explained that 'recovery' is an essential component of business continuity, but 'with a bunker you increase the likelihood that you won't get to the recovery stage because they are built to be resilient'. Further reinforcing his point, Longley stated: 'Why not reduce the need to recover in the first place by storing your data in a resilient infrastructure?' While definitions of resilience vary, in the domain of disaster management it is often understood as referring to 'a basic ability to withstand shock and survive disaster … while still retaining essential functionality' (Duffield 2013: 55). As 'resilient infrastructures', bunkers, Longley suggested, are built to withstand disaster and to continue operating through even the most extreme events, meaning there should rarely be a need to 'recover' or 'resurrect' data. For DataGarrison, the bunker's promise of future resurrection was secondary to its promise of resilience, endurance, and continuity in the present.

Fragile data futures

The durable materiality of the bunker jars with the limited lifespan of the digital hardware it contains, which operates on an altogether different timescale. Fish and Garrett (2019) have suggested that theorization of bunkers must necessarily address the relationship between 'the materiality of the bunker and temporality of its contents'. Indeed, the security a bunker offers is shaped – and sometimes subverted – by its contents. While the bunker endures, the hard disk drives, servers, and other technical computing components stored within are fragile and prone to failure, decay, and rapid obsolescence. Given the limited lifespan of digital technologies, the servers on which Fort store their clients' data might typically be conceived as 'future vulnerable' rather than 'future-proof' (Edwards, Jackson, Bowker & Williams 2009: 371). At Fort, however, the fragile materiality of the computing equipment provides another opportunity to

© 2021 The Authors. *Journal of the Royal Anthropological Institute* published by John Wiley & Sons Ltd on behalf of Royal Anthropological Institute

Figure 6. The more-than-human environs of the data hall. (Image provided by DataGarrison.)

promote the future-proof data security on offer, as I experienced when Bates and I entered one of the bunker's data halls.

Mid-way down one of the corridors, Bates waved his card in front of an e-reader next to an armoured door. The unlocking process was initiated with an electronic beeping sound. Releasing a gust of cold air, the door opened onto a room full of server cabinets: the data hall (Fig. 6). Configured and calibrated for the sole purpose of providing optimal conditions for data storage, the data hall is a decidedly nonhuman space. Air conditioners noisily circulate cold air around the rows of servers to prevent them from overheating. A room temperature of 18-23°C and a humidity level of 45-55 per cent must be maintained to provide ambient cooling and to prevent fires, ensuring that critical server components are not damaged. Whilst walking between the servers, Bates and I met Will Hartley, one of Fort's technicians. Hartley was wearing a thick North Face parka to avoid the breeze from the air conditioners and was busy installing a new server. He has worked at Fort for the past ten years and spends most of his time in the data hall, fixing and replacing servers. Hartley warned that the hard disk drives (HDDs) inside the servers are particularly fragile and prone to failure. He explained that these devices are therefore routinely replaced every twelve months. Much of Hartley's work involves what he called 'pre-emptive upgrading': the anticipatory retiring of servers, whether they are broken or not. 'We can't sit around and wait for a hard drive to fail', he told me, 'we have to act before it breaks'. By discarding servers before they have a chance to malfunction, Hartley 'proofs' the bunker against future hardware failure, removing hard drives from their trajectories of decay and deterioration. Through this anticipatory maintenance, whereby data is constantly migrated from discarded drives to new drives, data is made to endure across ephemeral hardware (Chun 2011).

Mindful of the excessive waste that pre-emptive upgrading produces, Hartley justified this practice as a standard future-proofing measure throughout the data centre industry and an unavoidable consequence of the fact that businesses, governments, and the lives of individuals are increasingly structured around a dependence on data stored on fragile media. To highlight the fragile materiality of digital storage media, Hartley prised open the casing of a decommissioned server and showed me the delicate mechanical parts of the hard drive housed within. He explained that a variety of contaminants can cause lasting damage to server hard drives. Dust, plant pollens, human hair, smoke fumes, and liquid droplets can all interfere with their fragile mechanisms, causing corrosion, oxide flake-off, or equipment failure. Photoelectric sensors are thus positioned at strategic points within the data hall to detect threatening particulate matter. Here we encounter what Garrett and Klinke have termed the 'more-than-human bunker' (2018: 1078).

Reverberations from passing traffic, especially heavy goods vehicles, can also damage hard drive mechanisms. The low traffic levels on the quiet country roads surrounding the Fort facility thus provide an additional layer of security. 'This is why location is so important when it comes to server storage', Hartley informed me. Another selling point of the facility in this regard is the 'vibration-proof' construction of the walls. One of Fort's online promotional videos provides viewers with extensive details about the composition of the walls, which are made from 'three metres of reinforced concrete, followed by one-and-a-half metres of fine-grade flint and tungsten rods, and then a rubber buffer strip'. The rubber buffer strip, we are told, helps absorb the shockwave associated with nuclear blasts and also protects the data centre from earthquakes.

Hartley drew my attention to one corner of the data hall, in which a number of servers were locked inside a Faraday cage: a metal enclosure that was installed during the Cold War to protect the bunker's computing equipment from EMPs generated by nuclear detonations. Now protecting the servers of clients that want to pay extra to ensure their data will survive an EMP event, the Faraday shielding reinscribes cloud storage within Cold War vectors of threat; a further reminder that, at the Fort data bunker, such threats are not past but actively structure its present technical configurations. 'Any and every data centre can upgrade hard drives to protect against equipment failure', Hartley explained, 'but only the most secure can ensure that hard drives aren't damaged if a bomb detonates nearby or an EMP goes off. Echoing Applegate, Hartley suggested that many organizations put their data at risk when they don't prioritize the physical security of their cloud provider's data centres. Despite the promise of placeless, transcendental, or dematerialized data storage, my time in the data hall with Hartley served as a reminder not only that cloud storage is emphatically material, but also that significant stakes are invested in *making* cloud storage material.

Conclusion: Re-materializing data storage

As a security framework, future-proofing constructs the future as a permanent threat-space against which Fort promise to protect clients' data. The impenetrability of the bunker barricades against external threats like bomb blasts and server heists, while offering a durable architecture to ensure the longevity of the data it contains. Anticipatory practices of pre-emptive upgrading further 'proof' data from futures of hardware failure and obsolescence. Future-proofing thus provides the data centre professionals at Fort with an elastic temporal framework with which they can navigate and negotiate shifting scales of security and threat across time. It is also an evocative marketing term that Fort frequently employ in their promotional material.

Back in the main office complex after my security safari with Bates, Applegate further elaborated on the marketing logics of the data bunker. 'The more we can make people realize that their data, their online services, and all the apps they use are stored in real, fragile buildings somewhere', he zealously told me, 'the more they'll want the best secured data centre to store their stuff'. Applegate presented the selling of future-proof data storage as less about producing (and profiting from) fear, and more about raising awareness of the material vulnerability of cloud storage. He explained that users have a right to what he called 'robust and resilient' data security – a right that he felt is obfuscated by the 'cloud' conceit.

If, as John Durham Peters has observed, the cloud metaphor evokes 'ideas of a heavenly record' (2015: 332), Fort strive to dismantle this vision of data transcendence by rendering cloud storage visible, material, and vulnerable. The security safari is just one tool through which they attempt to do this. Their website, their social media, and their online videos provide other promotional channels, as do the trade fairs and expo events that they attend. Through these different marketing platforms, they strive to render data materially vulnerable, offering the 'future-proof' bunker as a secure cloud storage solution. It is thus not only threats to data that are being conjured at Fort but also the threatening material fragility of cloud storage itself. In his forensic history of the hard disk drive, Matthew Kirschenbaum (2008) has traced how, over the course of the twentieth century, digital data storage became increasingly invisible. From punched card and magnetic drums, data storage gradually moved into the computer, becoming locked inside the plastic casing of desktop towers and laptop shells. As new paradigms of distributed computing, such as the cloud, normalize the storing and processing of data at a distance, the materiality of digital storage becomes 'ever more abstracted and removed from daily awareness' (Kirschenbaum 2008: 19). At Fort, considerable effort is invested in undoing this process. Online data storage must be made visible and material if it is to be made vulnerable, and it must be made vulnerable if bunkered data storage is to be sold. Through this double conjuring of threat and materiality, the spaces and places of cloud storage are made to matter, producing the conditions of possibility for the bunkered data centre's commercial continuity.

Journal of the Royal Anthropological Institute (N.S.) 27, 76-94
© 2021 The Authors. *Journal of the Royal Anthropological Institute* published by John Wiley & Sons Ltd on behalf of Royal Anthropological Institute

Fort's commitment to dispelling the 'myth of immateriality' (Appadurai & Alexander 2020: 76) that enshrouds the cloud aligns, if somewhat incongruently, with recent critical efforts to render cloud infrastructure visible. 'Making the invisible visible' and 'grounding the cloud' have become both mantras and methodologies for directing attention to the infrastructure that is rhetorically erased by the cloud metaphor. By materializing the digital through a variety of visual practices, scholars, journalists, and artists have highlighted the social, material, and environmental impact of cloud computing. The question now is not whether cloud storage is material but how, in what ways, and to what ends is the (im)materiality of online data storage established in different spatiotemporal and geographic settings? The ways that bunkered data centres themselves work to render cloud storage strategically visible and material invites further reflection on the multiple registers, negotiations, and performances of (in)visibility and (im)materiality involved in the marketing and securitizing of commercial data centres (Amoore 2018; Furlong 2021). While specific types of data centre, such as those operated by intelligence agencies, may strive to remain invisible, for many commercial data centres, which rely on attracting clients through marketing, strategic visibility is often essential. This is especially the case with data centres that have been retrofitted inside nuclear bunkers, where the security promised by the spectacular setting is a unique selling point that must be emphasized as a key factor of product differentiation in the data centre marketplace. As Applegate highlighted: 'If people think their data's just stored in some make-believe cloud, this is bad for our business'.

In this sense, the bunkered data centre departs from the visual logics that guided the Cold War bunker, when these defensive installations were required to remain hidden. As Beck (2011: 83) reminds us, 'a visible bunker is to a large extent disarmed'. In an attempt to address the vulnerability that accompanies visibility and locatability, Fort have removed their facility from 'street view' in Google Maps (but not from the 'satellite view'). Managing the contradictory imperatives of security and marketing is continuous work. Further vulnerabilities arise from the ageing architecture of the bunker itself, which requires Fort to invest considerable expense in maintaining the property.

The Fort data bunker thus appeals to a particularly security-conscious clientele who are attuned to the role that location, time, and materiality can play in 'proofing' digital data from a spectrum of scenarios that unfold across different scales of threat, ranging from server hijackings by hostile actors, to the failure of critical hardware, to regulatory incompliance. With cloud clients increasingly required to meet various security, regulatory, or sustainability mandates, the location and material impact of data centres is taking on heightened significance for both cloud providers and their customers alike. The operators of bunkered data centres capitalize on the spatial, temporal, and material security value of their subterranean fortresses, promising their clients that their data will survive any eventuality. In the future-proof data bunker, threats to the security and survivability of data are thus simultaneously things against which protection is offered and from which profit can be extracted.

NOTES

I would like to thank the Editors of this special issue, as well as the anonymous reviewers, for their insightful feedback on previous drafts. Funding for the research described in this essay was carried out with the assistance of a Sutasoma Award from the Radcliffe-Brown Trust Fund of the Royal Anthropological Institute.

[1] The material presented in this essay is drawn from ongoing fieldwork and interviews with data centre professionals that began in summer 2015. The names of individuals and companies have been changed to protect the privacy of interlocutors.

[2] Although relatively rare occurrences in comparison to digital breaches, there have been some major server heists: in October 2007, armed intruders broke into CI Host, a Chicago-based colocation data centre and stole twenty servers; in December 2007, five men dressed in police uniforms gained entry to a Verizon data centre in London, stealing £2 million worth of equipment; in July 2008, the *Financial Times*' web hosting equipment was stolen from a data centre in Watford (UK); in February 2011, thieves stole equipment from a Vodafone data centre in Basingstoke (UK); and in November 2015, five servers were stolen from the data centre of the charity Plan UK, containing the personal details of 90,000 donors.

[3] The data-centre-as-pyramid has recently found architectural expression in the pyramid-shaped facility operated by Switch and located near Grand Rapids, Michigan. Switch, who refer to themselves as 'a globally recognized leader in future-proof data centre design', turn to the pyramid to communicate the future-proof aesthetic.

[4] A similar feature has been highlighted by media theorists Peter Jakobsson and Fredrik Stiernstedt (2012) in their study of Pionen, a data centre located inside a former civil defence bunker built into the bedrock of Stockholm. They examine the role that the geological history of the site plays in staging the facility as a secure storage space 'constructed for eternity' (2012: 112).

[5] The data preservation company Piql (pronounced 'pickle') operate the Arctic World Archive from inside an abandoned coal mine on the archipelago of Svalbard, Norway. Modelled on the nearby Global Seed Vault, Piql combine the material endurance of their underground location with a digital data preservation service, whereby they transfer data onto a durable tape-based storage medium – a process they refer to as 'pickling' data (hence their name). Known as 'the digital world's Doomsday Vault', on their website Piql promise 'to keep data alive for centuries'. Elsewhere, the National Library of Norway archive and store their databanks in the mountain facilities at Mo i Rana. The US-based information management services company, Iron Mountain, preserve digital and analogue media in a nuke-proof underground vault in Pennsylvania. The Swiss-based data bunker complex Mount10 (pronounced 'Mountain') also specialize in the long-term storage of digital data.

REFERENCES

AMOORE, L. 2018. Cloud geographies: computing, data, sovereignty. *Progress in Human Geography* **42**, 4-24.

ANDERSON, B. 2010. Preemption, precaution, preparedness: anticipatory action and future geographies. *Progress in Human Geography* **34**, 777-98.

APPADURAI, A. & N. ALEXANDER 2020. *Failure*. Cambridge: Polity.

ARONOVA, E., C. VON OERTZEN & D. SEPKOSKI 2017. Introduction: Historicizing big data. *Osiris* **32**, 1-17.

BECK, J. 2011. Concrete ambivalence: inside the bunker complex. *Cultural Politics* **7**, 79-102.

BELL, D.F. 2008. Bunker busting and bunker mentalities, or is it safe to be underground? *South Atlantic Quarterly* **107**, 213-29.

——— 2011. The bunker: metaphor, materiality and management. *Culture and Organization* **17**, 155-73.

BENNETT, L. 2020. The bunker's after-life: cultural production in the ruins of the Cold War. *Journal of War & Culture Studies* **13**, 1-10.

BRATTON, B.H. 2015. *The stack: on software and sovereignty*. Cambridge, Mass.: MIT Press.

CARRUTH, A. 2014. The digital cloud and the micropolitics of energy. *Public Culture* **26**, 339-64.

CHARLES, E. 2016. White mountain (available online: *http://www.emma-charles.com/white-mountain*, accessed 18 January 2021).

CHUN, W. 2011. The enduring ephemeral, or the future is a memory. In *Media archaeology: approaches, applications and implications* (eds) E. Huhtamo & J. Parikka, 184-206. Berkeley: University of California Press.

DeNICOLA, L. 2012. Geomedia: the reassertion of space within digital culture. In *Digital anthropology* (eds) H.A. Horst & D. Miller, 80-98. London: Berg.

DEVILLE, J., M. GUGGENHEIM & Z. HRDLIČKOVÁ 2014. Concrete governmentality: shelters and the transformations of preparedness. In *Disasters and politics: materials, experiments, preparedness* (eds) M. Tironi, I. Rodríguez-Giralt & M. Guggenheim, 183-210. Chichester: Wiley Blackwell, for The Sociological Review.

DOURISH, P. 2017. *The stuff of bits: an essay on the materialities of information*. Cambridge, Mass.: MIT Press.

DUFFIELD, M. 2011. Total war as environmental terror: linking liberalism, resilience, and the bunker. *South Atlantic Quarterly* **110**, 757-69.

Journal of the Royal Anthropological Institute (N.S.) **27**, 76-94

——— 2013. How did we become unprepared? Emergency and resilience in an uncertain world. *British Academy Review* **21**, 55-8.

EDWARDS, P.N. 1996. *The closed world: computers and the politics of discourse in Cold War America.* Cambridge, Mass.: MIT Press.

———, S.J. JACKSON, R.G.C. BOWKER & R. WILLIAMS 2009. Introduction: An agenda for infrastructure studies. *Journal of the Association for Information Systems* **10**, 364-74.

FISH, A. & B.L. GARRETT 2019. Resurrection from bunkers and data centers. *Culture Machine* **18** (available online: *https://culturemachine.net/vol-18-the-nature-of-data-centers/resurrection-from-bunkers/*, accessed 18 January 2021).

FURLONG, K. 2021. Geographies of infrastructure II: Concrete, cloud and layered (in)visibilities. *Progress in Human Geography* **45**, 190-8.

GARRETT, B. & I. KLINKE 2018. Opening the bunker: function, materiality, temporality. *Environment and Planning C: Politics and Space* **37**, 1063-81.

GHERTNER, D.A., H. MCFANN & D.M. GOLDSTEIN 2020. *Futureproof: security aesthetics and the management of life.* Durham, N.C.: Duke University Press.

GOLDSTEIN, D. 2010. Toward a critical anthropology of security. *Current Anthropology* **51**, 487-517.

GRAHAM, S. 2016. *Vertical: the city from satellites to bunkers.* New York: Verso.

HOGAN, M. 2015. Data flows and water woes: the Utah Data Center. *Big Data & Society* **2**: **2** (available online: *https://journals.sagepub.com/doi/10.1177/2053951715592429*, accessed 18 January 2021).

HOLBRAAD, M. & M.A. PEDERSEN (eds) 2013. *Times of security: ethnographies of fear, protest and the future.* New York: Routledge.

HOLT, J. & P. VONDERAU 2015. 'Where the internet lives': data centers as cloud infrastructure. In *Signal traffic: critical studies of media infrastructures* (eds) L. Parks & N. Starosielski, 71-93. Urbana: University of Illinois Press.

HORN, E. 2018. *The future as catastrophe: imagining disaster in the modern age.* New York: Columbia University Press.

HU, T. 2015. *A prehistory of the cloud.* Cambridge, Mass.: MIT Press.

JACOBSON, K. & M. HOGAN 2019. Retrofitted data centers: a new world in the shell of the old. *Work Organization, Labor & Globalization* **13**: **2**, 78-94.

JAKOBSSON, P. & F. STIERNSTEDT 2012. Time, space and clouds of information: data centre discourse and the meaning of durability. *Cultural technologies: the shaping of culture in media and society* (ed.) G. Bolin, 103-17. New York: Routledge.

JHA, A. 2009. Secrets of the data bunker. *The Guardian*, 11 November (available online: *https://www.theguardian.com/technology/2009/nov/11/data-server-farms*, accessed 18 January 2021).

JOHNSON, A. 2019. Data centers as infrastructural inbetweens. *American Ethnologist* **46**, 75-88.

——— & M. HOGAN 2018. Introducing location and dislocation: global geographies of digital data. *Imaginations: Journal of Cross-Cultural Image Studies* **8**: **2**, 4-7.

KIRSCHENBAUM, M.G. 2008. *Mechanisms: new media and the forensic imagination.* Cambridge, Mass.: MIT Press.

LAKOFF, A. 2017. *Unprepared: global health in a time of emergency.* Oakland: University of California Press.

LOW, S. & M. MAGUIRE (eds) 2019. *Spaces of security: ethnographies of securityscapes, surveillance and control.* New York: University Press.

LUPTON, D. 2018. How do data come to matter? Living and becoming with personal data. *Big Data & Society* **5**: **2** (available online: *https://journals.sagepub.com/doi/10.1177/2053951718786314*, accessed 18 January 2021).

MAGUIRE, M., C. FROIS & N. ZURAWSKI 2014. *The anthropology of security: perspectives from the frontline of policing, counter-terrorism and border control.* London: Pluto.

MASCO, J. 2009. Life underground: building the bunker society. *Anthropology Now, Special Atomic Issue* **1**, 13-29.

MATTERN, S. 2015. Deep time of media infrastructure. In *Signal traffic: critical studies of media infrastructures* (eds) L. Parks & N. Starosielski, 94-114. Urbana: University of Illinois Press.

MINGARD, Y. 2014. *Deposit.* Göttingen: Steidl.

NIELSEN, M. & M.A. PEDERSEN 2015. Infrastructural imaginaries: collapsed futures in Mozambique and Mongolia. In *Reflections on imagination: human capacity and ethnographic method* (eds) M. Harris & N. Rapport, 237-61. London: Routledge.

PETERS, J.D. 2015. *The marvelous clouds: toward a philosophy of elemental media.* Chicago: University Press.

Journal of the Royal Anthropological Institute (N.S.) **27**, 76-94
© 2021 The Authors. *Journal of the Royal Anthropological Institute* published by John Wiley & Sons Ltd on behalf of Royal Anthropological Institute

PICKREN, G. 2018. The factories of the past are turning into the data centers of the future. *Imaginations: Journal of Cross-Cultural Image Studies* **8**: **2**, 22-9.

ROSSITER, N. 2016. *Software, infrastructure, labor: a media theory of logistical nightmares*. London: Routledge.

SEBALD, W.G. 1998. *The rings of Saturn* (trans. M. Hulse). London: Harvill.

SHRYOCK, A. & D.L. SMAIL 2018. On containers: a forum. Concluding remarks. *History and Anthropology* **29**, 49-51.

SNEATH, D., M. HOLBRAAD & M.A. PEDERSEN 2009. Technologies of the imagination: an introduction. *Ethnos* **74**, 5-30.

TAYLOR, A.R.E. 2019. The data center as technological wilderness. *Culture Machine* **18** (available online: *https://culturemachine.net/vol-18-the-nature-of-data-centers/data-center-as-techno-wilderness/*, accessed 18 January 2021).

TSING, A. 2001. Inside the global economy of appearances. In *Globalization* (ed.) A. Appadurai, 155-88. Durham, N.C.: Duke University Press.

VEEL, K. 2018. Uncertain architectures: performing shelter and exposure. *Imaginations: Journal of Cross-Cultural Image Studies* **8**: **2**, 30-41.

VIRILIO, P. 2009 [1975]. *Bunker archaeology* (trans. G. Collins). New York: Princeton Architectural Press.

VONDERAU, A. 2017. Technologies of imagination: locating the cloud in Sweden's global north. *Imaginations: Journal of Cross-Cultural Image Studies* **8**: **2**, 8-21.

ZIELINSKI, S. 2006. *Deep time of the media: toward an archaeology of hearing and seeing by technical means*. Cambridge, Mass.: MIT Press.

À l'épreuve du futur : les données bunkérisées ou comment vendre l'ultrasécurisation du nuage

Résumé

Laissés à l'abandon après la Guerre froide, des bunkers antiatomiques du monde entier trouvent une seconde vie en tant que centres de stockage de données ultrasécurisés pour les fournisseurs de services du nuage informatique. Les responsables de ces centres de données misent sur le potentiel spatial, temporel et de sécurité matérielle de leurs forteresses souterraines, en faisant d'elles des solutions de stockage « à l'épreuve du futur ». C'est au prisme de ce concept que l'auteur explore comment les professionnels du stockage de données exploitent l'imaginaire du bunker pour configurer les données comme des objets à protéger. L'article prend la forme d'une visite ethnographique dans un bunker de données britannique. Lors de cette visite, l'on agitera le spectre de matérialités fragiles et de menaces futures sur les données, afin d'assurer la continuité commerciale du bunker. Cette protection contre l'avenir, selon l'auteur, apporte une ouverture conceptuelle sur les impératifs entrelacés de la sécurité et du marketing qui régissent le marché du stockage de données.

5
From connection to contagion

CORI HAYDEN *University of California-Berkeley*

This essay proposes that we 'think data' with a complex legacy of work, once disavowed and now resurgent in social theory, on crowd formations. I propose this move because social media platforms' mobilization of data – the extractions, ever-shifting reaggregations, and micro-targeting, on the one hand, and our engagements, re-tweets, acts of sharing, and production of virality, on the other – has fuelled such anxious concern about the very things that animated much crowd theory in the first place. Key among these concerns are the force of emotional contagion and the threat of social dissolution; the composition of 'the social' by elements that well exceed the human; and pressing questions about the media through which energetic forces travel, often with lightning speed. What questions might be enabled by attending to the resonance between crowd theory's 'anti-liberal' preoccupations and contemporary concerns over how social media platforms crowd us?

Thinking data: crowds and clouds

With what tools might we 'think data'? In this essay, I suggest that we do so with the crowd, or, rather, with a complex legacy of work, once disavowed and now resurgent in social theory, on crowd formations. I have been thinking these two things (data, crowd) together for a while now under the rubric of 'crowds and clouds' (see also Hayden in press). I am certainly not alone in doing so. Among my fellow travellers, Lilly Irani, Chris Kelty, Nick Seaver, and a suite of collaborators laid the foundations for what compels me here in their 2012 issue of *Limn*, precisely under the title 'Crowds and clouds' (Irani, Kelty & Seaver 2012). The volume broached a crucial question: how was the cloud (as data aggregation, social media platforms, and algorithmic filtering, among other things) generating new kinds of collectives or aggregate formations? That question is no less crucial today, though its urgency has since taken another turn. In this essay, I want to pose again the question of how clouds crowd.

Let me clarify what I mean by each part of that question. First, the cloud: in much recent work, the cloud is many things. It is not just a usefully imprecise synonym for 'the internet', but a materialized imaginary, and a nexus of power and sovereignty (Hu 2015; Noble 2018); an infrastructure (see Starosielski 2015); and a medium or environment (Parks & Starosielski 2015; Peters 2015). Here, I am using cloud in a narrow sense to refer to social media platforms as engines for data production, data gathering (including by tracking our clicks, scrolls, likes, and shares), and data aggregation. These practices continually de- and re-compose their units (individuals, preferences-purchases, demographics, 'interests') into provisional, ephemeral, infinitely expandable, and highly partible collectives (see Besteman & Gusterson 2019; Boellstorff & Maurer 2015; Latour 2010; Seaver 2012). But what exactly, we might ask, is 'crowded' or crowding about these aggregating effects?

With this invocation of the crowd, in turn, I am pointing not to just any aggregation, but specifically to the crowds of crowd theory, an ambivalent conceptual and methodological archive including late nineteenth-century French work in psychology and the emergent sciences of the social (Gustave Le Bon, Gabriel Tarde, and Émile Durkheim), Freud's engagements therewith, Canetti's mid-twentieth-century meditations in *Crowds and power*, and quite a bit more. Much early crowd theory either articulated or generated an anxious concern with the ways that crowds, sutured together not by 'rational thought' but by the powers of imitation and suggestion, dissolved the boundaries of the autonomous individual. In this way, for Le Bon at least, crowds threatened to dissolve society itself. As Christian Borch has argued in a supremely careful account of this body of work, early crowd theory was banished from 'respectable' social science for much of the twentieth century (Borch 2012: 2). But the very reasons it was pushed to the margins – including what he calls its 'anti-liberal' epistemological commitment to notions of imitation, suggestion, and 'emotional contagion,' as well as its uncomfortable proximity or utility to authoritarianism – are, I will suggest, among the reasons why it (the crowd of crowd theory) beckons again. For multiple reasons, 'anti-liberal' crowd theory is no longer banished.

On the one hand, there has been a recent explosion of interest in crowd theory in anthropology, sociology, science and technology studies, political theory, and cultural studies, among other fields. Much of this work has been drawn to crowd theory's unorthodox vocabularies and its otherness vis-à-vis the tenets of liberal social and political thought, not least its decentring of the individual as the basic unit of analysis (see, among many, Borch 2006; Candea 2015; Chowdhury 2019; Dean 2016; Mazzarella 2010; Schnapp & Tiews 2006). In crowd theory, anthropologists and others have found what William Mazzarella (2017) calls a mimetic archive: a source of disavowed questions and sensibilities that in fact continue to seep back into frame and that may well help us animate other-than-liberal conceptualizations of the social and the political (Chowdhury 2019; Dean 2016). (We could think of affect theory as a closely related conversation here.)

But of course, there is another anti-liberalism or perhaps illiberalism that draws attention 'back' to crowd theory today. The rise of authoritarian, anti-democratic regimes in the United States and Europe, to take a very narrow view of the matter, has returned us to the close relationship between Le Bon's understandings of the crowd, in particular, and authoritarian rule or aspirations (Mussolini found him quite useful). Not for nothing did the UK newspaper *The Telegraph* pronounce that 'a 19th century Frenchman' had predicted the rise of Donald Trump, overlaying his profile picture with a choice quotation from Le Bon: 'A crowd is only impressed by excessive sentiments. Exaggerate, affirm, resort to repetition, and never attempt to prove anything by reasoning' (Ryan 2016).

There are certainly many reasons to re-attune to invocations of 'the crowd' and its 'surging energies, light and dark', as Mazzarella has memorably put it (2017: 2). One of

them, I suggest here, is how they might help us pose questions about 'data', in the
of social media. What follows is not a review of crowd theory, but a brief meditation on
why some of the questions that have animated and haunted that work might be good
for 'thinking data' today. To think data and crowd together is not to invoke a thinly
conceived return of the repressed (the crowd went away and now it's back!), or a project
of applying old theory to new data (which in this case is 'data'). My speculative proposal
hews more to the sense that there is quite a lot of seepage and contagion, a mutual
saturation, or a kind of persistence, in the questions that preoccupy (some of us) about
data and the questions that have long preoccupied (some of us) about crowds. In its
mobilization through and as social media, data carries crowds/crowd theory within.

There is something admittedly and explicitly dystopic about my interest here. I am
asking how the cloud crowds us (again) at a moment in which that question has taken
an explicitly anxious, arguably 'anti-liberal' turn. For it seems increasingly difficult to
disentangle various insurgent illiberalisms, from conspiracy theories to racist violence,
from the data that transits through and constitutes social media. How far we are
from those the heady days around 2012 and 2013, when the Occupy movement and
the Arab Spring, heralded (by some) as Facebook and Twitter Revolutions, allowed
some to hope that social media platforms might indeed be uniquely positioned to
unleash crowd potency in the service of radical, (small-d) democratic visons (see
Dean 2016; Milan 2015; Tufecki 2015). That story has of course changed dramatically.
As Facebook's algorithmic filters and revenue models (for example) have enabled
extreme forms of political polarization and disinformation (Vaidhyanathan 2018), it
is hard these days to countenance any necessary relation among crowds, the internet,
democratic emergence, or the 'wisdom of the crowd', as proponents of crowdsourcing
would have it, even as instances of all of the above persist. The role of Facebook,
WhatsApp, YouTube, Twitter, 4Chan, and other platforms in a growing catalogue of
'dark' surging energies (state genocidal campaigns 'waged on Facebook' [Mozur 2018],
the role of Cambridge Analytica's deceptions in both the Brexit and Trump campaigns
[Cadwalladr & Graham-Harrison 2018], the rise of the alt-right, and so much more)
have all made it difficult to hold onto any fantasy – which was of course always already
under critique (see Han 2017 and Hu 2015) – that social media companies, built up as
massive, private data-generating and data-gathering engines, would obviously serve as
the lubricants of liberal, much less radical, democratic crowd emergence.

I can think of no better shorthand for this arc than Facebook's own transformation
from self-branded engine of 'connection' to accused vector of 'contagion'. The latter,
highly charged term, which is so important to crowd theory, has become even
more charged in the context of the 2020 coronavirus pandemic. The World Health
Organization, the United States Centers for Disease Control and Prevention, and other
public health bodies have indeed issued warnings about an 'infodemic' fuelled by the
major social media platforms – an overabundance of information, much of it false,
racist, and dangerous, which, along with the other virus, must be contained.[1] Infodemic
and Cambridge Analytica, QAnon and 'memetic warfare' (Philips 2018), and white
nationalist marches have arguably supplanted Facebook and Twitter 'Revolutions' as
iconic instances of the cloud and its crowds. I might go so far as to venture that the
presence of the crowd in those early, celebratory imaginations of Twitter Revolutions
even anticipated the turn from hype to dystopia that Douglas-Jones, Seaver, and Walford
name in relation to 'data' more broadly, in the introduction to this issue.

But what kind of relation am I suggesting here? If crowd theory can be a conceptual resource for thinking data, it is not only because these platforms help generate crowds as aggregates in their various forms. Rather, this move is important because social media platforms' mobilization of data – the extractions, ever-shifting reaggregations, and micro-targeting, on the one hand, and our engagements, re-tweets, acts of sharing, and production of virality, on the other – has fuelled such anxious concern about the very things that animated much crowd theory in the first place. Not least of these concerns are the force of emotional contagion and the allied threat of social dissolution; the composition of 'the social' by elements that well exceed the human; and pressing questions about the media through which energetic forces travel, often with lightning speed.

Contagion, heterogeneity, medium

What is transiting through our preoccupations with social media as data extraction and aggregation right now? Another way to ask that question is: what transits through crowd theory's crowds? There are three points of contact on which I want to focus, drawing them out very briefly from crowd theory, and then, in the next section, turning to how these preoccupations might help us think data in social media. The first of these points of contact is *emotional contagion*. The term played a significant role in Gustave Le Bon's late nineteenth-century work *The crowd: a study of the popular mind*, which sounded his alarm about the ill-understood, 'barbaric' power of the crowds rising up against an elite order he was committed to preserving (Le Bon 2009 [1895]). This work is an easy target for understanding why crowd theory might have been shoved to the margins of respectable social science in the twentieth century. Le Bon's writings were a reaction to the century-long aftermath of the French Revolution, and in particular to the rise of socialism and workers' demands in late nineteenth-century Paris. These movements and these masses represented nothing less, in his view, than 'a determination to utterly destroy society as it now exists' (Le Bon 2009 [1895]: 7). His anxiety about the mysterious power of these crowds was infamously suffused with the stink of evolutionary racism: '[B]y the mere fact that he forms part of an organized crowd, a man descends several rungs on the ladder of civilization. Isolated, he may be a cultivated individual; in a crowd, he is a barbarian – that is, a creature acting by instinct' (Le Bon 2009 [1895]: 19).

But it was not the specific demands of these crowds, nor even their size, that ultimately defined their power and thus required study. What most drew Le Bon's attention was the force that held a crowd together, and here he and his fellow travellers become much more interesting. Not just any mass of people constituted a crowd: a group became a crowd only when 'emotional contagion' took hold of its members – a mutual susceptibility to ideas, images, emotions, or actions that, in a crowd, spread like fire from one person to the next, outpacing and indeed swamping reasoned thought or deliberation. In a crowd, Le Bon fretted and Elias Canetti later marvelled, we lose ourselves. Le Bon's version of this argument was drawn from late nineteenth-century experimental research on hypnotism and somnambulism, which suggested that vulnerability to influence and suggestion might be a generalized tendency, and not a weakness specific to pathologized subjects. He was not alone in finding this work interesting: if this argument lands us firmly in the zone of anthropology's 'primitive participation', late nineteenth-century psychology, sociology, and criminology, including the work of Gabriel Tarde, also drew heavily on these insights, committing to suggestion and imitation as prime movers for everything from market speculation to the constitution of society ('sociality') itself, as Tarde argued (Tarde 1903 [1890]; see also Candea 2015; Schnapp & Tiews 2006).

This commitment to imitation-suggestion, whether in Le Bon's overwrought sense of emotional contagion, or in Tarde's much more complex arguments about the entanglement of imitation and the social, is why Christian Borch has called crowd theory an anti-liberal formation. Late nineteenth-century French crowd theorists working in this idiom noted that suggestion, imitation, and contagion meant not only a 'loss' of rationality and capacity for discernment (Le Bon), but also, closely related, a dissolution of the individual as an autonomous, bounded, stable, and sovereign subject. It is this fundamentally de-individuating move that puts crowd theory at odds with the tenets of 'liberal' social theory (see Borch 2012: 17; Brighenti 2014; Candea 2015).

If emotional contagion, imitation, and suggestion are one key point of contact, a second, closely related idiom is crowd theory's insistence on the *heterogeneity* of the crowd. Le Bon noted repeatedly that a crowd is something distinctive and even new; the force of emotional contagion results in a recombination and hence an essential transformation of its constitutive elements. A crowd is, in this idiom, something different to, and far more than, a 'summing up-of or an average struck between its elements' (Le Bon 2009 [1895]: 16). More broadly, indeed, crowd theory produces a notion of crowds that are constitutively not-simply-human; there is, in much of this work, something peculiar, arguably 'more-than', about their nature. For Tarde, humans are not the only monads in the world, or even in the universe, through which the forces of imitation, vibration, and irritation bring about resemblances, nor is imitation a 'psychological' principle transiting between individual people and their individual minds (Tarde 2012 [1893]). Actions imitate actions, gestures imitate gestures, and ideas imitate ideas (Latour 2005; Tarde 2012 [1893]). Elias Canetti, writing in a very different idiom a half century later, evoked crowds at times as something almost alien, and hungry. 'Open crowds', he wrote, want to 'feed on anything shaped like a human being' (Canetti 1962: 16).

Third, among resonances for how we might think data and crowd together, I would suggest that many crowd theorists indeed already understood crowds as *media* through which transit palpability and urgency, in Le Bon's idiom, as well as the infinitesimal acts of imitation that generate both crowds and sociality more broadly, in Tarde's work. The mystery, for which imitation-suggestion served as both answer and further question, was: how? How to account for the ways that affect, impulses to action, ideas, even consumer preferences for commodities (such as coffee, over which Tarde marvelled) travel, at what seemed to be such uncontrollable speed? In much crowd theory literature, the media of suggestion did not exist in any one plane or register. Tarde wrote of the 'imitation rays' that transited through and within people, and molecules, and 'the ether' (1903 [1890]: 69-70). Le Bon saw the human mind as the medium of contagion. Canetti, writing in the mid-twentieth century in a way that only glanced off of the idiom of imitation-contagion, wrote of the transformative effect of physical touch, and the density of bodies, pressed against each other. But he also wrote of other elements and forces through which crowd dynamics manifest: fire, forests, and the sea, among them.

The rise of mass communication in the late nineteenth and early twentieth century was of course part of the ether within which such musings emerged, and which carry crowding firmly into questions of data as 'social' (i.e. as social media). Jackie Orr shows as much in *Panic diaries* (2006). Revisiting the many (after-)lives of Orson Welles's famous 1938 radio drama *War of the Worlds*, Orr traces a route forward from the induction of 'the Martian panic' to a war-time-driven, rationalizing US social science research programme seeking to experimentalize (and hence to harness, or at least mitigate) the forces of mass-mediated suggestibility and emotional contagion. In so doing, she also traces a thread directly from Le Bon and Tarde to a range of US social scientists whose concerns anticipate many of the conversations that have haunted fears about mass media, and that have attached to social media today. Robert Park, writing in 1904, hoped that the circulation of a new thing called 'facts' might rescue the public from its own mass-mediated vulnerability to suggestion, contagion, and panic (Orr 2006: 44). Edward Ross, writing in 1908, drew directly on Tarde to argue that mass media (the telegraph) produced unprecedented conditions for 'contagion without contact': that is, the ability for suggestion to travel even or especially through a crowd-at-a-distance (Orr 2006: 48-9). Crowds are media, Orr reminds us, not just for contagion at a distance, but for the conduct of experimental social science as well. We will return to this point below.

Meanwhile, I think it is important to note that in the first half of the twentieth century, 'cloud' was also not far from crowd-as-medium. In the concluding chapter to *Terror from the air*, Peter Sloterdijk introduces us to a conversation of sorts between the young Elias Canetti, who later went on to write the beautiful and unnerving book *Crowds and power*, and the German poet Hermann Broch. Writing during the toxic interwar years in Germany, Broch decried the ways in which Hitler's nationalist communications operations worked on the 'somnabulent' masses, as if these operations were an extension of the chemical warfare that had been deployed with such terrible effect in the First World War. Sloterdijk reads Broch to say that mass-mediated authoritarian nationalism created its own noxious bubble, enveloping its publics in a 'suffocating' fog in which, Broch implied, one could only breathe in the excrescence that one has just exhaled (Sloterdijk 2009: 96-105).

When I read this section of Sloterdijk with my students, they (we) are brought up short. Has he delivered us directly to the thick of toxic Twitter (French 2019), the danger of filter bubbles, a growing, palpable certainty that social media – especially, here, in the overt circulation of data in the form of tweets and posts – is the data-fuelled recirculation of 'our own' excrescence? In any event, media, cloud, and crowd have arguably been impossible to disentangle for over a century. And so it is time to ask again: how does data crowd?

Social media as crowd media

There is something striking about the way that crowd theory's distinctive preoccupations, from the potentially destructive but also generative force of emotional contagion and suggestibility, to the peculiarly more-than-human heterogeneity of crowds, to a concern with how ineffable energetic forces travel, have come so alive in recent discussions of what Facebook or YouTube (for example) have wrought. As matters of concern, crowd and social media seem in some respects to be one and the same. Through algorithmically filtered feeds of similarity, likes, and likeness, Facebook, Twitter, YouTube, and other platforms seem to have become highly effective suggestionizing (Le Bon's term) machines. These machines, moreover, are constitutively heterogeneous, feeding quite explicitly on that which 'looks like a human': bots, markets in Twitter followers, click farms, 'fake' accounts that might be automated or might be human-made. The notably efficient transit of affect and 'irrationality'

Journal of the Royal Anthropological Institute (N.S.) **27**, 95-107

('fake news,' extreme sentiment) through these networks *is* the problem named by Le Bon's concerns with emotional contagion. And 'emotional contagion', in turn, is a key principle on which social media platforms' revenue models are based (Kramer, Guillory & Hancock 2014). How do we think these relations or correlations without reproducing or intensifying a panicky breathlessness? Below, I offer a few reflections on what we might do with and within these suggestive proximities.

Crowds are made by suggestion, not scale

Perhaps social media's data *crowds* not simply because of how large or powerful the aggregations are, but because of the forces and dynamics that transit through them, and the effects thereof. The crowds of crowd theory are defined less by their numbers than by that which connects them: that is, by their modality. As with micro-targeting in advertising, electoral campaigning, or hate-spewing, crowding can evoke a process of suggestionizing, magnetizing, or gathering heterogeneous elements into Tardean 'similarity spaces', to invoke Nick Seaver's essay in this volume. This point matters to what it might mean to say that social media crowds us.

Certainly, one of the ongoing criticisms of social media as a form of datafication has been that it makes worlds so small – inducing, we fear or accuse, a kind of narcissism (from selfies to self-tracking [Wolf 2009]), shrinking people's and algorithms' news and information horizons into self-reinforcing bubbles, and otherwise radically disconnecting 'us' (Vaidhyanathan 2018). But crowd theory draws our attention to the heterogeneous scales of crowding that are at work in precisely those forms of 'atomization'. Indeed, if we take Tarde seriously, atoms, individuals, cells, and selves are already crowds – monads, in fact, that only become more complex the 'smaller' you go (Latour 2010). Thus, what crowds us even in such moments of presumed atomization is our embeddedness in algorithmic universes of suggestion and likeness. We might think of the role of Cambridge Analytica in the pro-Brexit and Trump campaigns: travelling through Facebook's homophilous 'friendship' networks (Kurgan, Brawley, House, Zhang & Chun 2019), the company used quizzes and surveys to gain access to the profiles of Facebook users and those whom they had friended. This extracted data was then mobilized in the form of 'psychographic' profiles of voters that were used, in turn, to micro-target electoral information at particular voters. Here we see the entanglement of social media's data practices: covert data extraction that is, in turn, enabled by the networks and relations of affinity produced through users' own engagements – sharing, Friendships, likeness – with the platform (see Cadwalladr & Graham-Harrison 2018). The scale of this operation was big (over 30 million profiles in the United States), but the point I am making is never only a question of scale. Perhaps we can say that a micro-targeting electoral campaign, even when it only 'targets' a small number of people, *crowds* because of the forms of similarity and even 'susceptibility' through which data points, people, ideas, suggestions, are both generated and brought into contact with each other.

Does social media crowd insofar as it incites violence, extremism, and lies?

The increasingly strong association between violence, misinformation, and social media is deeply relevant to the question of how data crowds us (Frenkel, Casey & Mozur 2018); it is certainly relevant to the arcs, or perhaps oscillations, I am sketching here from hype to dystopia, from connection to contagion. But how, again, might we think about this relation? With what confidence can we say that particular data practices – licit and illicit forms of data collection, aggregation, message sharing, liking, boosting, re-tweeting – *produce* particular political atmospheres, waves of violence, or other concretely atmospheric or affective modulations? In a 2018 article given the arresting headline 'A genocide incited on Facebook', the *New York Times* reported that members of Myanmar's military had created fake Facebook profiles and poured a great many resources into deliberately (and effectively) using the platform to set the conditions for its ethnic cleansing campaign against the Rohingya Muslim minority (Mozur 2018). A 2018 study in Germany conducted by two researchers at the University of Warwick and published by the Social Science Research Network concluded that 'social media can act as a propagation mechanism between online hate speech and real-life violent crime' (Müller & Schwarz 2018). In their report on the study, *New York Times* journalists Amanda Taub and Max Fisher describe its results – its own exercise in data mining – as follows:

> Towns where Facebook use was higher than average, like Altena [Germany], reliably experienced more attacks on refugees. That held true in virtually any sort of community – big city or small town; affluent or struggling; liberal haven or far-right stronghold – suggesting that the link applies universally. Their reams of data converged on a breathtaking statistic: Wherever per-person Facebook use rose to one standard deviation above the national average, attacks on refugees increased by about 50 percent (Taub & Fisher 2018).

Methodologically, this relation poses a problem, and politically, it does, too, but in neither sense are the problems completely new. Correlation or causation? Medium or message? How do we get inside and pin down the relation between the violence and the platform? Decades of work on media have wrestled with precisely these questions, of course. Will the masses do whatever masses do, regardless of the medium? Jean Baudrillard argued so, doubling down on the masses as the medium that matters:

> It has always been thought – this is the very ideology of the mass media – that it is the media which envelop the masses. The secret of manipulation has been sought in a frantic semiology of the mass media. But it has been overlooked, in this naïve logic of communication, that the masses are a stronger medium than all the media, that it is the former who envelop and absorb the latter (Baudrillard 2007 [1978]: 44-5).

Or, *pace* McLuhan (to whom Baudrillard is responding), does 'the medium' generate something particular, something of its own, *becoming* the message? In other words, is social media merely a monetized effect of, even a parasite on, extant forms of collective effervescence, or is it the source of palpable energies itself, a mode of configuring atmospheres and affective/informational environments? This is a question that, taken in the instrumentalized register of accountability and responsibility, animates a growing chorus of calls to more strongly regulate Facebook and Twitter. But it is also a question that animates much recent work on new/digital/social media and the cloud, in which media and the cloud are conceived of as environmental and even elemental: that is, as a robust surround, like air, or soil, and not merely as a source of semiotic inputs (and hence manipulation) (Parks & Starosielski 2019; Peters 2015).

I think crowd theory might suggest another, closely related way in, or perhaps a third question with which to contemplate this dilemma. I cannot help but think of Le Bon's anxious – and more than halfway noxious – understanding that if crowds are peculiarly 'receptive' to extreme sentiment, they are also the transformative medium through which such sentiment both travels and is animated. What, then, if the notions of suggestion-imitation and emotional contagion in crowd theory profoundly blur the line between message and medium, between input and environmental surround, between the violence and Facebook?

What connects is *contagion*

We cannot address this question of medium vs message without also pointing to the fact that Facebook is a platform that 'connects' precisely by instrumentalizing and monetizing emotional contagion itself (Kramer, Guillory & Hancock 2014; Lanchester 2017).[2] Indeed, until users and others objected too loudly, academic psychologists collaborating with Facebook's own research team had used the social network as a ready-made experimental platform for studying more or less the thing that concerned Edward Ross about the telegraph in 1908: contagion without contact (Orr 2006). In a now-infamous 2014 study, 'Experimental evidence of massive-scale emotional contagion through social networks', published in the *Proceedings of the National Academy of Sciences*, the study's authors took one step further in what was, at the time, a commonplace practice of using Facebook not just as a data source but also as a test bed for studying the psychology of emotional contagion (Kramer *et al.* 2014; see also Meyer 2014). Their particular innovation, enabled by collaboration with Facebook's own research team, was that they first manipulated user feeds and then tracked the results (Meyer 2014). With the spectacularly matter-of-fact tone of those accustomed to asking these kinds of questions, the study authors described their research results as follows:

> We show, via a massive ($N = 689,003$) experiment on Facebook, that emotional states can be transferred to others via emotional contagion, leading people to experience the same emotions without their awareness. We provide experimental evidence that emotional contagion occurs without direct interaction between people (exposure to a friend expressing an emotion is sufficient), and in the complete absence of nonverbal cues (Kramer *et al.* 2014: 8788).

The study was conducted by deliberately changing users' newsfeeds – omitting or hiding words of putative emotional valence – and tracking whether this affective modulation proved 'contagious': that is, whether the induced change in affect spread detectably to those users' Facebook friends' subsequent posts. The resulting proof of contagion was, others have noted, arguably quite small, only becoming visible, statistically, because of the massive scale of the experiment (Meyer 2014).

(Statistical) significance notwithstanding, perhaps it is not surprising that the study's publication generated quite a bit of outrage about the very idea of researchers manipulating users' feeds without their consent; others responded that this is in fact effectively what Facebook does all the time anyway (Meyer 2014). But I am intrigued by the 'obviousness' of using Facebook for such a study in the first place. This obviousness brings a few considerations into view. First, as Nick Seaver has suggested in an insightful comment on this essay, Facebook is not just a rich site of extant social data to be extracted. Rather, the platform is an experimental infrastructure itself, one that is already shaping social relations into data amenable to analysis. That is, our moments of contact with each other transit along quantifiable, already-defined channels, and, I would add, these channels themselves formalize and automate some fairly dense and non-innocent social and political histories. I am thinking particularly of Laura Kurgan and colleagues' brilliant 2019 account of the racialized history that gave rise to algorithmic formalizations of Facebook's 'like' and 'friend' functions (Kurgan *et al.* 2019).

That Facebook is indeed non-innocently and experimentally shaping what will count as 'social relations' is, in turn, a point that has been enlivened by critics who note that if it is an infrastructure for data extraction, it is also, therefore, an infrastructure for labour (and value) extraction. Artist and curator Laurel Ptak's manifesto 'Wages for Facebook' – a nearly word-for-word version of Sylvia Federici's 1973 'Wages against Housework' – says the following:

> To demand wages for Facebook is to make it visible that our opinions and emotions have all been distorted for a specific function online, and then have been thrown back at us as a model to which we should all conform if we want to be accepted in this society. Our fingertips have become distorted from so much liking, our feelings have gotten lost from so many friendships (Ptak 2014).

Contact, as friendship, likes, sociality itself, and even as 'emotional contagion', is thus not just an ancillary effect of Facebook's platform, to be studied after the fact. It is baked in to the platform as an infrastructure for data extraction (by Facebook) *and* data generation (by 'us'). Not incidentally, it is also the basis of Facebook's business model: the company sells attention, and hence sells advertising, by multiplying clicks and shares, which in turn accumulate and spread more effectively the more intense the emotional affect involved (Lanchester 2017; Vaidhyanathan 2018; Wu 2016). Facebook is certainly not unique in this regard. This principle is the business model of multi-platform, data-driven news and entertainment media more broadly (see Baldwin 2019).

In a 2018 report written for the Data & Society Institute on the challenges for journalists posed by the nexus of extremism, violence, misinformation, and digital and social media, Whitney Philips writes:

> In the social media age, the measurability and commoditization of content, in the form of traffic, clicks, and likes, has tethered editorial strategy to analytics like never before. The emphasis on quantifiable metrics stacks the news cycle with stories most likely to generate the highest level of engagement possible, across as many platforms as possible. Things traveling too far, too fast, with too much emotional urgency, is exactly the point (Philips 2018).

Things travelling too fast, too far, and with (too much) emotional urgency is the scenario that crowd theorists contended with, that early twentieth-century social scientists experimentalized, and that monetized data materializes and enables. That phrase is also pointed shorthand, for it's not just any 'thing' that seems to transit in this way. Elsewhere in the report, Philips advises journalists working in today's social media and data-driven news landscape to '[t]reat violent antagonisms as inherently contagious', in much the same way that standards have developed for covering 'suicide, mass shootings, and terrorism, all of which are known to inspire and even provide behavioral blueprints for future copycat attacks' (Philips 2018: 10).

The dynamic relation between contagious, destructive urgency and a business model that feeds on and hence amplifies exactly such urgency is, we might say, one of the most important sites of palpable intensification and more-than-social, crowded composition at work here. It has certainly provoked a series of concerns about the way Facebook in particular, though not alone, makes us into 'dopamine'-fuelled, emotionally driven users, ever more vulnerable to each other and to the redounding forces of irrationality, hatred, and contagious fakery (to paraphrase just a few of countless such laments). Le Bon argued that crowds, galvanized through the power of contagion and governed by extreme sentiment rather than measured reason, threatened to bring civilized society (i.e. aristocratic society) to its knees (2009 [1895]: 8). Critics of Facebook, including a chorus of former Facebook employees, have started talking about the way that social media (or just 'social') might well be destroying society itself, and with it, the substrate of rationality on which political equality (the opposite, of course, of what Le Bon desired) is based. As former Facebook engineer Chamath Palihapitiya has publicly lamented:

> It literally is a point now where I think we have created tools that are ripping apart the social fabric of how society works. That is truly where we are … The short-term, dopamine-driven feedback loops that we have created are destroying how society works: no civil discourse, no cooperation, misinformation, mistruth. And it's not an American problem. This is not about Russian ads. This is a global problem (Wang 2017).

I confess to being quite easily hailed by such laments, even as I try to stay, well, measured and reasoned about them. Saying that we have been here before – after all, isn't this an early twentieth-century problem? – can often be a move that counters, even de-fangs, a certain sense of urgency, or even panic, about what 'we' have wrought.

But that is not quite the move I want to make by trying to think 'data' with crowd. There are so many ways in which crowd theory's preoccupations seem to persist *in* and *as* data: that is, in and as social media and the forms of data production, data mining, filtering, virality, and targeted advertising or (mis)information around which they are organized. They are alive in more-than-human crowdings, in the potency of contagious suggestion even at the most micro-level, in the potential relation between the economies of emotional urgency and the (in)stability of a social or democratic order itself. The cloud crowds us, again, in the novel formations through which these questions persist and make insistent demands on us.

NOTES

I would like to thank Antonia Walford, Rachel Douglas-Jones, and Nick Seaver for convening this forum. My thanks to them, as well to Haidy Geismar, Marilyn Strathern, and two anonymous reviewers, for their generative and thoughtful comments and suggestions.

[1] See WHO Novel Coronavirus (2019-nCoV) Situation Report 13, February 2, 2020, available at *https://www.who.int/docs/default-source/coronaviruse/situation-reports/20200202-sitrep-13-ncov-v3.pdf* (accessed 20 January 2021).

[2] As Adam Curtis's 2002 documentary series *The Century of the Self* shows so clearly, there is a direct line from Le Bon and Sigmund Freud (who engaged with Le Bon's work seriously, but insisted that the missing link in the latter's explanatory apparatus was, of course, the force of libidinal desire) to the rise of propaganda, marketing, and public relations. It is a line that conveniently takes the form of lineage, in the person of Edward Bernays, Freud's US nephew, who infamously saw the vast potential of crowd psychology and psychoanalysis to serve as a manual for controlling the masses, in peacetime (marketing) as in war (propaganda, authoritarian rule).

REFERENCES

BALDWIN, T. 2019. *Ctrl Alt Delete: how politics and the media crashed our democracy.* London: Hurst & Company.

BAUDRILLARD, J. 2007 [1978]. *In the shadow of the silent majorities* (trans. P. Foss, J. Johnston & P. Patton). Los Angeles: Semiotext(e).

BESTEMAN, C. & H. GUSTERSON (eds) 2019. *Life by algorithms: how roboprocesses are remaking our world.* Chicago: University Press.

BOELLSTORFF, T. & B. MAURER (eds) 2015. *Data: now bigger and better!.* Chicago: Prickly Paradigm Press.

BORCH, C. 2006. The exclusion of the crowd: the destiny of a sociological figure of the irrational. *European Journal of Social Theory* **9**, 83-102.

——— 2012. *The politics of crowds: an alternative history of sociology.* Cambridge: University Press.

BRIGHENTI, A. 2014. *The ambiguous multiplicities: materials, episteme and politics of cluttered social formations.* Basingstoke: Palgrave Pivot.

CADWALLADR, C. & E. GRAHAM-HARRISON 2018. Revealed: 50 million Facebook profiles harvested for Cambridge Analytica in major data breach. *The Guardian*, 17 March (available online:

https://www.theguardian.com/news/2018/mar/17/cambridge-analytica-facebook-influence-us-election, accessed 29 January 2021).

CANDEA, M. (ed.) 2015. *The social after Gabriel Tarde: debates and assessments.* London: Routledge.

CANETTI, E. 1962. *Crowds and power* (trans. C. Stewart). New York: Farrar, Straus & Giroux.

CHOWDHURY, N. 2019. *Paradoxes of the popular: crowd politics in Bangladesh.* Stanford: University Press.

DEAN, J. 2016. *Crowds and party.* London: Verso.

FRENCH, D. 2019. Why Twitter is even more toxic than you think. *National Review* (blog), 2 January (available online: *https://www.nationalreview.com/2019/01/political-twitter-even-more-toxic-than-thought/*, accessed 20 January 2021).

FRENKEL, S., N. CASEY & P. MOZUR 2018. In some countries, Facebook's fiddling has magnified fake news. *The New York Times*, 14 January (available online: *https://www.nytimes.com/2018/01/14/technology/facebook-news-feed-changes.html*, accessed 20 January 2021).

HAN, B. 2017. *In the swarm: digital prospects.* Cambridge, Mass.: MIT Press.

HAYDEN, C. in press. Crowding the elements. In *Reactivating elements* (eds) N. Myers, D. Papadopoulos & M. Puig de la Bellacasa. Durham, N.C.: Duke University Press.

HU, T. 2015. *A prehistory of the cloud.* Cambridge, Mass.: MIT Press.

IRANI, L., C.M. KELTY & N. SEAVER (eds) 2012. Crowds and clouds. *Limn* 2 (available online: *https://limn.it/issues/crowds-and-clouds/*, accessed 20 January 2021).

KRAMER, A.D.I., J.E. GUILLORY & J.T. HANCOCK 2014. Experimental evidence of massive-scale emotional contagion through social networks. *Proceedings of the National Academy of Sciences* 111, 8788-90.

KURGAN, L., D. BRAWLEY, B. HOUSE, J. ZHANG & W.H.K. CHUN 2019. Homophily: the urban history of an algorithm. *E-Flux Architecture: Are Friends Electric?*, 4 October (available online: *https://www.e-flux.com/architecture/are-friends-electric/289193/homophily-the-urban-history-of-an-algorithm/*, accessed 20 January 2021).

LANCHESTER, J. 2017. You are the product. *London Review of Books*, 17 August, 3-10.

LATOUR, B. 2005. *Reassembling the social: an introduction to actor-network-theory.* Oxford: University Press.

——— 2010. Tarde's idea of quantification. In *The social after Gabriel Tarde: debates and asessments* (ed.) M. Candea, 145-62. London: Routledge.

LE BON, G. 2009 [1895]. *The crowd: a study of the popular mind.* New York: Classic Books.

MAZZARELLA, W. 2010. The myth of the multitude, or, who's afraid of the crowd? *Critical Inquiry* 36, 697-727.

——— 2017. *The mana of mass society.* Chicago: University Press.

MEYER, R. 2014. Everything we know about Facebook's secret mood manipulation experiment. *The Atlantic*, 18 June (available online: *https://www.theatlantic.com/technology/archive/2014/06/everything-we-know-about-facebooks-secret-mood-manipulation-experiment/373648/*, accessed 20 January 2021).

MILAN, S. 2015. When algorithms shape collective action: social media and the dynamics of cloud protesting. *Social Media + Society*, July-December, 1-10.

MOZUR, P. 2018. A genocide incited on Facebook, with posts from Myanmar's military. *The New York Times*, 15 October (available online: *https://www.nytimes.com/2018/10/15/technology/myanmar-facebook-genocide.html*, accessed 20 January 2021).

MÜLLER, K. & C. SCHWARZ 2018. Fanning the flames of hate: social media and hate crime. Rochester, N.Y.: Social Science Research Network (available online: *https://papers.ssrn.com/abstract=3082972*, accessed 28 January 2021).

NOBLE, S. 2018. *Algorithms of oppression: how search engines reinforce racism.* New York: NYU Press.

ORR, J. 2006. *Panic diaries: a geneaology of panic disorder.* Durham, N.C.: Duke University Press.

PARKS, L. & N. STAROSIELSKI (eds) 2015. *Signal traffic: critical studies of media infrastructures.* Chicago: University of Illinois Press.

PETERS, J.D. 2015. *The marvelous clouds: toward a philosophy of elemental media.* Chicago: University Press.

PHILIPS, W. 2018. The oxygen of amplification: better practices for reporting on extremists, antagonists, and manipulators online. *Data & Society*, 22 May (available online: *https://datasociety.net/output/oxygen-of-amplification/*, accessed 20 January 2021).

PTAK, L. 2014. Wages for Facebook (available online: *http://wagesforfacebook.com/*, accessed 20 January 2021).

RYAN, V. 2016. How a 19th century Frenchman predicted the rise of Donald Trump. *The Telegraph*, 8 September (available online: *https://www.telegraph.co.uk/news/2016/09/08/how-a-19th-century-frenchman-predicted-the-rise-of-donald-trump/*, accessed 20 January 2021).

SCHNAPP, J.T. & M. TIEWS (eds) 2006. *Crowds.* Stanford: University Press.

SEAVER, N. 2012. Algorithmic recommendations and synaptic functions. *Limn* **2** (available online: *http://limn.it/algorithmic-recommendations-and-synaptic-functions/*, accessed 20 January 2021).

SLOTERDIJK, P. 2009. *Terror from the air*. Cambridge, Mass.: MIT Press.

STAROSIELSKI, N. 2015. *The undersea network: sign, storage, transmission*. Durham, N.C.: Duke University Press.

TARDE, G. 1903 [1890]. *Laws of imitation* (trans. E.C. Parson). New York: Henry Holt and Company.

——— 2012 [1893]. *Monadology and sociology* (ed. & trans. T. Lorenc). Melbourne: re.press.

TAUB, A. & M. FISHER 2018. Facebook fueled anti-refugee attacks in Germany, new research suggests. *The New York Times*, 21 August (available online: *https://www.nytimes.com/2018/08/21/world/europe/facebook-refugee-attacks-germany.html*, accessed 20 January 2021).

TUFECKI, Z. 2015. *Twitter and tear gas: the power and fragility of networked protest*. New Haven: Yale University Press.

VAIDHYANATHAN, S. 2018. *Antisocial media: how Facebook disconnects us and undermines democracy*. Oxford: University Press.

WANG, A.B. 2017. Former Facebook VP says social media is destroying society with 'dopamine-driven feedback loops'. *The Washington Post*, 12 December (available online: *https://www.washingtonpost.com/news/the-switch/wp/2017/12/12/former-facebook-vp-says-social-media-is-destroying-society-with-dopamine-driven-feedback-loops/*, accessed 20 January 2021).

WOLF, G. 2009. Are self-trackers narcissists? *Quantified Self: Self Knowledge Through Numbers* (blog), 17 February (available online: *https://quantifiedself.com/blog/are-self-trackers-narcissists/*, accessed 20 January 2021).

WU, T. 2016. *The attention merchants: the epic scramble to get inside our heads*. New York: Knopf.

De la connexion à la contagion

Résumé

Cet article propose de « penser les données » à l'aune d'un héritage intellectuel complexe, jadis décrié et qui connaît actuellement un renouveau, celui de la théorie des foules. La démarche de l'autrice part du constat que la mobilisation de données des réseaux sociaux – extractions, réagrégations en mouvement constant et microciblage d'une part, et nos activités, retweets, partages et production de viralité de l'autre – inspire de très fortes préoccupations à propos des mêmes questions que se posait initialement la théorie des foules. Ces préoccupations sont notamment la force de la contagion émotionnelle et la menace de dissolution sociale, la composition du « fait social » par des éléments qui dépassent largement l'humain, ainsi que des interrogations persistantes sur les médias qui véhiculent les forces énergétiques, souvent à une vitesse fulgurante. Quelles questions pourrait-on résoudre en se penchant sur la résonance entre les préoccupations « antilibérales » de la théorie des foules et les inquiétudes contemporaines sur les méthodes qu'emploient les réseaux sociaux pour créer les foules ?

6
Hacking anthropology

HANNAH KNOX *University College London*

This essay outlines how the 'hack' might offer a model for anthropological research in the face of the distributed relations evidenced by digital data. The argument builds on fieldwork with citizens and activists and looks at their attempts to understand and make use of the data produced by energy sensors and monitors. Drawing on their experiences, I suggest that 'the hack' emerges as an important form of practice that helps people navigate the place of data in social relations. Taking the hack not just as ethnographic observation but also as a methodological proposition, I use my ethnographic material on the practice of the hack to reconsider the anthropological challenge of doing ethnography of processes that are only perceptible through numerical or digital data. To explore the value of the hack for anthropology, I introduce an example of an attempt to do ethnography in the mode of the hack. The essay ends with reflections on how the hack might provide us with new ways of getting to grips with the anthropological implications of systemic and emergent relations that are both brought to light and remade through data.

In this essay, I outline how 'the hack' might offer a model for ethnographic engagement in complex, emergent processes that are amenable to perception only through their traces in data. Computational infrastructures and data analytics have brought into view a host of new kinds of entities, big and small, from climate change, to DNA, to the viral patternings of online phenomena like memes and Twitterstorms or infrastructural imaginaries of smart networks of people, objects, and information. These phenomena are anthropologically fascinating, reassembling people and things in new configurations that challenge conceptual and practical boundaries between individuals and social groups, and between people and things. However, they also raise important conceptual and methodological questions about how to engage with such processes as objects of anthropological attention.

Researching data realities
I suggest that researching data realities specifically entails three key challenges. The first of these is the problem of *scale*. When we are confronted by emergent

Journal of the Royal Anthropological Institute (N.S.) **27**, 108-126
© 2021 The Authors. *Journal of the Royal Anthropological Institute* published by John Wiley & Sons Ltd on behalf of Royal Anthropological Institute

phenomena depicted in graphs, spreadsheets, visualizations, algorithmic effects, and digital traces, where is our ethnographer to locate themselves? Where should we be doing ethnography if we are interested in tracing the world-making capacities of environmental models or the operations of artificial intelligence? Any location can only provide a partial view on what are frequently referred to as global processes or networked systems.

This is not in itself a new problem for ethnographers. Nonetheless, as anthropologists of contemporary infrastructures (Abram, Winthereik & Yarrow 2019; Anand, Gupta & Appel 2018; Harvey, Jensen & Morita 2017) have pointed out, scale is central to issues which data makes newly available. Here the totalizing global (if not interplanetary) pretensions of discourses deployed to describe the value of digital systems depend on big numbers, total data, and extensive networks in conjuring these large-scale worlds (Tsing 2005). More prosaically, the very material infrastructures upon which the digital systems that make this large-scale world rely also, themselves, transgress national boundaries and connect places around the globe (Starosielski 2015). The discursive imaginaries and material infrastructures of digital data, then, serve to amplify and reframe longer-running concerns in anthropology regarding how to do local and situated ethnographies in the face of global networks and large-scale effects (Marcus 1995; Ong & Collier 2005).

The second problem concerns what we do with the idea of *representation*. As long as we see our job as ethnographers being the representation of other people's representational practices, then the problem of scale or data is tamed as simply another representational manoeuvre – and we can focus on the everyday practices of creating these kinds of graphs and depictions of distributed and large-scale processes. However, digital data traced in these graphs and charts self-evidently does more than represent. Like all methods of empirical science, digital data models are a world-*making* as much as a world-*framing* phenomenon. If we want to attend to the realities of these representations – in terms of both the 'realities' that they trace and the realities that they produce – how should we best do this? Anthropological theory has constantly flipped back and forth between making claims about epistemologies and representations and making reality claims. However, digital data worlds themselves seem to rework a distinction between representation and reality. Unlike intentionally generated representations that frame, delimit, or reduce reality through the act of description, the digital data practices I have in mind have to grapple with a representational excess. By this I mean that the assembly of data from sensors, in models, and across sources, creates pictures or diagrams of relations whose meaning is unclear and whose significance demands ongoing interpretation. Digital data worlds are less the 'thin simplifications' of plans and maps (Scott 1998) than thickening complexities through which vernacular and expert data analysts must find a way of navigating. Given this, I suggest that if we are to participate in conversations about the implications of digital data, we need to find our way out of the trap of *either* treating data uncritically as direct signs of an underlying reality, *or* treating it critically as socially constructed representations. In what follows, I ask: is there a way of reconceiving the realities of digital data worlds? And if so, how might we go about doing this?

This brings us to a third problem: what I am terming here the anthropological commitment to *analytical agnosticism*. Even if we do manage to gain some partial, post-dualistic insights into the social and cultural dynamics of digital data worlds, the

Journal of the Royal Anthropological Institute (N.S.) 27, 108-126
© 2021 The Authors. *Journal of the Royal Anthropological Institute* published by John Wiley & Sons Ltd on behalf of Royal Anthropological Institute

question remains of what we should do with this knowledge and where we should do it. One of the strengths of anthropology is that anthropologists require of themselves and their peers an acknowledgement of the provisionality of all knowledge claims, including our own. This agnosticism is what enables the operation of ethnographic critique, holding at bay the assumed superiority or universality of disciplinary or institutionally sanctioned ways of knowing that often inform our taken-for-granted understandings of the world. By setting these to one side, we allow space for other voices and perspectives to appear. But this same demand for provisionality also makes the moment of action a difficult one to countenance, for action demands justification and justifications generally demand a closure of the provisionality that allows for difference to emerge as a possibility.

At the same time, digital data worlds often seem to demand calls for action, born out of not a commitment to a particular ideology but rather a more post-political form of action that emerges from engagements with data read as signs of reality (Swyngedouw 2010a; 2010b; 2011). Here I am thinking of the climate scientist who finds themselves an 'accidental activist' as they listen to the signals of their experiments in which they see themselves and the infrastructures of their lives implicated, or the big technology companies and governments who realize that digital systems have unforeseen ethical consequences. When a 'position' or 'perspective' is produced by a machine, or actions are assembled and sustained by hybrid human/nonhuman infrastructures, I suggest that this potentially changes the terms upon which reflexivity and relativism are founded. For no longer is the issue the status of 'our' world-view vs the world-view of an 'other'. Rather, a new issue has emerged, namely the possibility that it is not only world-views that are relevant now, but also data-worldings – a more uncertain and emergent landscape of complex relations that come into view in relation to digital data and its unfolding and call forth a need to remake meaning (Massumi 2010). This raises the stakes for the commitment to analytical agnosticism, for what does it mean to abstain from taking a position in the face not of human world-views but of digital data worlds? What, in the face of biased algorithms or alarming climate models, are we remaining agnostic towards? Is it not more important that we 'take seriously' the algorithm or the computer model than render it provisional to allow other perspectives from outside the dominant techno-political order to appear?

This essay proceeds, then, from this threefold problem of how to do anthropology in the face of the systemic, emergent, and at times uncanny relations realized by new streams and assemblies of data. Still wedded as I am to the capacity of ethnography to inform anthropological understanding, my answers to these questions begin with my own empirical ethnographic research with others who have been working with and responding to data about distributed and emergent phenomena.

The challenges posed by these data worlds came into view in my own research in relation to an attempt to do an ethnographic analysis of climate models and their political effects (Knox 2020). Climate change as it appears in climate models is a phenomenon which is materialized in data traces of carbon, temperature, energy, humidity, economy, and ocean acidity. Climate change as described by climate science is not a description of weather in the here and now, but a phenomenon composed out of data on climates of the past from which projections of climates of the future are derived (Edwards 1999; 2010; Lippert 2015; Lövbrand & Stripple 2011). Climate change's life in data means that definitionally it takes place in no individual location and that its relevance is located more in the future than in the present. People who engage with the

Journal of the Royal Anthropological Institute (N.S.) **27**, 108-126

question of how to mitigate climate change thus engage not with phenomenologically present environmental processes, but with complex data models that recast everyday practices into a climatological register. One thing highlighted by an attention to climate change as a feature of data models is that just because climate change, as it is described in climate models, is never *here*, and not *now*, crucially this does not mean it is not *real*. Indeed, it is the alarming reality of traces of climatological change that have begun to shift climate change from a matter of scientific representation to a matter of public concern, moving people to think about and reflect on their material practices in the here and now in a new light.

In studying climate change as a phenomenon that manifests in and through data, and trying to understand the implications of data models for social practice, I have found myself forced to revisit and rethink long-running anthropological questions about what constitutes the real; the methods that we as anthropologists have of engaging with different kinds of realities; and the responsibilities that follow from the production of anthropological knowledge about these realities. It is to the central challenge that emerging forms of data pose to anthropological understandings of the real that this essay aims to respond.

In this essay, my focus is not on climate scientists or climate models per se, but on people whose practices have become framed and informed by climate change thus described. Specifically, the essay explores in the city of Manchester, where I did my research, how climate change as data model became grounded and experienced in people's engagements with the materiality of their everyday lives and how this proceeded through an ongoing and intimate attention to material relations made visible by data. In my research, this took the form of everyday engagements with environmental monitoring and energy data that operated as a proxy for measurements of carbon emissions and that served to link people to houses, energy infrastructures, political settlements, and planetary futures. Through an analysis of these practices, I derive a response to the questions posed above about the challenge of approaching digital data worlds as an anthropological problem, suggesting that one generative answer to this challenge might be to rethink data in the mode of the 'hack'.

Drawing on my experience of trying to understand the place of material sensors and energy monitors in people's engagement with an unfolding and distributed climate-changing world, 'the hack' emerges as a crucial concept. I propose the hack as a concept that has the capacity to denote a relationship with data that takes it not just as a stable representation that we need to deconstruct, but also as a means of engaging with relations that are imprecise and unknown and whose imprecision and unknowability become a frame for action. In this essay, the hack is taken not just as an ethnographic observation but also as a specific mode of practice that I use to reflect back on the practice of doing ethnography on digital realities. The final third of the essay moves the discussion away from an analysis of my ethnographic material to explore whether we might find in the practice of the hack a way of doing anthropology differently. Here I describe an experience of organizing and running a 'hack lab' as a form of ethnographic research. Far from disavowing a critical stance towards normative modes of action, I suggest that 'taking seriously' techno-political configurations in the mode of 'the hack' might offer anthropologists a useful perspective with which to rethink anthropology's place in the face of data relations, creating a form of anthropological practice appropriate to understanding the place of data as an increasingly central aspect of contemporary social relations.

Journal of the Royal Anthropological Institute (N.S.) **27**, *108-126*
© 2021 The Authors. *Journal of the Royal Anthropological Institute* published by John Wiley & Sons Ltd on behalf of Royal Anthropological Institute

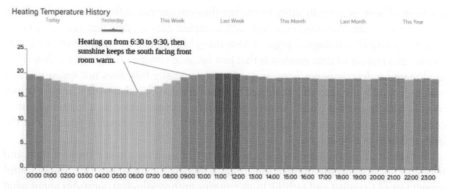

Figure 1. Graph of temperature from Hive heating system.

Data ethnography

In keeping with the focus on the anthropology of digital data worlds, I want to start not with a person, or a place, an event or a story, but instead with three graphs. The graphs are being shown to me by Alison,[1] a Manchester resident who has been monitoring the material properties of her home in preparation for energy efficiency work that she hopes to have done on the house in coming years. Alison is talking me through her experiences of monitoring the physical and energetic properties of her house and the different feeds of information that she uses to gain insights into her home environment. We are seated at her kitchen table, laptop open in front of us, and she opens the graphs one by one.

The first graph (Fig. 1) offers a dawn of bars, warm at first, then cooling to lime green, before darkening to deep orange and a long evening glow. This is yesterday's living room, as relayed by the thermometer of Alison's Hive™ heating system. Signals have been sent from the hive in the living room to a server via Wi-Fi and broadband to British Gas. The bits of information have then been dragged back into the kitchen where we are now sitting, and displayed on the computer screen. On the screen is a graphical read-out which Alison has captured and annotated for the various people to whom she has shown this data. There is no indication of the causes of the changes in temperature, so she has labelled the effect of her heating system on rising heat, and noted the effect of the sun on keeping the front room warm throughout the day.

The second graph (Fig. 2) that Alison shows me offers a multi-layered depiction of data. Down at the base of the data cut-through is the outside world – a feed of information from a weather service describing outside temperatures for the Manchester suburb in which she lives. Jagged intervals, first arrayed like a path along a valley, then step upwards as the afternoon sun warms the air, reaching a 12°C peak before stepping carefully, gradually, back down into the night. Laid upon this bottom stratum, in green, is the living room again. Here the room is depicted in energetic glory with information from an independent temperature sensor providing a more lively picture than the Hive data flow, with a sort of a rollercoaster feel as the heat falls at first, only to be caught by the thermostatic control of the central heating, which, then boosted by the radiated sunlight from the south-facing window, lifts the room up to a comfortable 20°C. As Alison describes how the sun moves on its inevitable course around the house, the temperature seems to enter into a cat-and-mouse game of boiler vs cold, hiccupping along until bed

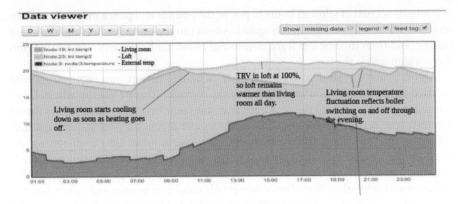

Figure 2. Graph of temperature from open energy monitor.

settles things down and the temperature is allowed to fall back to its early morning low. The final stratum has the aspect of a gentle swell in blue. Here insulation does its work, keeping the loft of the house, which also has its own temperature sensor, well apart from jagged landscape of the cool outdoors or the fluctuations of the downstairs room.

The final graph (Fig. 3) comes from Alison's user profile on the website of the energy company OVO. Here the cybernetic system of house and world and heating is replaced by a simple on/off, aggregated into towering heaps of energy used over time. Alison is a 'super-forum user', and has agreed with OVO that meter readings from the smart meter they installed can be sent back to them at five-minute intervals rather than the daily readings that come as standard. They learn about her habits. She learns too. Each

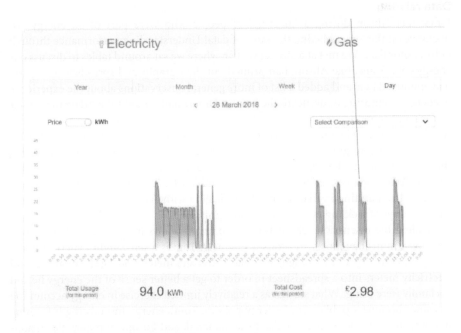

Figure 3. Graph of temperature from OVO energy company.

Journal of the Royal Anthropological Institute (N.S.) **27**, *108-126*
© 2021 The Authors. *Journal of the Royal Anthropological Institute* published by John Wiley & Sons Ltd on behalf of Royal Anthropological Institute

five-minute accrual of kilowatt hours of gas, or the pounds and pence that gas costs, can now be tracked, mapped, and interrogated. Alison can see when her heating is working hardest, and from this she can learn new things about her house, its costs, her life, and the world in which she lives.

Alison is not a typical smart meter user. Schooled in software engineering, and invested long term in transforming her home to make it more energy efficient, her sensibility to her house and the data feeds that now come from various sensors is that of someone who is comfortable with data analytics and driven for personal and political reasons to use this data to inform changes to her environment. Now semi-retired, she has both the time to turn her attention to her home and the need to do so as she is spending many more of her waking hours there. She lives in a part of the city with a vibrant social network of liberal environmentally conscious people, and so her desire to live a more ecologically sustainable life is also validated through her interactions with many people around her.

Alison was one of several people I spoke to about energy monitoring. Drawing on her monitoring experiences and that of others, I suggest that, far from providing a stable description of the world upon which decisions can be made, data from monitoring devices was experienced by those I met as something rather different. Data here was not simply descriptive or informational – not an 'immutable mobile' (Latour 1986) – but rather became actively constitutive of an experience of living in an environment characterized by complex, extensive, and often unknowable relations. Responding to this unfolding complexity, those who found themselves being required to engage with data as a way of proceeding in the world found themselves creating questions as to what might be a socially appropriate way of organizing and relating. It is this kind of data relationality that I term here the practice of the hack.

Data relating

I first met Alison during a 'meet-up' of people who were part of an energy co-operative on the topic 'Making the most of data! Understanding performance through bill/monitor data'. We met at a city centre bar, where we sat around tables to discuss our energy data. Some, like Alison, had printed out their graphs and spreadsheets. Alison had annotated hers and added a list of more general observations about the experience of energy monitoring underneath the graphs. Others had brought their data in on their laptops and some needed to connect to Wi-Fi to access it directly from their energy supplier's website. The meeting was an opportunity to make sure that the spreadsheets were properly configured, to learn from others about different kinds of monitoring (both digital and analogue) that were possible, and to talk about the difference that data made to people's experiences of engaging with the techno-politics of environmental change – from finding insulation installers, dealing with energy companies, to finding effective ways of tackling ever-rising carbon emissions.

Leading the discussions about how to go about analysing energy data was Tom. Employed in his day job as an acoustic engineer, Tom is a self-taught expert in home energy monitoring. Ten years ago, he began to transfer meter readings from his gas and electricity meters into a spreadsheet in order to get a better sense of the energy he and his family were using. What started as a relatively limited exercise in energy accounting has since become a public act of energy politics, Tom's energy monitoring informing not only his own energy use but also local, national, and European policy discussions on energy and climate change and an international network of followers on Twitter.

Journal of the Royal Anthropological Institute (N.S.) **27**, *108-126*
© 2021 The Authors. *Journal of the Royal Anthropological Institute* published by John Wiley & Sons Ltd on behalf of Royal Anthropological Institute

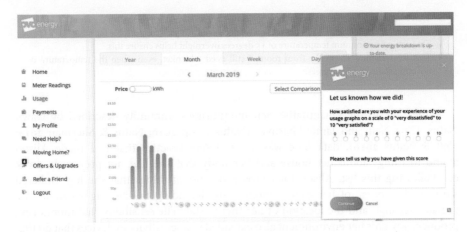

Figure 4. Pop-up box asking for user feedback on author's OVO energy account.

Before this meet-up, I had already gone to talk to Tom at his home, largely because of his reputation among others I was doing research with as someone who knew a lot about home energy monitoring. During my conversations with Tom, he conjured an image of himself as a kind of energy detective. Data created puzzles that Tom found himself needing to investigate. Data on his home seemed to open up more and more questions which he set out to answer by further monitoring and through conversations with others interested in his monitoring activities. This included other members of the energy co-operative of which he was a member, environmental activists, monitor developers, bike shop experts, friends, and colleagues.

This effect of monitoring data was similar for others I spoke to. Data was not so much a consistent source of information about how people's houses were performing, but was rather a prompt for conversations, a trigger for questions, and an impetus for understanding complex relations that cut across professional, institutional, and social boundaries. During my interview with Alison, I discussed with her a new feature on the OVO website that auto-generated a profile of energy using 'habits' from the signals from the smart meter. She was sceptical about the conclusions this algorithm came to about how much energy was being used in categories such as 'standby', 'entertainment', or 'refrigeration'. When I went to my own OVO account as I was writing this essay to remind myself of the categories that were being used, a pop-up box appeared (Fig. 4), as if anticipating the argument I am making here, asking me if I was satisfied with my experience of usage graphs on a scale to 1 to 10, and to ask me to tell them why I had given them the score!

A similar relation with data was also articulated in other conversations at the meet-up. Alison had brought with her the graphs described above, as well as an A4 sheet of paper with some further reflections on things that occurred to her as she was putting the data together. On the A4 sheet, she listed 'some of the things I've discovered through monitoring':

Some of the things I've discovered through monitoring are:

- That the front room heats up far more slowly than the living room – both external walls have hard to fill cavities, and the double glazed bay window is approaching 30 years old.

Journal of the Royal Anthropological Institute (N.S.) **27**, 108-126
© 2021 The Authors. *Journal of the Royal Anthropological Institute* published by John Wiley & Sons
Ltd on behalf of Royal Anthropological Institute

- That I wake up with a cold nose in the night if the temperature drops below 13 degrees.
- That heating the house up to 17 degrees on work day mornings is comfortable for me.
- That setting a minimum temperature of 15 degrees overnight helps ensure this.
- That for watching TV in the front room, I still need a blanket, even when the temperature is hovering at around 19 degrees.

Rather like in the Quantitative Self monitoring community described by Dawn Nafus, Gina Neff, and Jamie Sherman (Nafus 2014; 2016; Nafus & Sherman 2014; Neff & Nafus 2016), data here was a sensitizing practice that had made Alison attend to things about her house and her body that she had not previously dwelt on. Following this list, Alison then provided a list of things that she has 'tinkered with' in the course of her energy monitoring, including the heating schedule, the radiator settings, and the location of her thermostat. The sensibility that monitoring produced towards her environment also extended to a sensitivity to devices that do that monitoring.

Alison had highlighted these things and circulated them in advance of the meeting because she was interested in talking with other people at the meet-up about whether they had experienced the same. She described her response to data not in engineering or managerial terms but in more tentative language of 'things I've discovered' and 'things I've tinkered with'. Others at the meeting came with a similar range of semi-formed reflections, examples, and questions, ranging from how to detect the movement of air in the house using the smoke from a joss stick, to queries about how data is transmitted between different devices and what communications protocols are used. The relationships that were interrogated in these conversations were undisciplined, transgressing boundaries between science and engineering, IT and energy, devices and blankets, bodies and numbers.

What data seemed to produce, then, for these people was not so much a representation that stabilized a picture of the reality in which they lived, and which in turn informed decisions about how to behave differently, but rather a collection of signals that called out for new kinds of engagement. Data did not so much reveal truths as reveal ambivalences that necessitated collaborations like the meet-up, or negotiations with companies and technology providers to make sense of the 'reassembly of the social' that they effected. The capacity of data to not only describe but also demand the creation of new relations means that data seemed to do more than work within the parameters of already-existing, habitual forms of participation with existing social groups. Rather, it enabled the constitution of new social relations that opened the world up for people in new kinds of ways. Here, what was important was not simply tweaks to the habitual rituals and practices of everyday life, but an opening up of individual practice that required a questioning of the taken-for-granted cultural and social parameters within which people were living, a questioning that I suggest is productively captured in the language of 'the hack'.

Hacking energy

Many of the people I spoke to who were actively monitoring their energy use had been involved in face-to-face events that had used the language of the hack to capture the form of interaction and practice that these data-orientated interactions encouraged. Some of those whom I spoke to attended a regular monthly technical meet-up called EcoHome Lab, where they had learnt how to build their own energy monitors, discussed the use of these energy monitors, and expanded into other topics such as how to use batteries or how to build their own air quality monitor.

EcoHome Lab took place monthly at a maker space called MadLab. MadLab describes itself as 'a grassroots site for innovation', its mission being 'to help people make things better, together'. On its mission page, it elaborates its philosophy:

> We believe that the best way to understand fast-paced technological innovation is by getting involved, through experimentation and play. In particular, MadLab is an advocate of hacking – taking things apart, figuring out how they work and re-purposing or re-imagining them. This is a principle we apply to everything we do, whether it's designing new digital devices and services or finding improved ways of working with our partners and communities.[2]

EcoHome Lab was understood both by its organizers and by their friends at MadLab to be very much aligned with the latter's philosophy. It brought together programmers, hardware developers, and people involved in ecological activities to fashion their own bottom-up technical interventions to tackle environmental issues. Building these technical objects had the effect of 'white boxing' energy infrastructures (cf. Corsín Jiménez 2014b) and helped people better understand systemic social and environmental change in often unexpected ways.

EcoHome Lab was not the only energy-related event that worked in this way. In 2013, another event had been run at MadLab where people had been invited to 'hack the DECC 2050 calculator'. The DECC 2050 calculator was a tool developed by the Department for Energy and Climate Change to model the effects of different policy choices to tackle climate change on economy and society. Users of the calculator could enter in their choices for how to reduce carbon emissions and the calculator would illustrate the likely implications of each intervention (Fig. 5).

At this event, people interested in climate change, energy, and policy had met civil servants who had been involved in the design of the calculator tool and together they had worked to try to break apart its assumptions in order to improve it – both in terms of its technical operations and in terms of its capacity to positively influence policy around climate change.

In 2017, two more energy-focused events were organized that were also explicitly framed in terms of hacking. The 2017 annual 'Hack Manchester' event brought programmers together for an intensive twenty-four-hour technology hack and asked the energy co-operative, the Carbon Co-op, who also ran EcoHome Lab to provide

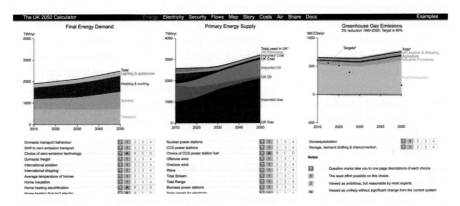

Figure 5. Screenshot of DECC 2050 calculator (classic edition).

one of the challenges for the event. In response, the Carbon Co-op came up with a challenge where programmers at the event were asked to design an energy information display. The same year, a very different event – a conference to discuss changes in energy infrastructure – was organized, with the title 'Hacking the Future of Energy'.

The hack, then, in this setting, was a way of describing a form of interaction that took place in a semi-public gathering, in which things – be they policies, technologies, theories, or concepts – would be taken apart, figured out, and repurposed or reimagined. This is somewhat different to the way that hacking has predominantly been discussed to date in anthropology. In recent anthropological work on hacking, the hacker has been a term used to denote someone who is involved in forms of computer programming and particularly the reverse engineering of programming for the purposes of espionage, crime, or vigilantism. Christopher Kelty and Gabriella Coleman capture this well in the preface to a special issue of *Limn* on 'Hacks, leaks, and breaches', where they write:

> '[H]acker' clearly means many different things – from adolescent boys to criminals on the 'Dark Web' to nation-state spies. And one might add: from makers of Free Software to certified information security researchers to cool television characters like Eliot Alderson, to wardens of privacy and promoters of encryption to those helping secure the work of journalists and dissidents (Kelty & Coleman 2017).

'Hackers' here means many things but it does not seem to mean people tinkering in rather mundane ways with the interface between sensors, data, and devices in their homes.

Whilst data, digital networks, and computation offer a technological plane of affinity between Kelty and Coleman's hackers and our data subjects, the idea of the hack in the cases I present here denotes something rather different to what they describe – both as a form of practice and as a claim to expertise. For Kelty and Coleman, hackers are people who playfully and creatively deploy the logics of computer coding to craft interventions. Coleman writes in her book *Coding freedom* of how 'the tension between individualism and collectivism, in particular, is negotiated through the extremely well-developed and common penchant that hackers have for performing cleverness, whether through technological production or humour' (2013: 94). She also elaborates elsewhere that hacking is a performative form of liberal, often techno-libertarian political ideals (Coleman 2009; 2010; 2011; Coleman & Golub 2008). Whereas Coleman's hackers are therefore experts who performatively express their superior technical expertise through craftiness, humour, and play, those with whom I spent time enacted hacking as a much more modest, tentative, and collaborative practice of questioning and unfolding realities through data. To 'hack' energy data involved an explicit attempt to do away with hierarchies and to demonstrate the necessity of collaborative modes of learning how to become effectively attuned to opaque and changing infrastructures. Hackathons or hack labs were not just sites for an open and participatory form of technology design but were also beginning to be seen as organizational forms through which social transformation might be achieved.

There is a clear parallel between what I am describing as hacking and design practices existing across various fields of activity that have been described in anthropology under the umbrella of 'prototyping' culture. In the attention to open source information sharing, the development of open hardware, and the production of new kinds of artefacts that might have the potential to draw forth new social formations, these practices of hacking captured many of the same preoccupations and cultural assumptions as those explored in descriptions of prototyping advanced by scholars like Christopher Kelty, George Marcus, Alberto Corsín Jiménez, and Adolfo Estalella (Corsín Jiménez 2014a; 2014b; Estalella & Corsín Jiménez 2017; Kelty, Corsín Jiménez & Marcus 2010). Like prototyping, the hack as a mode of practice created its understanding by actively creating material propositions or interventions into the field of distributed relations that data was tracing out. These interventions could be technological (the open source energy monitor, the DECC 2050 calculator, the Hive thermostat), political (policy propositions), ludic (games), numerical (gathering data in a spreadsheet), or artistic (staged art/activist interventions), but they all used intervention as a way of simultaneously *acting on* and *producing new knowledge* about opaque, complex, and emergent digital data worlds.

However, as I spent more time participating and engaging in the mode of the 'hack', I began to understand it as a practice that was less about designing prototypes that might ultimately be taken up as future models for general social and technical practice. Instead it was better understood as a critical, materialist, post-disciplinary mode of critiquing and deconstructing existing social relations and material infrastructures. If prototyping focuses on the production of provisional artefacts that would be put into circulation as experiments orientated to the making of a possible future, hacking was more of a disruptive, analytical practice, orientated to the reordering of complex technical infrastructures. Rather than bringing design preoccupations to the fore, what hacking seemed to offer was a means of doing a critical social and cultural analysis through the collaborative deconstruction of contemporary socio-material infrastructures that were self-evidently composed out of and revealed by data. As such, I shifted my understanding of hacking from an activity primarily concerned with experimental design to one that was preoccupied with the radical possibility of seeing otherwise – a realization that opened up an unexpected bridge to the practice of anthropology.

Like anthropology, the hack was an attempt to see the world differently. It was an act of conceptual deconstruction through material participation and one that required listening to different viewpoints and technical practices on their own terms. Like work informed by science and technology studies and ethnographic studies of infrastructure, it was also tolerant of the crossing of boundaries between the social and the technical, investigating social problems through attention to technical artefacts and framing technical challenges in terms of their social implications. In the hack as a practice of material deconstruction, people seemed to have devised a way of productively engaging with data realities, appreciating them as both socially constructed *and*, simultaneously, real. This introduced the possibility that the hack might offer a form of practice through which we as anthropologists might rethink our own conceptual and methodological relationship with data. Was there a way, I wondered, of not only doing an anthropology of the hack, but also learning from it to hack anthropology itself? What could anthropology look like if it were to not only analyse, describe, or critique the practice of the hack, but also embrace it as an alternative way of producing anthropological insight in the face of relational complexity foregrounded by digital data infrastructures?

Hacking anthropology

In the summer of 2018, I had the opportunity to put these thoughts into practice. As I neared the end of my research on energy monitoring, I talked to some of the people I had been doing the research with about 'impact and communication'. Although at this point I had not begun to think explicitly in the language of the hack, it nonetheless seemed entirely logical, when Jonathan Atkinson, project manager of the Carbon Co-op, suggested that one option could be to organize a 'hack lab' to continue and extend the research. Jonathan told me that he had wanted to do a hack lab for a while but had not had the chance. For him, it would be a way of extending work that the Carbon Co-op were already doing to unpack and understand energy systems by stimulating investigations and ongoing conversations about the relationship between energy, infrastructure, data, and equity. For me, the suggestion was intriguing. Could this be a way of experimenting with a form of research which moved beyond the stable distinction between world and representation in which I felt trapped? I wondered what we might learn through this form, both about 'the hack' as a practice and about the complex and changing world of digital energy infrastructure.

We therefore set about organizing the hack lab. As we began to put the event together, it turned out that the hack lab was not a fixed or clear format for any of the organizers, but one that came into being as we looked at other examples of hack labs and hackathons and spoke to people who had attended these kinds of events. We applied for funding and the funding we received also helped determine how it was structured. The hack lab that we eventually designed took place over a weekend in November 2018. It was conceived and organized by myself, Britt Jurgensen, a community practitioner and performance artist, Jonathan Atkinson, and Laura Williams, also from the Carbon Co-op. The title of the event was 'Hacking the Future of Energy: How Can We Make the Future of Energy More Equitable?' – a question that was posed as a direct challenge to potential participants to engage with a highly technical, data-informed energy infrastructure as a problem of collective social life. People were invited to apply through a mail-out to our networks and a Facebook advert. The advertising for the event was targeted at community energy activists, technical experts, people working in energy industries, and social scientists, and participants were asked to say either what idea they would like to work on, or what they thought they could bring to the discussion in terms of skills, interests, or enthusiasm for getting involved in a just energy transition. There was to be a prize of £2,000 for the winning team with the best solution to the challenges of energy equity.

As an intervention into digital data worlds, the event description specifically invited people to respond to the digitalization of energy infrastructure with suggestions for technologies, projects, or experiments that would capitalize on these changes to make energy 'more equitable'. The call for participants set out the terms of the hack:

> The generation, distribution and supply of energy is changing with more renewables, battery storage and developments in smart metering and smart grid technology. These changes create the opportunity to rethink who energy is for and who controls it. New technological tools and changing sources of electricity might enable alternative ways of managing, sharing, buying and distributing electricity. What would this look like? And what would the social effects of such a system be?

It also specifically requested that people consider their response as a critical engagement with technological systems and their propensities, stating that: 'Open source standards and systems, solar generation, EV charging, battery storage, DIY renewables, Blockchain technology, social enterprises, co-operative platforms – all these elements may have a role to play in your idea'.[3]

Journal of the Royal Anthropological Institute (N.S.) **27**, *108-126*
© 2021 The Authors. *Journal of the Royal Anthropological Institute* published by John Wiley & Sons Ltd on behalf of Royal Anthropological Institute

This framing for the event emerged out of collaborative research I had been involved with into energy monitoring and its extended implications for grid operators, electric vehicle manufacturers, solar panel developers, communities, and policy-makers. It intervened by inviting people to respond, with me and my research partners, to the landscape of relations that was emerging and appearing through my ethnography of/with energy and carbon data.

The event started with two presentations from external speakers that put forward propositions as to the socio-technical challenges of a changing and digitalizing energy infrastructure told from the perspective of social science, energy justice, and sociology. Following these presentations, people pitched their ideas for how they thought they could intervene in the energy system and five teams were formed. On the second day, the teams worked intensively on their ideas. People shifted teams as ideas fell apart and other ideas were strengthened. A 'slack channel' was set up to run alongside the event – gathering resources, photos, tweets, and video clips into a stream of information that people were encouraged to interact with. Facilitators reminded people of the question they were meant to be answering. Thea Nguyen, an anthropology student, took notes and photographs of the event. On the third day, there were just three teams left, and they pitched the proposals that they had worked up to a panel of judges. Comparing the proposals against a set of criteria, a winning team was chosen. The winning team were a group who proposed to create a proof-of-concept model for an open source peer-to-peer energy trade. This was a technological proposition which held in place fragile threads connecting the possibility of open and direct exchanges of energy between householders; the creation of a form of economic activity without excessive accumulation; and the creation of an incentive for more people to become involved and invested, both emotionally and financially, in a future without fossil fuels. The proposal was to create a data model which could prove that a single transparent exchange of electricity was possible between a citizen in one part of the country with a solar panel on their roof and a citizen in another part of the country in need of power. In imagining how to re-channel power so as to make renewables more viable, and in doing so reconnect people in new ways, the winning project was not only proposing a technological solution to a problem of energy transfer, but was also proposing a means of reimagining and redescribing the socio-technical relations through which climate change was manifesting and through which both climate and society might be reshaped.

There is much more to be said about the event, but for our purposes here, I want to bring the essay back to the three challenges of studying data realities with which I began to consider how designing an event in the model of the hack offered a response to some of the ethnographic challenges of doing research in/of digital data worlds.

First, the problem of method. One of the challenges that ethnographers face is how to speak back to the scalings of digital data infrastructures. By definition, the ontological presence of globally interconnected digital data worlds as mega, global, transnational entities, or what Timothy Morton (2013) has called 'hyperobjects', means they exceed that which can be studied ethnographically. Yet spending time talking about and participating in the data practices of people who were monitoring their energy and houses and asking questions about these relations revealed that the hack, as a mode of engagement, has the potential to operate as a scale-transforming practice. To hack one's own energy bills and to post the results on Twitter was to open up the domestic home as a site not just of local energy practices but also of public participation in energy and data infrastructures. In hacking energy data, inviting others who might be located

Journal of the Royal Anthropological Institute (N.S.) **27**, 108-126
© 2021 The Authors. *Journal of the Royal Anthropological Institute* published by John Wiley & Sons Ltd on behalf of Royal Anthropological Institute

in the same city, or on the other side of the world, for their reflections, the hack did not create sites of participation that scaled relations along a trajectory of local to global wherein an ethnographer might need to place themselves, but rather assembled entities of different orders around an issue. What matters in the act of hacking is not the forging of relations of alliance with proximate others, but a practice of gathering and sifting, shuffling and reorganizing, in order to work out where social and material alliances are possible and where they are likely to fail. The hack does not so much create a microcosm of the world that can be imagined so as to be scaled up, but instead creates a cluster around which more and more people, things, and ideas can accrete. Success in the model of the hack is not a prototype that provides a scale model for a technological future, but an artefact, project, or idea around which the world is gathered and, in the process of that gathering, remade. Ethnography in the mode of the hack, then, offers a form of understanding that is not about finding out what a particular group of people are doing in a particular place and why, but about discovering, through a 'staging' of relations, the possibility or impossibility of different forms of relating. Ethnography in this mode does not seek to represent all of the different existing views on the world, but rather seeks to understand how views and worlds are made, formed, reinforced, and dismantled.

This brings us to our second challenge, which concerned studying processes that do not bifurcate neatly into a world and a representation of that world but continually 'fold' into one another. The hack offers a relationship to representation that is instructive for anthropology, for it shifts representation from the end-point of a process of knowledge production to the starting point upon which a process of understanding proceeds. In hacking data, we saw that data was not the end-point of a representational process. Data traces could be representational, but they could also be unstable signifiers. Signals could be errors, statistical inferences could be wrong, measurements could be improved upon, data infrastructures could always be 'inverted' (Bowker 1994). Treating data not as a text to be read but as a thing to be 'hacked' shifted representation from a form of description to a site of action.

In recent years, there have been other anthropologists who have begun to explore the virtues of a form of anthropology that takes place in this moment where representations become a site for action rather than claims for truth. Sarah Pink and colleagues have been exploring how to develop design anthropologies that seek to shape the future, rather than just describing the present (Akama, Pink & Fergusson 2015; Pink & Salazar 2017; Salazar, Pink, Irving & Sjöberg 2017). Building on the ground laid by anthropologists such as George Marcus (1995; 2000), Michael Fischer (2007), Paul Rabinow (Rabinow, Marcus, Faubion & Rees 2008), and Douglas Holmes (Holmes & Marcus 2005; 2008), the collaborative ethnography collective COLLEEX has also begun to explore how to do ethnography that is more interventionist and collaborative in its design (Estalella & Sánchez Criado 2018). Similarly, Alberto Corsín Jiménez's work to reflexively develop an open source architecture for urban participation and for anthropology publishing also arguably operates in precisely this mode of ethnography as hack that I am outlining here (Corsín Jiménez 2017). In each of these cases, ethnographic understandings are recast not as stabilizations and settlements but rather as propositions that both emerge out of and enact a critique. As propositions, they invite a response but they do not determine from whom or from what that response might emerge. Responses can take the form of opinion, of nonhuman reconfigurations, of data glitches, or even of silences or gaps.

Journal of the Royal Anthropological Institute (N.S.) **27**, *108-126*
© 2021 The Authors. *Journal of the Royal Anthropological Institute* published by John Wiley & Sons Ltd on behalf of Royal Anthropological Institute

This brings us to our third challenge, which is that of analytical agnosticism and a critical attention to difference. If anthropology in the mode of the hack is not a stabilization of truth but rather a proposition orientated to the possibility of change, then what does this do to ethnography? Where data hacks are concerned, the answer to the proposition (a statement, a technology, a game) demands a collective rather than an individual response. Propositions become the impetus for devising forms of social organization adequate to understanding the problem, gathering people and things as resources to map out and address the contours of the 'thing' with which they are confronted. Unlike conventional ethnography, where an intervention might be deemed to fix or position the ethnographer as coming with an immutable position, might intervening in the mode of the hack not help relieve our ethnographer of the demand that all actions require justifications, and all justifications must be seen as truth claims? In the mode of the hack, an intervention would no longer require that the ethnographer decide in advance of acting whether they were assuming a particular truth or making a demarcated truth claim that would position them in such a way as to close down other ways of seeing. Instead, ethnography in the mode of the hack offers an alternative status for ethnographic knowledge. Here an intervention is not pre-justified but rather deploys evidence in a way that says: this is my ethnographic evidence that I have crafted to tell the best story I can – what do you know that might disrupt or extend that? The question posed in this way invites an answer without prejudice to the kind of evidence that could be brought to bear on the issue thus described. The hack therefore creates the possibility of opening anthropology up beyond a conversation between anthropologists, and beyond current discussions of how anthropology might be refashioned as a practice of design, allowing our own interpretations to be troubled, disrupted, and questioned by people with other stories, data, or materials to bear on the problem that we propose.

When technical projects are so often dominated by propositions that emerge from questions of engineering, a proposition that emerges from ethnographic, anthropological, or sociological sensibilities not only adds the 'social' back into technical projects, but also creates an alternative set of questions about what 'the problem' even is. Rather than asking how can we improve the carbon-intensive energy system revealed by climate models, the hack lab proposed the question: how can we make the energy system more equitable? Far from assuming that equity, fairness, and equality were unproblematic or transparent concepts, raising them to the status of a proposition (i.e. that the energy system is unequal), rather than an afterthought to a project aiming at technical functionality, meant that the question of what equality looked like in the face of a changing climate and changing energy infrastructure, or even if it was a good thing, became the focus of collective discussions over the efficacy of the solution. An engineer who participated in the event began the weekend by very vocally stating that he couldn't see what the fuss was about and in his view there were simple technical solutions that would resolve inequality in the energy system. On the second day, and deep into discussions about how to navigate geographical boundaries and regulatory controls over the transfer of both electricity and data between different people, different organizations, and different parts of the country, he expressed surprised frustration at just how complicated it all was. Yet rather than end with the conclusion that 'it is complicated', the format of the hack moved this observation onto the question of how to make these complicated relations anew. Critique and creation here proceeded hand-in-hand.

Journal of the Royal Anthropological Institute (N.S.) **27**, 108-126
© 2021 The Authors. *Journal of the Royal Anthropological Institute* published by John Wiley & Sons
Ltd on behalf of Royal Anthropological Institute

Conclusion

In this essay, I have tried to explore what an anthropology of data worlds could look like if we were to explore the hack not just as an incidental discovery of a contemporary, even neoliberal practice of competitive experimentation (Jones, Semel & Le 2015; Powell 2016), but also as a model for doing anthropology in the face of digital data worlds. We are living in unsettling times. Border-transgressing processes – from globalization to migration, climate change to technological hybridity – dominate social relations, undercutting explanations and re-modulating knowledge. Anthropological responses to this emergent, unsettling relationality have often tended to ground the abstractions of data by filling in the gaps with ethnographic descriptions of the local social processes from which data traces are abstracted. I am not advocating doing away with more familiar modes of ethnographic knowledge production, but I am arguing that adherence to this way of producing understanding risks putting limits on what we understand ourselves as legitimately being able to do and know as anthropologists. Faced with digital data worlds that pose ongoing challenges to the relevance, transportability, and translatability of ethnographic understanding of issues ranging from climate change to artificial intelligence to post-truth politics, I have argued that the hack might offer an opening to a different kind of anthropology.

In some ways, anthropology in the mode of the hack makes more central what ethnographers have always known: that knowledge production is collective; that truths are stabilized as a result of social practice and not as a result of their inherent 'truthfulness', but that neither are these stabilizations disconnected from the substance out of which they are made. Hacking anthropology is meant as an opening to new questions about how contemporary anthropological knowledge might be formed, a call to consider whether we might do better in acknowledging its own capacities for socialization and the role that digital data might play in this process. It is proposed as a way of attuning us to questions about where our representations sit within ecologies and materialities of knowledge. In order to engage with digital data worlds, it is clear we need new ways of redescribing what anthropology is and what it can be. Otherwise anthropology risks becoming an anachronism, an authorially powerful study of discrete cultures, an extractivist project that aims to stabilize world-views and align them as so many parts of a global human ecumene. Pushing back against this, hacking anthropology, far from closing down anthropological thinking into a single world-view that silences others, proposes a way of acknowledging the material relationality of all knowledge, including anthropological knowledge. Building on the understanding I have gained from others about what it means 'to hack', I have suggested how we might redesign our methods so as to make more explicit the invitation to others to join us as we attempt to understand the anthropological implications of unfolding data realities.

NOTES

I would like to thank all of the research participants and partners who supported and helped with this project. The research upon which this essay is based was generously funded with grants from the British Academy (Award Number: MD160038), the ESRC Festival of Social Science, and the UCL Grand Challenges Fund.

[1] All names of research participants who were interviewed for this research have been pseudonymized. For research collaborators who participated directly in the co-design of the energy hack event, and who I consider research partners rather than research subjects, their full names have been given and they have not been pseudonymized.

[2] See https://www.artscatalyst.org/artist/madlab (accessed 21 January 2021).

[3] See https://carbon.coop/portfolio/hacking-the-future-of-energy/ (accessed 22 January 2021).

REFERENCES

ABRAM, S., B.R. WINTHEREIK & T. YARROW (eds) 2019. *Electrifying anthropology*. London: Bloomsbury.

AKAMA, Y., S. PINK & A. FERGUSSON 2015. Design + ethnography + futures: surrendering in uncertainty. In *CHI 2015: Crossings, 2015*, 531-42. New York: Association for Computing Machinery (ACM).

ANAND, N., A. GUPTA & H. APPEL 2018. *The promise of infrastructure*. Durham, N.C.: Duke University Press.

BOWKER, G.C. 1994. *Science on the run: information management and industrial geophysics at Schlumberger, 1920-1940*. Cambridge, Mass.: MIT Press.

COLEMAN, E.G. 2009. Code is speech: legal tinkering, expertise, and protest among free and open source software developers. *Cultural Anthropology* **24**, 420-54.

———— 2010. The hacker conference: a ritual condensation and celebration of a lifeworld. *Anthropological Quarterly* **83**, 47-72.

———— 2011. Hacker politics and publics. *Public Culture* **23**, 511-16.

———— 2013. *Coding freedom: the ethics and aesthetics of hacking*. Princeton: University Press.

———— & A. GOLUB 2008. Hacker practice: moral genres and the cultural articulation of liberalism. *Anthropological Theory* **8**, 255-77.

CORSÍN JIMÉNEZ, A. 2014a. Introduction: Special issue: Prototyping cultures. *Journal of Cultural Economy* **7**, 381-98.

———— 2014b. The right to infrastructure: a prototype for open source urbanism. *Environment and Planning D: Society and Space* **32**, 342-62.

———— 2017. Auto-construction redux: the city as method. *Cultural Anthropology* **32**, 450-78.

EDWARDS, P.N. 1999. Global climate science, uncertainty and politics: data-laden models, model-laden data. *Science as Culture* **8**, 437-72.

———— 2010. *A vast machine: computer models, climate data, and the politics of global warming*. Cambridge, Mass.: MIT Press.

ESTALELLA, A. & A. CORSÍN JIMÉNEZ 2017. Ethnography: a prototype. *Ethnos* **2**, 846-66.

———— & T. SÁNCHEZ CRIADO 2018. *Experimental collaborations: ethnography through fieldwork devices*. New York: Berghahn Books.

FISCHER, M. 2007. Culture and cultural analysis as experimental systems. *Cultural Anthropology* **22**, 1-65.

HARVEY, P., C.B. JENSEN & A. MORITA (eds) 2017. *Infrastructures and social complexity: a companion*. London: Routledge.

HOLMES, D. & G.E. MARCUS 2005. Cultures of expertise and the management of globalization: towards the re-functioning of ethnography. In *Global assemblages: technology, politics, and ethics as anthropological problems* (eds) A. Ong & S.J. Collier, 235-52. Malden, Mass.: Blackwell.

———— 2008. Collaboration today and the re-imagination of the classic scene of fieldwork encounter. *Collaborative Anthropologies* **1**, 81-101.

JONES, G.M., B. SEMEL & A. LE 2015. 'There's no rules. It's hackathon.': negotiating commitment in a context of volatile sociality. *Journal of Linguistic Anthropology* **25**, 322-45.

KELTY, C.M. & E.G. COLEMAN 2017. Preface. *Limn* **8** (available online: *https://limn.it/articles/preface-hacks-leaks-and-breaches/*, accessed 21 January 2021).

————, A. CORSÍN JIMÉNEZ & G.E. MARCUS (eds) 2010. Prototyping prototyping. *Limn* **0** (available online: *https://limn.it/issues/prototyping-prototyping/*, accessed 21 January 2021).

KNOX, H. 2020. *Thinking like a climate: governing a city in times of environmental change*. Durham, N.C.: Duke University Press.

LATOUR, B. 1986. Visualisation and cognition: drawing things together. *Knowledge Society: Studies in the Sociology of Culture Past and Present* **6**, 1-40.

LIPPERT, I. 2015. Environment as datascape: enacting emission realities in corporate carbon accounting. *Geoforum* **66**, 126-35.

LÖVBRAND, E. & J. STRIPPLE 2011. Making climate change governable: accounting for carbon as sinks, credits and personal budgets. *Critical Policy Studies* **5**, 187-200.

MARCUS, G.E. 1995. Ethnography in/of the world system: the emergence of multi-sited ethnography. *Annual Review of Anthropology* **24**, 95-117.

———— 2000. *Para-sites: a casebook against cynical reason*. Chicago: University Press.

MASSUMI, B. 2010. The future birth of the affective fact: the political ontology of threat. In *The affect theory reader* (eds) M. Gregg & G.J. Seigworth, 52-70. Durham, N.C.: Duke University Press.

MORTON, T. 2013. *Hyperobjects: philosophy and ecology after the end of the world*. Minneapolis: University of Minnesota Press.

Journal of the Royal Anthropological Institute (N.S.) **27**, *108-126*
© 2021 The Authors. *Journal of the Royal Anthropological Institute* published by John Wiley & Sons Ltd on behalf of Royal Anthropological Institute

NAFUS, D. 2014. Stuck data, dead data, and disloyal data: the stops and starts in making numbers into social practices. *Distinktion* **15**, 208-22.

——— 2016. *Quantified: biosensing technologies in everyday life.* Cambridge, Mass.: MIT Press.

——— & J. SHERMAN 2014. This one does not go up to 11: the Quantified-Self movement as an alternative big data practice. *International Journal of Communication* **8**, 1784-94.

NEFF, G. & D. NAFUS 2016. *Self-tracking.* Cambridge, Mass.: MIT Press.

ONG, A. & S.J. COLLIER 2005. *Global assemblages: technology, politics, and ethics as anthropological problems.* Malden, Mass.: Blackwell.

PINK, S. & J.F. SALAZAR 2017. Anthropologies and futures: setting the agenda. In *Anthropologies and futures: researching emerging and uncertain worlds* (eds) J.F. Salazar, S. Pink, A. Irving & J. Sjöberg, 3-22. London: Bloomsbury.

POWELL, A. 2016. Hacking in the public interest: authority, legitimacy, means, and ends. *New Media and Society* **18**, 600-16.

RABINOW, P., G.E. MARCUS, J. FAUBION & T. REES 2008. *Designs for an anthropology of the contemporary.* Durham, N.C.: Duke University Press.

SALAZAR, J.F., S. PINK, A. IRVING & J. SJÖBERG (eds) 2017. *Anthropologies and futures: researching emerging and uncertain worlds.* London: Bloomsbury.

SCOTT, J.C. 1998. *Seeing like a state: how certain schemes to improve the human condition have failed.* New Haven: Yale University Press.

STAROSIELSKI, N. 2015. *The undersea network.* Durham, N.C.: Duke University Press.

SWYNGEDOUW, E. 2010a. Apocalypse forever? Post-political populism and the spectre of climate change. *Theory, Culture & Society* **27**, 213-32.

——— 2010b. Impossible sustainability and the post-political condition. In *Making strategies in spatial planning: knowledge and values* (eds) M. Cerreta, G. Concilio & V. Monno, 185-205. New York: Springer.

——— 2011. Depoliticized environments: the end of nature, climate change and the post-political condition. *Royal Institute of Philosophy Supplements* **69**, 253-74.

TSING, A.L. 2005. *Friction: an ethnography of global connection.* Princeton: University Press.

Hacker l'anthropologie

Résumé

Cet article donne un aperçu de la manière dont le hackage informatique pourrait représenter un modèle pour la recherche anthropologique face aux relations distribuées que les données digitales mettent en évidence. L'argument s'appuie sur un travail de terrain auprès de citoyens et de militants qui tentent de comprendre et d'exploiter les données produites par des moniteurs et des capteurs d'énergie. À partir de leurs expériences, l'autrice suggère que la pratique du « hack » aide les individus à naviguer parmi les données dans les relations sociales. Menant une observation des pratiques de hack tout en formulant une proposition méthodologique, elle met son ethnographie au service d'une réflexion sur le défi anthropologique que représente l'étude ethnographique de processus perceptibles uniquement à travers des données numériques ou digitales. Dans le but d'explorer la valeur du hack pour l'anthropologie, l'article présente l'exemple d'une tentative de réaliser un travail ethnographique à la manière du hackage. L'autrice conclut en s'interrogeant sur la manière dont cette pratique pourrait nous apporter de nouvelles solutions, pour comprendre les implications anthropologiques des relations systémiques et émergentes qui sont à la fois révélées et refaçonnées à travers les données.

© 2021 The Authors. *Journal of the Royal Anthropological Institute* published by John Wiley & Sons Ltd on behalf of Royal Anthropological Institute

7

Data – ova – gene – data

Antonia Walford *University College London*

In this essay, I observe that data is valuable not only for what it is, but also for what it will become: that is, that data is a form of potential. I explore two aspects of this by drawing two comparisons with other forms of potential: ova and genes. First, building on ethnographic fieldwork with environmental scientists and technicians in the Brazilian Amazon, I compare data processing with ova donation in the United Kingdom in order to explore how data processing might be considered a form of reproductive labour. I then turn to emergent big data infrastructures in the environmental sciences, and compare the environmental sciences with genomics, in order to gesture towards some critical questions that need to be asked of such open data initiatives. I end with a reflection on comparison as a privileged means of drawing out the forms understood to be latent within data.

Potential

The possibilities and promises of big data have been getting a lot of attention over the past decade or so, be it in academic research, businesses keen on making a profit, or a Euro-American press animated by the spectre of an 'Orwellian state' (Iliadis & Russo 2016; Watts 2018). On the other hand, data also remains conspicuously unspecified: something that is extracted from people without them even knowing, an informational artefact that is both 'raw' and technically opaque, apparently worth billions dollars but valued as such on elusive markets by data brokers who remain in the regulatory shadows. Data is everywhere, but at the same time strangely absent.

I want to suggest in this essay that, far from being an obstacle to analysis, this incapacity to grasp data is actually a function of one of its specific properties, namely that data is understood to be valuable because it can be transformed into something else.[1] No wonder it is hard to get a hold of; and no wonder it is not always obvious what or where data is. The metaphors about big data that are in general circulation are telling here (Awati & Shum 2015; Raicu 2015): data is the new oil

Journal of the Royal Anthropological Institute (N.S.) **27**, 127-141
© 2021 The Authors. *Journal of the Royal Anthropological Institute* published by John Wiley & Sons Ltd on behalf of Royal Anthropological Institute

This is an open access article under the terms of the Creative Commons Attribution-NonCommercial License, which permits use, distribution and reproduction in any medium, provided the original work is properly cited and is not used for commercial purposes.

(*The Economist* 2017), the new gold (Peck 2017) – a resource from which wealth can be extracted, a raw material to be 'mined' (see, e.g., Lupton 2013; Puschmann & Burgess 2014; Seaver 2015). But aside from what the specific terms of these metaphors are, it is interesting that there has been so much metaphorical work around big data at all. This is not coincidental. Metaphors work exactly through the capacity for one thing to be – partially at least – something else.

If data is often coveted exactly because it is understood as something that will transform into something else (even if 'there's no such thing as raw data', Gitelman 2013), another way to say this is that data is constituted by its potential; what Marilyn Strathern has pointed to in a different context as a 'capacity for development as yet unrealised' (1996: 17). In fact, taking my lead from Strathern, I want in this essay to suggest that data is in some aspects very like other forms of potential property which are 'difficult to recognise' (1996: 17) in this way: ova, genes, ideas – amongst other forms.

There is a third way in which data metaphors matter, then: it matters what ideas we are using to think data through. This essay is an experiment in thinking data not through metaphors of resource extraction, but through other forms of transformative potential, specifically ova and genes. I will be building on another of Strathern's astute observations regarding the analogical relationship between kinship and knowledge – how, in the English imagination at least, they have always served as resources for thinking each other (Strathern 1995; see also Maurer 2015). However, moving away from metaphors of resource extraction and towards alternative ways of recognizing data is not to move away from the questions of value, appropriation, and rightful ownership that animate current public data debates. On the contrary, it is exactly the entanglement and disentanglement of what we might call 'production' and 'reproduction' that I want to focus on in order to unravel the ways in which data comes to be valued as a form of social relation that has not happened yet.

The essay is structured around two comparisons which allow me to refract the idea of data's potential in two different directions. Drawing on my own ethnographic material from fieldwork conducted with earth system scientists in Brazil, in the first of these I compare the work of small-scale scientific data processing with ova donation in the United Kingdom in order to examine potential as inhering in the tension between what something is and what it will become. In the second, I compare the emergence of transnational big data environmental science with genomics, focusing on how the idea of open data functions in each as a form of potentiality that rests on the tension between the possibility of becoming anything, and the necessity of having to become something. Heeding the remit of this special issue to demonstrate not only how anthropology can contribute to our understanding of 'the data moment', but also how taking data as an ethnographic object might ask us to analytically reshape anthropology, in the conclusion of the essay I reflexively focus on anthropological comparison as a revelatory technique. Comparison has traditionally been understood to work in anthropology by bringing together disparate sets of materials in order that they might show each other in a different light (Strathern 2005; Walford 2021; cf. Candea 2018). Here, I explore the idea that, rather than bringing together elements understood to be distant or previously unconnected, comparison can also work by disarticulating or disentangling internal aspects of an entity or phenomenon that are understood to be imbricated in each other – and as such, I argue that comparison is a privileged technique for drawing out the latent forms that 'data' carries within it.

Journal of the Royal Anthropological Institute (N.S.) **27**, *127-141*
© 2021 The Authors. *Journal of the Royal Anthropological Institute* published by John Wiley & Sons Ltd on behalf of Royal Anthropological Institute

Data means, data ends

The first comparison I will be making rests on ethnographic work completed with the Large-Scale Biosphere-Atmosphere experiment in Amazonia (LBA), a long-term international scientific programme led by Brazilian researchers at the National Institute for Amazonian Research (INPA) to investigate the role of the Amazon forest in the global carbon cycle. To this end, the LBA has numerous experiments set up throughout the Amazon region, which are collecting large amounts of data on all sorts of variables, from carbon flux to hydrology to photosynthetic activity. The LBA has built several meteorological towers, as well as a 300 m tower in order to measure CO_2 and different sorts of trace gases and their flux, including carbon dioxide. It does this in real time, with the data sent to the HQ in Manaus, and then stored or disseminated to the wider LBA community. There are many different scientists from different disciplines working in it at any one time, as well as a basic team of researchers, technicians, and students. I spent around thirteen months in total with the LBA, conducting ethnographic research, in 2007, 2010, and 2011.

At the time of my research, within the LBA an economy of exchange had grown up centred on the collection and movement of data. The LBA provides infrastructural support for foreign (*estrangeiro*) – non-Brazilian – researchers to set up data collection campaigns in the Amazon, using the LBA's basecamp, paths, quad bikes and the labour of the technicians, often in return for either sharing that data, giving lectures, lending instruments, supervising students, or putting names on published papers; and this data is also then taken back by foreign researchers to funders in their home countries, and used to request further funding, set up new projects, and so on. Although each of these exchanges had its own specific duration and features, most of them were aimed at obtaining or collecting, in the end, more data. As one researcher told me, there is always too much data, but also never enough.

What became clear to me over the course of my research was that there were (at least) two different conceptions of data that people were working with. Very early on in my fieldwork, I had a conversation with a well-known researcher who impressed upon me in no uncertain terms that he considered the flow of data to be in one direction only – from Brazil to the rest of the world – with very little recompense in return. When I asked why, he said:

> Yes, some people say, 'Oh, the data in itself doesn't have any value. It needs a certain amount of intellectual work'. But data has a value. There's an enormous amount of work done on the data already – collection, treatment, and so on – each part is not a single thing … The data can be very different in a complex environment. To install the instrument is already a lot of work, as much intellectual as any other.

On the other hand, the head of the LBA database and IT department who was responsible for the LBA data management had a different idea of data. He told me:

> Data, yes, it generates knowledge … It's extracted, by the sensor, or observations … but looking at this data, it doesn't make much sense … you have 40 MB of data from an experiment but it won't give you any scientific answer. What is there in this data?

The difference he was pointing to, he told me, was between 'data and knowledge. Data doesn't tell you anything. I can get the data and analyse it, but the number isn't going to tell me anything. The data is just a number, it doesn't have a nature (*natureza*). It can be in various scales. The number is not knowledge'. In fact, he explained to me, the point of a database is to keep the data in constant use by someone, anyone – the more used it

Journal of the Royal Anthropological Institute (N.S.) **27**, *127-141*
© 2021 The Authors. *Journal of the Royal Anthropological Institute* published by John Wiley & Sons Ltd on behalf of Royal Anthropological Institute

is, the better kept the data is and the less 'entropy' sets in; the more your data circulates, I was told, the more 'visible' and 'valuable' it is.

Between these two positions, then, we see that data emerges quite differently. On the one hand, the labour invested in the product of data means that it already has value, and it can certainly belong to someone such that its collection demands recompense – here, data is an end in itself. On the other hand, data's value is exactly in its capacity to be constantly made into something else, and to be kept in constant circulation so that it can be used and reused by as many people as possible – data as means, here a means to 'knowledge'. Where, on the one hand, there is an awareness of the value of data being in what it already is, on the other, it is in what it will, endlessly, become.

Another way in which this tension appeared, more dramatically, was through the idiom of property, specifically through suspicions that data had been 'stolen' (*roubados*). Several members of the LBA knew someone whose data had been unfairly taken or stolen by a foreign research partner: that is, either not shared during a collaboration, or published without any forewarning or acknowledgement of the partnership. These stories of data theft sometimes drew on other forms of theft, like biopiracy, and seemed to be a concern for several of the researchers I spoke to. As one told me: 'Imagine, I've got some raw data, and I'm not working on it. And then someone comes along from Scotland[2] and uses it to write something – you can't do that, that's stealing … Officially, I'm the owner of the data'. At the same time, other researchers expressed confusion as to accusations of stealing; yet others suggested that there were only certain conditions under which stealing data was at all possible. When I asked one researcher based in the United States, for example, about the accusations of stealing data, he was a little nonplussed. 'You can't really steal data like that', he said. This was because the data is free – it belongs to everyone, he said, and he told me how surprised he had been that he had such an unexpectedly hard time getting data from certain institutions in Brazil. Another researcher told me that although he might be considered unconventional for it, he would not have any qualms using someone else's data from an online repository – if it is available online, as far as he is concerned, it's free, and he'll use it whether they had published or not. I was often told it was not really possible to steal data because the data's collection was funded by government bodies or taxpayers' money; or that the data itself didn't have any value, data was just data; or that the person who had collected the data wasn't using it, it was just sitting there doing nothing. The conflict here is not over whose rightful property the data is, but whether data should be considered property at all (see Walford 2012).

The appropriation of data from the Brazilian Amazon, as the comparisons with biopiracy indicate – and especially under the auspices of common knowledge and unrealized property rights – places data clearly within an extractive relationship that characterizes science as a colonial enterprise (Safier 2008; Walford 2018). Rather than simply a reiteration of historical inequalities, however, this relationship is a complex lived experience for those who work with the data, and different inflections of it could appear in any particular researcher's practice or speech, whether Brazilian or *estrangeiro*. Data, in this context, is something valuable in its own right, an object of personal property in part because of the labour of its production; but at the same time, its value is also framed as being exactly because it is common property, and as such can, and should, be continually transformed into something else. Data is both end and means, simultaneously. Although as I have said, these two ways of understanding data could appear together, I want to hold them apart for now as a useful heuristic. This is

Journal of the Royal Anthropological Institute (N.S.) **27**, *127-141*
© 2021 The Authors. *Journal of the Royal Anthropological Institute* published by John Wiley & Sons Ltd on behalf of Royal Anthropological Institute

because whereas the former, what we might call 'data as ends', is comprehensible within conventional frameworks of labour and ownership, the latter – 'data as means', or data as the potential to become something else – is more difficult to recognize and therefore requires further analytical attention.

In order to give it this attention, I will now turn back to the LBA data 'economy'. Although I initially described scientific data as an exchange object, or an item of barter, that circulates within a singular micro-economy at the LBA, there are in fact different ways in which different LBA data circulates. In the case of campaigns or one-off collaborations, the researchers in question generally collect and clean their own data; they are formally governed by data policies depending on what funding body finances them, which means they have a limited amount of time before they must upload their data to a public database. However, in terms of the informal data economy I described earlier, they can choose whom to share it with and how. Under almost any policy, they are given the chance to publish with it first: that is, to transform it into something else, normally an article or what the database manager above might call 'knowledge'. It is very rare for anyone to share their raw (unprocessed) data (dados crus). In the case of the LBA tower data, on the other hand, which is long-term monitoring data, the raw data is collected from the instruments in the forest by technicians, or sent in real time to the LBA HQ in Manaus. It is then processed by the LBA data curators or cleaners and turned into certified data (dados certificados), before being made available to the wider LBA community, either on request or automatically. Unlike the individual data collection drives or campaigns, this long-term monitoring data does not officially 'belong' to anyone – the LBA has to be acknowledged when the data is used, but the language of ownership is expressly avoided when talking about it.

However, although the LBA data was often framed, both in terms of regulation and in everyday discourse, as belonging to no one, in the sense that no person or group has exclusive property rights over it, the situation was not as clear-cut as that. This was in part because there are of course people whose labour goes into this LBA tower data, preparing it for others to use. Joana and Raquel,[3] responsible for 'cleaning' (limpar) the data, spend hours with the data from two of the LBA's towers, teasing out the errors and flaws in it. They painstakingly go through each variable in the data, trying to piece together whether the errors in the dataset are due to a problem in the battery supply, an unfortunate frog that met its fate in a pluviometer, or a lightning strike. They deal with requests for the data from researchers all over the world. They are paid to do this labour, and so from one perspective, any relation of ownership they might feel towards the data because of the fact they have worked on it, in the Lockean sense, is severed through monetary exchange (Locke 1980 [1690]; Strathern 2012). As Raquel told me, 'Look, I … no, I'm very clear. I don't have any link to this data. Whenever [the head of the group] or anyone says that I do, I say – no, that this doesn't belong to me. This is not my property'. Joana and Raquel exchange their work on the data for money so that others may use the data – as several people told me, 'It's just their job'.

But severing their relationship to the data is not that easy. In fact, even though the data cleaning is 'their job', I discovered over time that Joana and Raquel did still feel some sort of claim over the data, a sentiment that was made apparent during one trip to the forest. Several people were discussing a recent field trip by students and researchers from the LBA and other Brazilian institutions, and from a university in the United States, who had come to the tower to learn about data collection campaigns. In the discussion, people made comments like the following: 'Well, they'll write an article quickly from that data. No one considers that someone worked on that data, or will include her', and 'The data is used so much but no one includes who treated the data … if everyone did, Raquel's CV would be amazing!' Although it had been made clear that the visiting group would not publish anything from the data without permission, that was not enough to satisfy the group. Their concern was, on the one hand, with the value of the data itself, not just the knowledge that would emerge from it; but, on the other, their comments also point to an understanding of data's value well beyond economic remuneration, and rather in terms of professional and social recognition. Raquel's labour on the data was eclipsed, and her name did not get attached to the data. She was, in a sense, made anonymous in order for others to be able to use the data to make themselves known.

The problem of eclipsed labour is of course well rehearsed. Here, the fact that Raquel is paid means that she is excluded from the benefits of her labour: she is alienated from the thing she produces; she does not get the credit she deserves. As the hydrological researcher explained to me, the concern is with data as a valuable object that can travel well beyond its context of production, and the lack of fair recompense for this; it is exploitation. However, in the discussions between the technicians, data also seems to oscillate between being both alienable and inalienable. The scientific knowledge economy is extremely complex when it comes to authorship and ownership, as has been well documented (Biagioli 2008; Biagioli & Galison 2003); and this oscillation hints at the way in which data does not sit easily within the parameters of an alienable/inalienable framing. This is because Raquel's labour is in fact towards producing a specific sort of phenomenon: *potential*. To argue that Raquel is being denied her just deserts requires data to be understood as something of inherent value already as data. But the other side of data's value is held within the idea that it is not yet what it will become. What is in fact eclipsed is that, far from being innate, the crafting of this potential, too, requires work; what is missing is an analysis of the labour that goes into producing something that is not yet anything – what might be called the reproductive labour of data.

Data – ova

There are in fact two senses in which Joana and Raquel might be said to be performing a sort of reproductive labour. In the first sense, it can be argued that their paid work is directed exactly at the social reproduction of the LBA community. Such an analysis rests on decades of feminist scholarship around the relationship between waged labour and reproductive labour: that is, between the formal, public labour market and informal, private, or domestic forms of work (see Duffy 2007 for an overview). Within this body of scholarship, the distinction between the formal and informal economy, or productive and reproductive labour, is being continuously dissolved and refigured (see Bear, Ho, Tsing & Yanagisako 2015; Dalla Costa & James 1972; Hardt 1999), such that it becomes clear that formal or productive labour can have aspects of intimacy, affect, and nurture, and, more generally, can reproduce forms of sociality. In this sense, the 'paid labour' itself of data cleaning – that is, the production of data as an end – has socially reproductive effects. The data exchanges and negotiations going on all the time at the LBA are the material and specific means by which the LBA community – and sociality – is generated (Walford 2012; cf. Hilgartner & Brandt-Rauf 1994). I described this earlier in the essay as an 'economy of exchange' featuring data, names, instruments, access to research sites, and from which collaborations, partnerships,

© 2021 The Authors. *Journal of the Royal Anthropological Institute* published by John Wiley & Sons Ltd on behalf of Royal Anthropological Institute

friendships, enmities, and institutions emerge. Joana and Raquel's work is thus not only about producing data as a knowledge object, but also about producing data as a form of social relation – as a way to build and sustain the LBA community. Furthermore, Joana and Raquel developed an intimate, embodied relation with it – what they called a 'feeling' (*feeling*) for the data. As I was told, they had to learn how to 'woo' (*namorar*) the data, get to know all its idiosyncrasies and quirks. Although they rarely visited the towers themselves, they would get to know the capricious instruments, and they would pore over instruction manuals for the notoriously troublesome dataloggers, the small computers on the towers which store the data ready to be downloaded. Through this intimate work, then, it can be argued that Joana and Raquel are quite literally providing the means by which scientific communities are made and constantly remade, as data circulates between people (or does not), acting to suture them together (or drive them apart). Shifting into an understanding of the socially productive effects of data labour is the first step towards expanding our understanding of what the value of the so-called data economy is.

But there is another form of reproduction hidden within this one. Beyond this general sense in which Joana and Raquel's work with data is socially generative lies a much more specific way in which the work they do is about reproducing personhood. Joana and Raquel are producing a very particular sort of entity or effect: potential. This often gets overlooked in debates about data's value, because there is a presumption that data has to already be 'something' to be valuable, socially or otherwise. Data as means – potential – then gets folded into data as ends.

In order to disentangle data as means from data as ends, I want to propose a comparison between data and an apparently very different form of reproductive potential: ova. Specifically, a comparison between Joana and Raquel, the data cleaners, and British ova donors, as investigated in the work of Monica Konrad. Here, too, there is a tension between what something is and what it will become, but it is framed as that between ova and the people they might grow into. This comparison allows me to shift into a different idiom to that of labour, ownership, exploitation, and economies; it allows us to think of the value of potential through ideas that have already been hovering at the edges of my analysis and which are often contrasted with the language of economy: kinship and the making of persons.

Konrad's study examines how British egg donors, as 'partible persons', detach parts of themselves so that their agency can circulate, making these parts of themselves into 'substance for others' (1998: 645). This detachment is very clear in the way they talk about it: in the words of one of the women Konrad spoke to, 'I don't think the eggs are mine, they're not something physical that they're my eggs. I don't even think of them as eggs'; others told her, 'It's not the eggs that are the actual thing, they're not like a physical thing that have come from my body', or 'They're just like a fingernail or something … they're just a normal part, like any other part' (1998: 650). This detachment, Konrad argues, is crucial to the efficacy of their social agency and to the nurturing of a certain kind of kinship. The egg donors she speaks to are often unable to put into words the relation that they feel towards the women they donate their ova to; but it is exactly this 'diffuseness' that 'is the form of the relatedness making up the connection' (1998: 650). In Konrad's analysis, the donors' circulating ova thus become a form of 'redirected social relation' (1998: 655), but a relation that is governed by anonymity, because their identity will always be kept a secret from the women in question, and their children. Konrad thus develops a notion of what she calls 'transilient kinship': a 'spiritual kinship where connexions and disconnexions between persons are to be recognized as forms of extensional relatedness dispersed through multiple (exteriorized) persons. These persons cannot always be located, or even nameable, and, most importantly of all, do not have to be grounded in specific, discreetly bounded persons' (1998: 659). Their anonymity, the open-ended nature of their donations, is at the basis of this form of relatedness.

What the egg donors do not lay claim to is the future of the egg they produce; they might start the process off, but another person takes it on. It is this very diffuseness and anonymity, this eclipsing of their agency as the origin of the process, that generates the sense of kinship they feel. But also important is the way they relate to the ova. Understanding ova as ends, as the final product of their (bodily) work which someone else gains from, would allow us to argue that these donors are being exploited – donors are not paid for their donations, for example;[4] but it would hide from us that what generates the affective attachment that animates the donors is the fact that their ova are constituted exactly by being 'not yet' (persons).

Returning to Joana and Raquel, they, too, give away potential without any claim to its realization. Here, too, 'what signifies is being the origin of a process that another carries forward' (Strathern 2003: 185). The data they produce is 'not theirs', they say, or only theirs incidentally – it belongs to those who will go on to transform it, for example by writing an academic paper based on it. Furthermore, as we have seen, their work on the data allows it to travel well beyond them and, in so circulating, elicit an LBA 'community'. If my comparison turns implicitly on the fact that both data and ova are in a sense difficult to recognize, however, it also demonstrates that there are different ways, or effects, of being unrecognizable. Konrad can argue that the unrecognized position of the British egg donors in her study – their anonymity, the inchoate forms they donate – generates a sense of diffuse, affective attachment. But although in one sense Joana and Raquel know they are instrumental in sustaining the LBA 'family' (a term I heard used several times), the effect of producing the means of reproduction is very different for them. Gametes hold within them the potential to turn into people, but data can also 'make' certain kinds of people, albeit in a very different way: the data cleaners are also reproducing the potential for (other) people to grow. The different ways in which data is transformed into knowledge contribute substantially not only to making 'humans into particular kinds of subjects called scientists' (Haraway 1997: 142), but also to making them into particular kinds of scientist subjects. This is a notion of a scientific subject based on the fact that what scientists produce gives them the ability to relate in certain ways, and it is this relational agency that allows them to grow as researchers, to amass value to their name, to make the claims that they do, to circulate. What they grow through is the ability to transform data, to take the potential and realize it.

However, this access to data's potential was denied to Joana and Raquel themselves. At the time of my research, they both had master's degrees, and they both expressed an interest in doing a Ph.D. Both of them had been struggling during the period of my fieldwork to find the time to write an article based on the data from the towers. Their frustration was quietly held, and rarely surfaced explicitly. If I asked them about it, they often avoided the question, but it was clear that they felt in some way stuck where they were, 'doing the work of technicians', as one person put it: that is, without the chance to turn the data into knowledge. The 'technical' work they do (trabalho do técnico) is understood to be simply a means to something else more important; they have master's degrees but no time or support to do a Ph.D. or to publish themselves, and as

© 2021 The Authors. Journal of the Royal Anthropological Institute published by John Wiley & Sons Ltd on behalf of Royal Anthropological Institute

such, following a sentiment I often heard, 'at the LBA, people with master's degrees do the work of technicians' (*No LBA, quem tem mestrado faz trabalho de técnico*). It was often aired as an expression of frustration, and it signifies the difficulty in classifying or categorizing Joana and Raquel as scientific subjects; they did not see themselves as technicians, but neither were they researchers. They are therefore stuck in what might be thought of as an 'unrecognizable' position – in the sense of unfamiliar, but also in the sense of unrecognized by others. Whereas in Konrad's analysis, it is through the nameless flows of donated ova to unknown others that 'women themselves can make their procreative powers into an ovular economy of intersubjective (cross-corporeal) agency' (1998: 653), what Joana and Raquel experience is rather different: a sense of truncated growth and a lack of agency. The data bestows upon them the potential of relating, but they cannot fully transform it (cf. Walford 2019). The promise of potential's endless transformativity is also always the possibility of not transforming at all.

Approaching the social world of the ova donors through a framing of labour and ownership, or alienability and inalienability – how can a person detach from themselves in this way? we might ask – obscures the generative effects of their reproductive labour, and the kinship that their anonymous donations reproduce. Likewise, trying to contain Joana and Raquel's relationship to data within the frame of waged labour, understanding data as an alienable object, is equally insufficient; but what it obscures is the extent to which a form of agency and personhood which they give to others is denied to them. Understanding data as a form of reproductive potential, as a means for persons to grow, is necessary to understand better not only how data has the value it does, but also how highly valued those who work with data, often in ways that are ignored, should be.

Opening data out

If in my first comparison I was interested in holding apart data as means and ends just long enough to allow a different set of concerns to emerge, in this final section it is another aspect of data as potentiality that I want to explore: not the tension between what data is and what it will become, but the tension between the possibility of becoming anything at all and the necessity of becoming something in the end – between potential and its realization.

I will be moving away from the LBA to look at what feels like a very different scale of data practice. Across the sciences, there has been an increasing imperative to operate policies of open data, where the data collected is free to anyone who wishes to download it. This pervasive and powerful imaginary of 'open data' is not new in the sciences by any means, and can be attributed to a number of different initiatives that resulted in widely followed guideline and principles.[5] Several scientific funding bodies make continued funding reliant on putting your data in public databases: this has been the case for some time for projects funded by the National Science Foundation in the United States, for example. In the environmental sciences specifically, there is emerging what might be thought of as a new data 'paradigm' (Gabrys 2016; Hey, Tansley & Tolle 2009) that relies heavily on the promises of open data. A striking example of this is the Group on Earth Observation (GEO), a partnership of 103 nations, the European Commission, and ninety-five participating organizations 'that envisions a future wherein decisions and actions for the benefit of humankind are informed by coordinated, comprehensive and sustained Earth observations and information'.[6] To this end, the GEO community is creating a Global Earth Observation System of Systems (GEOSS).[7] On one of the original demos on the GEO website, called 'GEO in Action',[8]

Journal of the Royal Anthropological Institute (N.S.) **27**, 127-141
© 2021 The Authors. *Journal of the Royal Anthropological Institute* published by John Wiley & Sons Ltd on behalf of Royal Anthropological Institute

we are confronted by the slogan 'Countries have borders. Earth Observations don't'. As I have written elsewhere (Walford 2018), the imaginary of the GEOSS frames data as an endless flow that observes no barriers and is in constant circulation. As the press statement for the GEO 2015 summit in Mexico City reads: 'GEO commits to unleash the power of open data to address global challenges'.[9]

However, despite its pervasiveness, as several scholars have pointed out, there are problematic assumptions woven into the implementation of open data systems. There are issues of differential access and different technological capabilities: that is, how open data actually is tends to be dependent on infrastructural capacities that the Global North takes for granted (Bezuidenhout, Leonelli, Kelly & Rapper 2017). As we have seen in the previous section, open data policies also tend to eclipse the labour that goes into the production of that data, as if it emerges already as part of the commons. Several of the concerns about open data in the sciences intersect partially with debates in other domains about accessibility to data and transparency. Although these latter often have more to do with changing forms of governmentality and surveillance (Ruppert 2015) and the recursivity and performativity of audit cultures (Carrier & Miller 1998; Strathern 2000), there is also shared concern that open data might be a proxy for other, more ominous practices: for example, how calls for open data, particularly in the environmental sciences, might be used as a form of political obstacle to environmental policy reform (Levy & Johns 2016).

With these critiques in mind, I wish to pause here at what it means for data to be 'open' in the first place. Again, there is something about data which lends itself to being opened up in this way. Several of the factors we saw in the ethnographic material I presented previously (at least from one side of the debate) play a role here: that data is 'not yet' knowledge; that it has been publicly funded; that it is a resource that should belong to everyone. But there is also a sense that, with the right infrastructures and platforms, the data could become anything; opening data is aimed at multiplying the possibilities presumed to be contained within it. Opening data is, as the GEO put it, 'unleashing' its power – understood, until then, to be hidden, inert, or contained. The idea of openness thus carries with it a number of implicit aspirations, ambitions, and understandings. In the next section, I want to use a comparison to make some of these explicit; and to think about what might happen when the openness of open data comes up against its realization – when anything become something, and how that is decided. This necessitates we shift from thinking of data as means, to questions of meaning.

Data – ova – gene

To end, I want now to turn to another science that has seen an explosion in data – genomics – in order to gesture towards where this argument might take us. Jenny Reardon (2017) has charted the development of genomics over recent decades, from lab-based small-scale genetics, where people collegially pipetted DNA samples into micro-arrays, to the massive inhuman infrastructures of automated sequencing producing petabytes of data that characterize genomics today. What she is particularly interested in is what happened after the Human Genome Project (HGP) was completed. In 2003, geneticists, faced with the map of the human genome, were also faced with the question: now we have it, what does it mean? It is this turn to social meaning that Reardon flags as characteristic of her object of inquiry: the *postgenomic condition*. Reardon points us towards the realization that dawned on geneticists that mapping the genome was not going to provide the sorts of answers they expected. Instead, she says, a much richer terrain opened up, made up of spaces where the 'meanings and values of the genomic data are being forged' (2017: 4), or, as she later puts it, 'in-formed'. The absence of meaning therefore simultaneously seemed to engender a potential excess of it.

Particularly relevant for my concerns here is Reardon's description of what she calls 'genomic liberalism' (2017: 7), the way the genome has come to stand for, or 'mean', a set of liberal ideals, such as participation, openness, transparency, and inclusion. The genome was framed as knowledge for all 'mankind', revealing 'our common humanity' (2017: 8) and often touted as heralding the 'end of race', in a deliberate attempt to move away from its roots in eugenics and the race controversies that dogged twentieth-century genetics (see also M'charek 2005). Importantly, data and data infrastructures were a crucial element in constructing this new face of genetic science, which drew on 'turn-of-the-millennium hopes for justice through data and democracy' (Reardon 2017: 8). But exactly how those hopes were to be realized became the sticking point. This is because, Reardon tells us, data is not meaning (2017: 174). What Reardon finds herself exploring, then, is not so much the information of life, but the life of information: 'Rather than reveal meaningful knowledge about life itself, genomics instead has given life to a deluge of data. How to make anything of value out of this data is now, quite literally, the million dollar question' (2017: 13).

What Reardon returns to throughout her description is what happens when the open-ended potential of the genome comes up against its own realization: genomes contain/become/already are specific persons. The quest for a generic human genome that could be shared by all was thwarted again and again by this realization: by the 'particular bodies, histories, and constraints of the people asked to provide their genomes' (2017: 21). That is to say, the postgenomic condition is characterized by the conflict between infinite potential and its necessary manifestation. This moment of tension is generative in Reardon's account. She examines how the hopes contained within genomic knowledge hover between different sets of meanings, and the conflicts this engendered – and in so doing, she shows how the genome is an ongoing site for the playing out of this dynamic: the opening up and closing down of meaning.

There is then a double imaginary, a resonance, of potentiality here. Although, as Donna Haraway has argued, genes are in one sense 'another kind of thing, a thing-in-itself where no trope can be admitted' (1997: 134) because they reduce life to a lowest common denominator, it is nevertheless true that genes are also understood as a form of potential: as the blueprint for life, they function through endless possibility for recombination, and, of course, they contain persons within them. Genes, then, both close down and open out meaning – it is not surprising that understanding people genetically led to both eugenics and the means to push back against it by allowing for the possibility for alternative futures, however utopian they may sound (the 'end of race'). And data in turn is also both decried for being reductionist, and pregnant with hopes for alternative political forms – openness, as we have seen, being one of them.[10]

Drawing a comparison with genomics as Reardon describes it, we might say that the environmental sciences are likewise entering into a 'post-environmental condition'. The 'environment', like the genome, is a potent symbol which has shifted its signification over time, carrying with it in its singular form ('the environment', as with 'the genome') notions of a shared commons, a 'global consciousness' that overcomes local concerns (Jasanoff 2001). Like genomics, in the environmental sciences we now see technological revolutions ushering in enormous amounts of data; partnerships with

Journal of the Royal Anthropological Institute (N.S.) **27**, 127-141
© 2021 The Authors. *Journal of the Royal Anthropological Institute* published by John Wiley & Sons Ltd on behalf of Royal Anthropological Institute

private companies and Big Tech; and the flourishing of liberal ideals of openness, democracy, and freedom through information – 'Countries have borders. Earth Observations do not', as the GEO tells us confidently. But a comparison with Reardon's account also forces us to ask about what all this data means, and for whom. This is not an obvious question from the perspective of open data initiatives, which are aimed precisely at deferring such questions endlessly. Contrary to Reardon's claim, it is not so much that data has no meaning that is the problem; rather, it is that its meaning lies exactly in its lack of immediate interpretation, its potential, and its capacity to carry latent forms within it. An unreflexive commitment to open data, therefore, does not allow us to ask whom exactly this data is benefiting and how. The environment in this new data-driven landscape is a site for both the opening out and closing down of new meanings, commodification by big tech companies, reinscriptions of colonial hierarchies, as well as claims for grass-roots environmental justice, via citizen science initiatives, for example (Gabrys, Pritchard & Barratt 2016). Like the genome, there is suddenly a space for new or different meanings to be forged. How to make sense of this 'post-environmental' moment is exactly what now requires careful and critical analysis.

Data – ova – gene – data

Anthropological comparison is often understood as a practice of bringing together different sets of material so that one might cast a different light on the other (see Candea 2018 for a comprehensive account). So in this essay, for example, I have developed a comparison between data and biological reproductive material in order to move away from what feels like an obvious analogy between data and natural resources; I make a comparison with reproduction rather than production, one might say. However, another way to understand comparison is almost the opposite to this: that it allows us to disentangle analytical elements that have become seemingly inextricably tangled up in each other. For example, here my comparisons are also intended to draw out the way that 'production' and 'reproduction' already participate in each other. Take my comparison between data and gametes, which relies implicitly on the way in which knowledge and kinship are always already implied in each other, at least historically in Euro-American understandings: the 'repeated echo between intellectual propagation and procreative acts' (Strathern 1995: 8). But such entanglements can also be seen in the resonances between scientific framings of reproductive processes and capital extraction (Martin 1992), or in the way that gametes and other forms of tissue like stem cells are increasingly understood explicitly as resources of biovalue and biocapital (Franklin & Lock 2003; Rajan 2006; Rose 2006); or how genetic imaginaries are understood through reference to ideas of information or code. That is to say, it can seem as if gametes *already are* capital, or genes *already are* knowledge – they somehow contain these forms latently within them, as Stefan Helmreich has argued in the context of the biotechnological imagination, in which 'biological process itself already constitutes a form of surplus value production' (2007: 293). In the material I have analysed, data and datafication are both explained by and contribute to this effect: data is understood to already contain hidden forms within it, and transforming phenomena into data is also to impute to them this potential for future realization and transformation. My comparisons in this essay are intended to make these imbrications explicit by disarticulating different imaginaries of data that are otherwise hidden inside itself. In this way, the comparisons turn data inside out – not by bringing data into relation with totally different imaginaries, but by holding the elements contained within data apart for just long enough to make it differently recognizable.

Comparison has therefore worked in my description to disentangle different aspects of data. Data, on the other hand, seems to, potentially at least, contain almost anything within it. This might be why it is so easily understood as an analogue to currency, or money (e.g. Eggers, Hamill & Ali 2013; cf. Holbraad 2005). This has led to critiques of data that push back against quantification and datafication, on the grounds that there are things in life that cannot be contained or captured in this way (much like, of course, the critiques of money or monetization). My approach, however, proposes a new form of critical engagement with data. Data's power comes not just from voracious encompassment, in the way capitalism is understood, but also from its *reproductive* framing, how it is understood to contain other forms already within it. It is this we must also learn how to question.

NOTES

I would like to thank the two anonymous reviewers for their supportive engagement with this essay, as well as those others who read it and generously commented: Alice Elliot and my co-editors Rachel Douglas-Jones and Nick Seaver. The ethnographic research on which this essay is based was funded by the IT University of Copenhagen.

[1] As when we are told cryptically in a *Harvard Business Review* article from 2013 that 'the value of big data isn't the data' (Hammond 2013).

[2] A deliberate reference to where I grew up.

[3] I have used pseudonyms throughout on the request of my interlocutors.

[4] In the UK, it is illegal to pay for egg donation (Cooper & Waldby 2014; Stoeckle 2018; see Strathern 2012 for a similar discussion around organ donation).

[5] See, for example, the widely cited Panton Principles from 2010 (*https://pantonprinciples.org/about/index.html*, accessed 22 January 2021):

> By open data in science we mean that it is freely available on the public internet permitting any user to download, copy, analyse, re-process, pass them to software or use them for any other purpose without financial, legal, or technical barriers other than those inseparable from gaining access to the internet itself. To this end data related to published science should be explicitly placed in the public domain.

[6] https://www.earthobservations.org/geo_community.php (accessed 22 January 2021).

[7] https://www.earthobservations.org/geoss.php (accessed 22 January 2021).

[8] Subsequently taken down.

[9] https://www.doi.gov/blog/geo-commits-unleash-power-open-data-address-global-challenges (accessed 22 January 2021).

[10] Of course, information was also there all along in our ideas about genes: genes were understood explicitly as a code, a form of information that needs deciphering to be comprehensible. This might also explain why it made so much sense to place 'the free flow of information and knowledge at the moral heart of genomics' (Reardon 2017: 29); in a sense, genetics and information – kinship and knowledge – have served as means to understand each other already for some time in Euro-America (Strathern 1995), to the point where they are sometimes hard to distinguish. Data and genes, then, share a longer history than might be imagined from Reardon's time-frame.

REFERENCES

AWATI, K. & S.B. SHUM 2015. Big data metaphors we live by. *Towards Data Science*, 14 May (available online: *https://towardsdatascience.com/big-data-metaphors-we-live-by-98d3fa44ebf8*, accessed 22 January 2021).

BEAR, L., K. HO, A.L. TSING & S. YANAGISAKO 2015. Gens: a feminist manifesto for the study of capitalism. *Theorizing the Contemporary, Fieldsights*, 30 March (available online: *https://culanth.org/fieldsights/gens-a-feminist-manifesto-for-the-study-of-capitalism*, accessed 27 January 2021).

BEZUIDENHOUT, L.M., S. LEONELLI, A.H. KELLY & B. RAPPER 2017. Beyond the digital divide: towards a situated approach to open data. *Science and Public Policy* **44**, 464-75.

Journal of the Royal Anthropological Institute (N.S.) **27**, *127-141*

BIAGIOLI, M. 2008. Documents of documents: scientists' names and scientific claims. In *Documents: artifacts of modern knowledge* (ed.) A. Riles, 127-57. Ann Arbor: University of Michigan Press.

———— & S. GALISON (eds) 2003. *Scientific authorship: credit and intellectual property in science*. London: Routledge.

CANDEA, M. 2018. *Comparison in anthropology: the impossible method*. Cambridge: University Press.

CARRIER, J.G. & D. MILLER (eds) 1998. *Virtualism: a new political economy*. New York: Berg.

COOPER, M. & C. WALDBY 2014. *Clinical labor: tissue donors and research subjects in the global bioeconomy*. Durham, N.C.: Duke University Press.

DALLA COSTA, M. & S. JAMES 1972. *The power of women and the subversion of the community*. Bristol: Falling Well Press.

DUFFY, M. 2007. Doing the dirty work: gender, race and reproductive labour in historical perspective. *Gender & Society* **21**, 313-36.

THE ECONOMIST 2017. The world's most valuable resource is no longer oil, but data. *The Economist*, 6 May (available online: *https://www.economist.com/leaders/2017/05/06/the-worlds-most-valuable-resource-is-no-longer-oil-but-data*, accessed 22 January 2021).

EGGERS, W.D., R. HAMILL & A. ALI 2013. Data as the new currency: government's role in facilitating the exchange. *Deloitte Review* 13 (available online: *https://deloitte.wsj.com/riskandcompliance/files/2013/11/DataCurrency_report.pdf*, accessed 27 January 2021).

FRANKLIN, S. & M. LOCK (eds) 2003. *Remaking life and death: towards an anthropology of the biosciences*. Santa Fe, N.M.: School of American Research Press.

GABRYS, J. 2016. *Program Earth: environmental sensing technology and the making of a computational planet*. Minneapolis: University of Minnesota Press.

————, H. PRITCHARD & B. BARRATT 2016. Just good enough data: figuring data citizenship through air pollution sensing and data stories. *Big Data & Society* **3**: **2** (available online: *https://journals.sagepub.com/doi/full/10.1177/2053951716679677*, accessed 27 January 2021).

GITELMAN, L. (ed.) 2013. *'Raw data' is an oxymoron*. Cambridge, Mass.: MIT Press.

HAMMOND, K.J. 2013. The value of big data isn't the data. *Harvard Business Review*, 1 May (available online: *https://hbr.org/2013/05/the-value-of-big-data-isnt-the*, accessed 22 January 2021).

HARAWAY, D. 1997. *Modest_Witness@Second_Millennium.FemaleMan©_Meets _Oncomouse*^{TM}. London: Routledge.

HARDT, M. 1999. Affective labour. *boundary 2* **26**: **2**, 89-100.

HELMREICH, S. 2007. Blue-green capital, biotechnological circulation and an oceanic imaginary: a critique of biopolitical economy. *BioSocieties* **2**, 287-302.

HEY, T., S. TANSLEY & K. TOLLE (eds) 2009. *The fourth paradigm: data-intensive scientific discovery*. Redmond, Wash.: Microsoft Research.

HILGARTNER, S. & S.I. BRANDT-RAUF 1994. Data access, ownership, and control: toward empirical studies of access practices. *Science Communication* **15**, 355-72.

HOLBRAAD, M. 2005. Expending multiplicity: money in Cuban Ifá cults. *Journal of the Royal Anthropological Institute* (N.S.) **11**, 231-54.

ILIADIS, A. & F. RUSSO 2016. Critical data studies: an introduction. *Big Data & Society* **3**: **2** (available online: *https://journals.sagepub.com/doi/pdf/10.1177/2053951716674238*, accessed 2 January 2021).

JASANOFF, S. 2001. Image and imagination: the formation of global environmental consciousness. In *Changing the atmosphere: expert knowledge and environmental governance* (eds) C.A. Miller & P.N. Edwards, 309-37. Cambridge, Mass.: MIT Press.

KONRAD, M. 1998. Ova donations and symbols of substance: some variations on the theme of sex, gender and the partible body. *Journal of the Royal Anthropological Institute* (N.S.) **4**, 643-67.

LEVY, K.E.C. & D.M. JOHNS 2016. When open data is a Trojan Horse: the weaponization of transparency in science and governance. *Big Data & Society* **3**: **1** (available online: *https://journals.sagepub.com/doi/full/10.1177/2053951715621568*, accessed 27 January 2021).

LOCKE, J. 1980 [1690]. *Second treatise of government* (ed. C.B. Macpherson). Indianapolis: Hackett.

LUPTON, D. 2013. Swimming or drowning in the data ocean? *This Sociological Life*, 29 October (available online: *https://simplysociology.wordpress.com/2013/10/29/swimming-or-drowning-in-the-data-ocean-thoughts-on-the-metaphors-of-big-data/*, accessed 22 January 2021).

MARTIN, E. 1992. The end of the body? *American Ethnologist* **19**, 121-40.

MAURER, B. 2015. Principles of descent and alliance for big data. In *Data, now bigger and better!* (eds) T. Boellstorff & B. Maurer, 67-86. Chicago: Prickly Paradigm Press.

Journal of the Royal Anthropological Institute (N.S.) **27**, *127-141*

© 2021 The Authors. *Journal of the Royal Anthropological Institute* published by John Wiley & Sons Ltd on behalf of Royal Anthropological Institute

M'CHAREK, M. 2005. *The Human Genome Diversity Project: an ethnography of scientific practice*. Cambridge: University Press.

PECK, R. 2017. Mark Cuban: 'Data is the new gold'. *Credit Suisse*, 22 June (available online: *https://www.credit-suisse.com/about-us-news/en/articles/news-and-expertise/mark-cuban-data-is-the-new-gold-201706.html*, accessed 22 January 2021).

PUSCHMANN, C. & J. BURGESS 2014. Metaphors of big data. *International Journal of Communication* **8** (available online: *https://ijoc.org/index.php/ijoc/article/view/2169*, accessed 22 January 2021).

RAICU, I. 2015. Metaphors of big data. *Vox*, 6 November (available online: *https://www.vox.com/2015/11/6/11620416/metaphors-of-big-data*, accessed 22 January 2021).

RAJAN, K.S. 2006. *Biocapital: the constitution of postgenomic life*. Durham, N.C.: Duke University Press.

REARDON, J. 2017. *The postgenomic condition: ethics, justice, and knowledge after the genome*. Chicago: University Press.

ROSE, N. 2006. *The politics of life itself: biomedicine, power and subjectivity in the twenty-first century*. Princeton: University Press.

RUPPERT, E. 2015. Doing the transparent state: open government data as performance indicators. In *A world of indicators: the making of governmental knowledge through quantification* (eds) R. Rottenburg, S.E. Merry, S.-J. Park & J. Mugler, 127-50. Cambridge: University Press.

SAFIER, N. 2008. *Measuring the New World: enlightenment science and South America*. Chicago: University Press.

SEAVER, N. 2015. Bastard algebra. In *Data, now bigger and better!* (eds) T. Boellstorff & B. Maurer, 27-47. Chicago: Prickly Paradigm Press.

STOECKLE, A. 2018. Rethinking reproductive labour through surrogates' invisible bodily care work. *Critical Sociology* **44**, 1103-16.

STRATHERN, M. 1995. *The relation: issues in complexity and scale*. Cambridge: Prickly Pear Press.

––––––– 1996. Potential property: intellectual rights and property in persons. *Social Anthropology* **4**, 17-32.

––––––– 2000 *Audit cultures: anthropological studies in accountability, ethics and the academy*. London: Routledge.

––––––– 2003. Emergent relations. In *Scientific authorship: credit and intellectual property in science* (eds) M. Biagioli & P. Galison, 165-94. London: Routledge.

––––––– 2005. Useful knowledge. *Proceedings of the British Academy* **139**, 73-109.

––––––– 2012. Gifts money cannot buy. *Social Anthropology* **20**, 397-410.

WALFORD, A. 2012. Data moves: taking Amazonian climate science seriously. *Cambridge Anthropology* **30**, 101-17.

––––––– 2018. If everything is information: archives and collecting on the frontiers of data-driven science. In *Ethnography in a data-saturated world* (eds) H. Knox & D. Nafus, 105-27. Manchester: University Press.

––––––– 2019. The properties of property: scientific data. *Theorizing the Contemporary, Fieldsights*, 29 March (available: *https://culanth.org/fieldsights/the-properties-of-property-scientific-data*, accessed 22 January 2021).

––––––– 2021. Analogy. In *Experimenting with ethnography: a companion to analysis* (eds) A. Ballestero & B.R. Winthereik, 209-18. Durham, N.C.: Duke University Press.

WATTS, R. 2018. Hack, spy, swing an election: Orwell game sums up life in a tech dystopia. *The Guardian*, 2 July (available online: *https://www.theguardian.com/games/2018/jul/02/orwell-game-hack-spy-tech-dystopia-government-surveillance*, accessed 22 January 2021).

Donnée – ovules – gène – donnée

Résumé

Cet article fait observer que la donnée a de l'intérêt non seulement pour ce qu'elle est, mais également pour ce qu'elle est amenée à devenir : en ce sens, la donnée est une forme de potentiel. L'autrice en explore deux aspects, en établissant deux comparaisons avec d'autres formes de potentiel : les ovules et les gènes. En premier lieu, à partir d'une étude ethnographique réalisée dans l'Amazonie brésilienne auprès de chercheurs spécialistes et de techniciens en environnement, l'autrice compare le traitement des données avec le don d'ovules au Royaume-Uni, afin d'explorer en quoi le traitement des données peut être considéré comme une forme de travail reproductif. En second lieu, l'article s'intéresse aux infrastructures émergentes des mégadonnées dans les sciences de l'environnement, et compare ces dernières à la génomique, afin de soulever des questions critiques nécessaires au sujet de ces initiatives de données ouvertes. L'autrice conclut par une réflexion sur le recours à la comparaison comme moyen privilégié de déceler les formes perçues comme latentes que comportent les données.

Journal of the Royal Anthropological Institute (N.S.) **27**, 127-141
© 2021 The Authors. *Journal of the Royal Anthropological Institute* published by John Wiley & Sons Ltd on behalf of Royal Anthropological Institute

8
Strategic translation: pollution, data, and Indigenous Traditional Knowledge

SARAH BLACKER *York University*

This essay examines the role of data practices in the making and refuting of settler colonial environmental science. Investigating the epistemic contestation surrounding environmental contamination produced by the oil industry in Alberta, Canada, I discuss an alternative approach to toxicology: a community-based monitoring programme that uses a 'three-track' methodology to present data in three distinct forms. Using this method, First Nations communities engaged in strategic translation, balancing their aim of rendering Traditional Knowledge and community needs legible to policy-makers against their desire to protect Traditional Knowledge from being assimilated into the dominant data paradigm. This translation, I argue, enacts a form of resistance in an era of relentless datafication: making-things-into-data can reflect the exercise of agency rather than submission to external pressure. In this way, the three-track methodology models how marginalized communities can leverage data's productive capacities for their own ends and produce scientific knowledge on their own terms.

Decades of industrial bitumen extraction from 'oil sands' have resulted in the extensive contamination of the Peace-Athabasca Delta in Alberta, Canada, home to the Mikisew Cree First Nation and the Athabasca Chipewyan First Nation. While it is estimated that millions of litres of contaminated wastewater leak from tailings ponds into the groundwater each day (Ross *et al.* 2012), measurements of contaminants and their relation to elevated rates of disease are contested, and Indigenous communities and their knowledges have largely been sidelined in environmental and health impact studies (Baker & Westman 2018). This essay examines how a community-based monitoring programme and a collaboratively produced report sought to bring First Nations' Traditional Knowledge (TK) into conversation with the dominant quantitative approaches used by Canadian scientists and policy-makers. I argue that the production of this report exemplifies a 'data practice' of strategically – and only partially – translating TK in order to enable First Nations communities to make a knowledge claim in a settler colonial context. Based on a 'three-track' methodology, the report enacts a form of resistance to the dominance of quantification, demonstrating that making-things-into-data can be an agentive practice.

Journal of the Royal Anthropological Institute (N.S.) **27**, 142-158
© Royal Anthropological Institute 2021

The report, '"Water is a living thing": environmental and human health implications of the Athabasca oil sands for the Mikisew Cree First Nation and the Athabasca Chipewyan First Nation in Northern Alberta', was based on a 2011-14 study that was funded by Health Canada and the Social Sciences and Humanities Research Council of Canada, and was peer reviewed by Health Canada's scientists. The study measured levels of polycyclic aromatic hydrocarbons (PAHs), as well as arsenic, cadmium, mercury, and selenium in groundwater, plants, and animals, and it documented elevated rates of cancer in Indigenous communities affected by the chemical contamination. Stéphane McLachlan, the environmental scientist selected by the First Nations communities to guide the collaborative project, states that the study design, the identification of collection and sampling sites, and the data analysis were all carried out by First Nations community members themselves (rather than trained scientists) and that they were trained in the necessary scientific techniques (McLachlan 2013). McLachlan's own role, he said, was that of an assistant, rather than director, taking a 'back seat' and acting as a translator to ensure that study results would be legible to policy-makers (Blacker, interview with McLachlan, 7 May 2015). The final text was designed to be accessible to non-specialists, and was authored by McLachlan in consultation with members of both First Nations. McLachlan characterizes this collaborative approach as a form of participatory epidemiology, which he believes can 'link environmental, animal, and human health' and 'address gaps in scientific data' by 'bridging local knowledge and Western science' (2014: 132).

In this essay, I show how the knowledge produced by this Indigenous-led project, one that refuted settler colonial science that had been conducted in the Fort Chipewyan area earlier, was enabled to travel and to influence policy-makers and other resistant audiences.[1] The story of the making of the 'Water is a living thing' report – including why it was needed; what it was expected to accomplish; and its design, production, and distribution – offers a valuable model for other collaborations. Most importantly, it suggests that the decision to pursue a *strategic, partial* translation of TK, in order to place it in dialogue with Western science and thus bolster a knowledge claim in a settler colonial context, should be understood as an expression of Indigenous agency made on TK's own terms.[2]

Measurement, datafication, and colonialism

This analysis draws on anthropological and science and technology studies (STS) scholarship on measurement, datafication, and colonialism, combining the three to approach data as a boundary object (Star & Griesemer 1989) in the making of knowledge claims about environmental contamination in Alberta. A growing body of work on public participation in science and the politics of measurement (Brown 1997; Frickel *et al.* 2010; Gabrys, Pritchard & Barratt 2016; Kimura 2016; Kinchy 2020; Kinchy, Parks & Jalbert 2016; Lave 2012; Li 2009; Matz, Wylie & Kriesky 2017; Ottinger 2010) shows that, just like analysis, measurement is not a neutral act. The practices through which data is collected are informed by the social and political context where the science is being carried out as well as by the assumptions and positionality of the scientists themselves. As Maggie Walter and Stephanie Russo Carroll write, the making of data and statistics is shaped by 'the social, racial and cultural standpoint of their creators ... Data are created and shaped by the assumptive determinations of their makers to collect some data and not others, to interrogate some objects over others' (2021: 2).

Journal of the Royal Anthropological Institute (N.S.) **27**, *142-158*
© Royal Anthropological Institute 2021

Because government metrics of contamination are framed as objective and politically neutral (Hoover 2013), they are difficult to challenge, particularly for economically marginalized and racialized communities that are disproportionately affected by environmental contamination.[3] Furthermore, nation-states that are committed to continued industrial development may have invested in the use of metrics that show minimal contamination (Barandiaran 2015; Pine & Liboiron 2015; Tecklin, Bauer & Prieto 2011). Community-led projects that produce alternate measurements of contamination can throw the supposed objectivity of state metrics into question (Kimura & Kinchy 2019; Ottinger & Cohen 2011).

Further shaping the context of data production are the reductive, coercive, and exploitative processes of 'datafication' that help produce asymmetrical power relations between those who (sometimes unwittingly) provide the raw material used to make data and those who control, interpret, own, and profit from it (boyd & Crawford 2012; Lupton 2016; Lyon 2014; Sadowski 2019; West 2019). Many scholars working in the field of data studies, particularly those who focus on data capitalism and data colonialism, have identified important spaces of resistance to datafication. This essay contributes to this line of inquiry by discussing how communities' participation in data projects can also be part of a strategy of resistance (Kovach 2009), rather than always entailing coercion or victimhood. In the case of 'Water is a living thing', the two First Nations communities *chose* to partially translate their knowledge into data because doing so enabled them to enter into dialogue with policy-makers – with data as the lingua franca – to participate in science, and to retain control over their own data.

The First Nations' strategic use and protection of TK, as a means to avoid assimilation into the data paradigm, must be seen in the context of the ongoing violence of the settler colonial state, as it is perpetrated through multiple institutions and practices. Candis Callison (2014; 2020), Denielle Elliott (2019), Max Liboiron (2021), Deborah McGregor (2013), Michelle Murphy (2017), Reena Shadaan and Michelle Murphy (2020), Kim TallBear (2013), Zoe Todd (2016; 2018), and Kyle Powys Whyte (2018) emphasize the importance of naming colonialism as the fundamental and persistent context that informs the production of scientific knowledge in settler colonial states. As Callison writes, '[C]olonialism is not an event in the distant past but, rather, a persistent disruption and dispossession of lands and waters that seeks to erase Indigenous presence, histories, knowledge, and people' (2020: 133). Moreover, in the current case study, colonialism is also the common context shaping the continued dominance of scientific, industrial, economic, governance, and assessment regimes in settler colonial Canada.

It is difficult to overstate the extent of the violence towards Indigenous peoples, knowledges, and lifeways enacted through settler colonialism, or the measures needed to undo these harms. This harm is perpetrated both materially and epistemically (Whyte 2018). Ecological destruction threatens Indigenous communities not only through contaminating water, air, soil, and food, but also by diminishing their relations to the land, and thus their TK. As Whyte writes, '[A]ctual environmental changes themselves hasten the undermining of qualities of relationships – such as loss of knowledge and Indigenous legal/juridical systemics coupled with the loss of landscapes from which those knowledge and legal/juridical systems came' (2018: 135-6).

Building on the foregoing insights regarding the politics of measurement, the power dynamics of datafication, and the continuing material, cultural, political, and epistemic threat of colonialism, this analysis centres the agency of First Nations communities in protecting TK and Indigenous lifeways against settler colonial scientific practices and norms through their strategic participation in the 'Water is a living thing' data project.

The ethnography of documents

Rather than the more common method of participant observation, I have carried out document-based ethnography, supplemented by interviews with McLachlan. In taking this methodological approach, I have drawn inspiration from many other scholars who are thinking about documents ethnographically, including Angela Garcia, Annelise Riles, Helen Verran, Matthew Hull, Chris Kelty, and Hannah Landecker. Riles writes that documents can act as 'artifacts of modern knowledge practices, and, in particular, knowledge practices that define ethnography itself' (2006: 7). John Law's work on remaking ethnographic practices, given the larger recognition that 'intimacy no longer necessarily implies proximity' (2004: 3), has also been influential in my thinking.

Document-based ethnography is well suited for conducting ethnographic research in situations of restricted access, particularly when access to fieldsites and other research is hampered by state policies and censorship. Governmentality is increasingly enacted through the proliferation of documents and reports as 'governmental technologies' (Rose and Miller 2010), but in the outsourcing of the making of these documents to consultancy firms, researchers lose access to these sites. When faced with these barriers, ethnographers can learn to glean more from the documents that they do have access to, by studying the conditions of their making and their circulation, and the politics of the knowledge claims they are making. As Hull writes, '[D]ocuments are not simply instruments of bureaucratic organizations, but rather are constitutive of bureaucratic rules, ideologies, knowledge, practices, subjectivities, objects, outcomes, and even the organizations themselves' (2012: 253).

Applying these insights, I focus here on the role of documentary practices in the refuting of settler colonial environmental science in Alberta. Following Kelty and Landecker's suggestion to position 'the literature as an informant', I have sought to illuminate data practices that are 'not necessarily visible through the lens of single actors, institutions or key papers' (2009: 177). The central practice analysed here is the adoption of McLachlan's three-track method, which was used in a collaboration between the two First Nations communities and non-Indigenous scientists in order to produce a document that could be circulated in the form of data. Closely examining this methodology, as we will see, can produce a more nuanced understanding of the kinds of measures that Indigenous communities have often needed to take to have their knowledge recognized in colonial contexts in which significant resources are mobilized towards delegitimizing it. The 'Water is a living thing' report, then, reflects a strategic translation – one that enabled the sharing of TK without its assimilation – rather than a straightforward reflection of how these communities know contamination.

Climates of evidence

The decision to produce the 'Water is a living thing' report was made in response to the particularly pro-industry stance taken by the Canadian federal government at the time. The 'politics of evidence' (Berland 2015) at work in Conservative Stephen Harper's government between 2006 and 2015 meant that extraordinary efforts were made to restrict the circulation of data that showed industry-caused evidence of harm to humans or the environment. The Harper government was criticized for 'science muzzling', as it monitored and censored the communications of scientists who conducted research as part of Canada's federally funded research institutions (Ghosh 2013). Some of the most highly censored research topics under this government included climate change, environmental and health impacts of the oil industry, and pollution of waterways. Journalists wishing to interview Canadian scientists were required to submit interview questions for government approval (Buranyi 2015). The Harper government also destroyed scientific data held at federally funded libraries and archives, which federal scientists only reported after resigning, for fear of losing their jobs. To counter this crackdown, Natasha Myers and Max Liboiron (Myers 2015; Myers & Liboiron 2015) launched the influential 'Write2Know' campaign, which drew public attention to the deleterious consequences for public knowledge. The public's ability to critique policy – and to resist it – was significantly hindered by this restricted access to scientific data.

Facing rapidly rising rates of disease in the community of Fort Chipewyan, a town of about 900, members of the Athabasca Chipewyan First Nation and the Mikisew Cree First Nation needed a way to render their experience into a form of evidence that would be recognized by the federal government, which would allow the community to gain access to much-needed resources. McLachlan had already earned a reputation as a trusted advocate and collaborator based on his previous work with Cree First Nations in Manitoba, which resulted in a 2013 report on the environmental impacts of a hydroelectric project on food and water sources. In that document, McLachlan juxtaposed qualitative data based on TK with quantitative environmental science data.[4] In his analysis, McLachlan wrote that the data contributed by the First Nations community members was 'rich and experienced-based' (2013: 4), while the data produced by the environmental scientists employed by Manitoba Hydro was 'largely specialized and inaccessible techno-scientific information' (2013: 5).[5] Importantly, the First Nations' data also reflected different temporal and spatial premises, with attention to impacts across multiple sites and multiple temporal scales, which made 'the shortcomings of the [industry-funded] science' evident (McLachlan 2013: 5).

Beyond these divergences, McLachlan also emphasized, were different interpretations of the data, which led each group to envision different futures for the land and its inhabitants. Perhaps unsurprisingly, the scientists' interpretation was 'generally much more optimistic about the nature of project-associated impacts'; more revealingly, they anticipated future contamination that could be countered by 'mitigation and rehabilitation measures' (McLachlan 2013: 5). In contrast, rather than presuming the inevitability of future contamination, the First Nations' interpretation characterized contamination as something new and alterable.

McLachlan was invited to visit the Athabasca Chipewyan First Nation and the Mikisew Cree First Nation, and to propose possible methods of producing credible evidence of harm from the oil sands industry. The First Nations wanted to work with an external toxicologist who could help them make a case for urgently needed medical resources after the loss of their community doctor. Building on the 2013 study in Manitoba, McLachlan again sought to position Indigenous TK as the epistemological equal of Western science in processes of producing knowledge. The method would place TK in relation to the type of data recognized as evidence by the federal government and industry actors, rather than allowing it to be cast off as a 'quaint artefact' that would ultimately be subservient to the Western science (Blacker, interview with McLachlan, 7 May 2015).[6] McLachlan's insistence upon non-hierarchical knowledge production was also an attempt to guard against the tendency for collaborations to 'scientize' TK (see Agrawal 2002) by 'testing and validating relevant knowledge using scientific criteria'

(Ellis 2005: 72). In this way, the three-track method is both a material object and an epistemic tool designed to foreclose scientization and dismissal.

The resulting report is methodologically exceptional in the field of environmental science in that it presents evidence in three distinct forms: the first articulates TK about environmental contamination (in narrative form);[7] the second provides measurements of contamination levels using current industry standards (in numerical form); and the third synthesizes the first two. But there is an important tension at the heart of this methodology: it aims to strategically translate TK into the language of data *just enough* to enable recognition while still holding back from total translation, thereby preventing the assimilation of TK and reserving space for it to speak autonomously in its own track. In this sense, the three-track methodology can be understood as a 'conceptual structure' designed to work against what Kristie Dotson calls 'epistemic oppression' by opening up participation in science to 'other epistemological accounts and commitments' (cited in Braun & Kopinski 2018: 559). Indeed, McLachlan describes the methodology as 'cross-cultural':

> [O]ne of the unintended benefits of collaborative, cross-cultural research involving both outside scientists and community members, is that there is much more interest in and support of these techniques, which in turn tends to generate quantitative data that are more acceptable to the relevant governmental agencies (2013: 27).

What this quote makes evident is that, despite collaborating with Western scientists, the knowledge and experiences of the First Nations communities would continue to be marginalized and delegitimized unless they were *articulated through the language of data*. Sally Engle Merry argues that quantification of data universalizes through the production of commensurability; local knowledge is altered when it is removed from 'its embeddedness in a holistic cultural and political context' so that it can be made comparable, classifiable, and commensurable (2016: 212). So what were the epistemic consequences of this methodology? Was the three-track method successful in protecting TK from universalization and in formulating a knowledge claim that would be credible to the state?

Politics in evidence

In Canada under the tenure of the Harper government, quantified data was privileged; it likely appealed to the policy-makers due to its aura of objectivity, which enabled the smoothing out of frictions and complexities, 'appearing pragmatic and instrumental rather than ideological' (Merry 2016: 4). Collaborations between Western science and TK – and particularly the three-track methodology – faced significant barriers that prevented the study's results from attaining credibility and legibility in this political climate.[8] Government and industrial actors, as well as some academic scientists, doubted that 'amateur' scientists could be producing valid toxicological data, suggesting that the community participants were 'biased' and incapable of producing 'objective' data (Natcher, Brunet, Bogdan & Tchir 2020).[9] McLachlan countered that the participants' scientific training was robust, but also that the First Nations participants' findings would inevitably reflect their knowledge and world-views to some extent, as is the case for all scientists' data collection as well as their interpretations (2014: 193).

The First Nations communities' decision to work with McLachlan using the three-track methodology must be understood in relation to earlier studies of contamination in the area, none of which proved a correlation with disease rates.[10] For example, the report commissioned by Alberta Health Services found no correlation between the documented contamination (Cantox Environmental Inc. 2007; Timoney 2007) and increased cancer rates, instead suggesting that 'the likely explanations for the changes in pattern of cancer incidence were thought to be related to lifestyle, socio-cultural factors, and genes' (Chen 2009: 32).[11] The difficulty of proving causation strongly shapes the interpretation of toxicological data. Establishing causation from correlation in the context of cancer rates is particularly difficult due to the complex aetiology of cancer and the scientific uncertainty that arises from the inability to isolate and test individual risk factors (whether chemical, environmental, or genetic). It is precisely this uncertainty and the difficulty of establishing causation within this paradigm that polluting industries mobilize in their arguments against regulation (Roiss 2019).

The findings of these four studies were viewed with suspicion by members of the First Nations communities; as McLachlan notes, '[M]any community members distrust data that originate from government and especially industry' (2014: 87). The studies did not incorporate TK into their data collection, nor did the scientists spend enough time in the region to gain adequate knowledge of the land to gain the ability to contextualize their findings (Tenenbaum 2009; Timoney 2007). The First Nations participants in the three-track collaborative study made it clear that they could not endorse a study of regional contamination that did not engage with TK. As one participant said:

> The government certainly isn't looking out for our best interests, so it's time that we look out for our own best interests. We are going to find out what's going on and we're going to talk to our Elders and listen to what they are saying, and we are going to design a monitoring programme around that (Tyas & McLachlan 2014).

McLachlan explains why the incorporation of TK into studies of contamination should guide data collection and its interpretation:

> The TK provides a very clear depiction of the nature of these changes and how wildlife, environmental, and human health combine and interact with one another. It also helps direct the scientific data collection and provides a strong socio-environmental context for any lab-based outcomes. This context in turn helps make both types of data more accessible and credible with community members. The scientific data, on the other hand, help support the TK in ways that might have more resonance with governments and industry, at least in the short-term (2014: 211).

In an interview, he emphasized that there are compelling *scientific* reasons to design a study led by TK, as doing so will produce more reliable data. This is not only the case in Fort Chipewyan: *any* Western scientific collection of environmental data in communities affected by industrial contamination needs TK to direct the study, to show scientists where to take measurements and how to read them within their local context (Blacker, interview with McLachlan, 7 May 2015).

As evidence accrues of associations between exposure to environmental contamination and adverse human health consequences, many scientists are calling for new methodologies in toxicology and epidemiology. To name one example, Peter Sly and colleagues critique epidemiologists' and statisticians' use of a 'conservative methodology' that restricts the possibility of showing correlation between the presence of environmental hazards and environmental disease, claiming it demands 'a very high level of evidence before a risk factor can be included' (2016: 4). The difficulty in proving correlation only increases when measuring chronic low-dose exposure to environmental contaminants that enter the body through the ingestion of food, water, or air; when interpreting quantified data in this context, '"proving" causation is almost impossible' (Sly *et al.* 2016: 6). Sly and colleagues also explicitly warn against Chen's (2009) interpretation, stating that:

> [T]he current methodology fails to consider emerging evidence that behaviors currently classified as caused by 'lifestyle' are, in fact, the result of much more than personal choice and are profoundly shaped by the social and cultural environment, genetics, and parts of the natural and the manmade environment (Sly *et al.* 2016: 4).

To address these limitations, Sly and colleagues call for 'a new approach' that 'considers environmental risks and redefines environmental diseases' (2016: 5). Indeed, the three-track methodology stands to gain evidential authority when considered from within a new framework for causal thinking in toxicology and epidemiology that allows the relation between environmental contamination and human health to be more readily seen and evidenced. This is a hopeful vision, but for the time being, Indigenous communities are still contending with Western scientific standards that make it extremely difficult to establish causation. It is within this paradigm that I situate data as an artefact of what can 'count' as scientific knowledge, and argue that it remains a form of political representation that Indigenous communities may strategically engage with in the settler colonial context.

Data as a language: translating knowledge into data

Well aware that their own interpretation of the Health Canada data would have no scientific standing under the Harper administration, the First Nations communities sought to translate TK into the language of data that would be legible to conventional toxicologists. Still, the communities suspected that unless they took extraordinary measures to prevent it, their TK would ultimately be subsumed within the dominant toxicological framework. In order to avoid this, the First Nations communities decided, together with McLachlan, that any translation of knowledge into data would need to be *led* by the communities' TK, placing the Elders' insights at the forefront. The Western scientists with whom the communities collaborated would act merely in a supporting role, rather than directing the study design or the interpretation of data collected.

If we consider data as a language, we see that the production of data, like language, can entail both a revealing and a holding back. Sharing data does not necessitate revealing everything or providing total access. Data can be curated so that it *holds back* that which is of the most value. Furthermore, figures can speak in cryptic ways. The third track was the space in which a strategic unveiling of data effected its calculated holding back, which was designed to protect TK and to retain Indigenous control over the data. In this process, the TK was never entirely translated into numerical data; it remained unassimilable, an inconvenient reminder of the epistemic alterity that the settler colonial state aimed to eradicate.

The first track documented the First Nations' evidence of contamination through TK presented in narrative form, while the second track documented the toxicological measurements of contamination presented in bar graphs. At first glance, it is not evident how the findings of the first track can be brought to bear on the findings in the second track (see Fig. 1). In the first track, evidence is presented as based in oral knowledge, held collectively, through references to how community members have experienced changes over time, and through descriptions of how these changes manifest visually. Documenting changes in beavers, for example, one programme participant observes that the animal's flesh 'wasn't rich and red like it used to be'; it was 'just kinda pale'

6.3.2 BEAVER

Generally speaking, some community members had noticed a decline in the health of beaver, to some degree in the Peace Athabasca Delta but especially in closer proximity to the Oil Sands,

> Nov 13: "And like Lawrence said, even the animals don't taste the same. He noticed that. That's all from Industry. Even McKay, my son-in-law, killed a beaver there. And then we smoked the beaver meat. And the meat wasn't rich and red like it used to be? It's just kinda pale. And then we smoked it, and then we had some of it, and it didn't even taste the same. Way different. And then they took another beaver there – I left it over there, I didn't bother."

Typically, beaver kidneys had the highest contaminant levels followed by liver. In contrast, beaver meat (muscle) typically showed the lowest levels of contaminants.

BEAVER MEAT (CONSUMPTION LIMITS RELATED TO ARSENIC)

Typically, beaver kidneys had the highest arsenic levels followed by liver (Fig 6.6). In contrast, beaver meat (muscle) typically showed the lowest levels of contaminants.

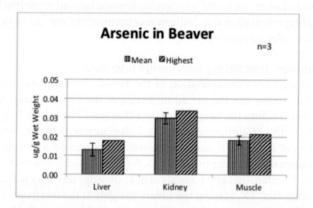

FIG 6.6. Concentration of arsenic in beaver liver, kidney and meat (muscle) (n=3). Standard error bars indicated for each mean value. Also indicated is maximum concentration observed.

Figure 1. Tracks one and two documenting contamination in beavers. (Published in McLachlan, S.M. 2014. 'Water is a living thing': environmental and human health implications of the Athabasca oil sands for the Mikisew Cree First Nation and Athabasca Chipewyan First Nation in Northern Alberta', p. 60. Reprinted with permission.)

and 'didn't even taste the same' (McLachlan 2014: 60). This documentation of TK on contamination in beavers is placed alongside a bar graph presenting the levels of arsenic found in the beavers' liver, kidney, and muscle that were tested. While the report makes an effort to contextualize these arsenic measurements, the significance of the data is difficult to assess for people who are not trained as toxicologists. Conversely, the meaning of the TK is immediately clear, even to readers unfamiliar with the region. This difference in the legibility of the data resonates with the findings of a study that showed that people who are provided with numerical data on their exposure to contaminants are often unsure how to make sense of this data and the level of risk it constitutes (Altman *et al.* 2008). The study concludes, as well, that people's interpretations of numerical measurements are mediated by various forms of social knowledge.

The third track creates a space of synthesis between this narrative and numerical data, enabling dialogue between the 'incommensurable' first two tracks. In the third track, quantified data gains flexibility, as it is situated as a necessarily partial form of accounting for a level of complexity that cannot be captured by numbers alone. In this sense, the third track enables exchange and transformation: the numerical data presented in the bar graphs can be altered in the third track to reflect the insights provided by the TK in the first track, just as the numbers can be made to speak to the narrative, sometimes lending additional specificity to the TK in terms of timelines, concentrations, and site specificity. As McLachlan notes, the TK contextualizes or even 'corrects' the numerical data presented in the second track.

The reasons why numerical data might need to be 'corrected' speak to fundamental points of divergence between TK and toxicological ways of knowing: TK brings pasts and futures to bear on the assessment of the present, while toxicology takes snapshot measurements; TK allows for the long-term observation of environmental changes and the interactions between different types of changes taking place, deeming them to be relevant guides in the selection of a sampling site, while toxicology considers this informed selection of sites to constitute bias.

Conventional toxicological practices can also play a role in the production of ignorance (McGoey 2019; Proctor & Schiebinger 2008) through the strategic selection of sampling sites known to provide *less* evidence of contamination than others. But the problems with conventional toxicological practices might also be more benign: scientists lacking the insights provided by TK may be less able to make connections between separately observed, but interrelated processes. One of the First Nations participants in the community-based monitoring programme expressed this incisively:

> [S]cientists look at very thin slices of stuff. They don't look at the whole book, they look at one word on a page and try to define. Somebody's got to put the book together. But if you can't see the whole book, you can't do it. That's the trouble with scientists. Where the traditional knowledge is like you have the whole book. You may not be able to say exactly why, what causes this, what causes that. But you can sure see the changes. The scientists can't explain the changes, because they can't see what the changes are (McLachlan 2014: 162).

I now turn to more closely examine this disjunction between the temporal scale of contamination that is visible to 'fly-in' scientists and the ability to 'see the whole book' through the lens of TK.

The temporal incommensurability of data

One of the questions investigated using the three-track methodology was: how can we know the concentrations and speeds at which PAHs are travelling downstream? Existing measurement techniques are inadequate to assess the massive scale (across hundreds of kilometres through groundwater) at which these toxins are travelling. Like radiation, PAHs are invisible to the human eye. They become visible only through their effects on plants, animals, and humans. Uncertainty about their effects will likely persist for some time to come. For one thing, there is epidemiological delay: human cancers are slow to develop and become statistically significant. Is the production of empirical evidence the best way to understand the effects of PAH contamination? The three-track methodology wagers that it is not, and highlights the value of TK in registering subtle changes in the environment that precede and cause the development of human cancers.

The TK reflects community Elders' ability to observe changes in the land, waterways, plants, and animal behaviour relationally, and in the three-track method this knowledge

6.3.4 DUCKS

All participants had observed a decline in waterfowl, both with respect to migrating but also resident populations,

> "There used to be thousands of ducks in the delta. Like I was saying, we used to live off the land. What we would do in the morning is start our little boat and go up the beach and be able to shoot 5 or 10 ducks. It was nothing to make a pot of soup or something and that was almost like daily. Every other day besides from fishing, we would be able to do that. Now, we go out and we can't even get a duck. Come home with nothing. The numbers just aren't there. Just not thriving in the that area as much, as previous years, that is what I noticed in this area."
>
> David Campbell, MCFN

However, some had also observed a decline in the quality of the meat of those birds that were harvested in Peace Athabasca Delta,

> Nov 13, 2012: "You know, you know years ago I remember when am young when I kill a duck it taste so good. Now it does not taste the same. Its kind of taste not like it use to, it doesn't taste good."

Although five different species were harvested by community members, we decided to combine all of the species together when analysing for heavy metals in order to increase sample sizes. Typically, contaminant concentrations were greatest in duck kidneys and livers and lower in duck muscle (meat). Of all the species tested, duck tissues tended to be most contaminated. Although these ducks tended to be migrants and so could have amassed these heavy metals elsewhere, young of the year that had been born in the region also had high levels of these concentrations.

Figure 2. Track one documenting contamination in ducks. (Published in McLachlan, S.M. 2014. 'Water is a living thing': environmental and human health implications of the Athabasca oil sands for the Mikisew Cree First Nation and Athabasca Chipewyan First Nation in Northern Alberta, p. 80. Reprinted with permission.)

of change over time informs the selection of sampling sites. For example, in one part of the first track, David Campbell, a member of the Mikisew Cree First Nation, references multiple temporal perspectives from which to understand how environmental contamination is affecting ducks in the region (see Fig. 2). The number of ducks present in the region has fallen rapidly, he explains, but this kind of change over time may not be evident in a toxicological snapshot. Members of the Athabasca Chipewyan and Mikisew Cree First Nations have expressed concern over the scientific practices of scientists who visit Fort Chipewyan very briefly to take measurements without speaking to community members or making an effort to understand the changes that have been taking place on the land.[12]

Despite Western scientists' charges of 'bias' against the First Nations study participants, McLachlan maintains that knowing the land is not the same as biased data collection, and that claims about the objectivity of conventional forms of toxicological data are fallacious (2014: 193). Such data is not only not impartial but it also has significant limitations: it is formally impossible for the bar graph in track two to represent change over time. Current data practices for measuring contaminants take a snapshot of a moment in time, and translate that measurement into a 'representative sample' that is then circulated, with an aura of objectivity, as a knowledge claim. The contingency embedded in such knowledge claims is rendered invisible.

The First Nations communities' need to produce data in a form that would be credible and legible to government policy-makers led to a collaboration that bridged epistemological differences. The urgency to translate TK into the language of data also took precedence over existing divisions that might have prevented people from working together towards this shared goal. While the communities were united in the need to produce data that could convince the government to provide needed medical resources, some community members worried that incriminating data could lead to the end of oil production in Alberta. As one of the participants said:

> We're not here to shut down the oil sands. If we shut it down, then people will be out of jobs and they'll have no income for their families. We want to work with industry, and with government. Without the Community-Based Monitoring programme, we wouldn't be finding this. Involve us more, and we could effectively manage the environment together (Tyas & McLachlan 2014).

Conclusion

While the 'Water is a living thing' report ultimately failed to persuade policy-makers under the Harper government, the First Nations communities were undeterred, well aware that the work of changing cultural and political norms and scientific standards is slow, and particularly so in the settler colonial context. Over the last five years, some collaborations between TK and Western science have been awarded funding in the Canadian context. However, the potential for TK to retain autonomy within such collaborations remains to be seen.

The three-track methodology mobilizes the divergence of incommensurable knowledges (rather than attempting to smooth these tensions over) with the aim of developing new ways of producing evidence of harm, ones that can be recognized as legitimate knowledge claims in settler colonial Canada. My aim has been to shed light on how regimes of imperceptibility (Kuchinskaya 2014; Murphy 2006) operate in this case study: not only are certain knowledges more readily recognized as forms of evidence and others actively delegitimized, but First Nations communities may also strategically seek to share some knowledge while keeping other knowledge obscured.

The three-track methodology enables a form of strategic participation in – and resistance to – this era of relentless quantification and datafication, demonstrating that making-things-into-data can be an exercise of agency rather than merely a succumbing to external pressure. It is not a 'giving in' to the demands of evidence-based science. Furthermore, the methodology troubles simplistic stereotypes of TK as premodern, technophobic, and void of agency. It models how marginalized communities can produce scientific knowledge on their own terms, even as incommensurabilities persist. There are also important implications for scholarship in the anthropology of data: this essay demonstrates that the demand for open data is not simple; it is a demand that can exacerbate existing inequities through the loss of data sovereignty as well as through the loss of knowledges that are inextricable from health, cultural well-being, and political sovereignty. This case study shows that the act of giving data and the act of holding it back – disclosure and refusal – are not mutually exclusive.

The three-track methodology is a strategic response to a politico-scientific context that largely silences Indigenous voices and epistemics altogether. This strategy is salient because such silencing does not happen only in Canada, but in many colonial, postcolonial, and settler colonial states (see, among many others, Creary 2018; Hoover 2017; Tuhiwai Smith 2012). While the three-track methodology is not the only model to be followed, it is a promising example of how to develop new methodologies that go beyond normative quantitative forms of data production. Most urgently, the work of developing methodologies that serve the needs of chronically marginalized communities must be prioritized as we continue the unfinished work of dismantling colonial knowledge regimes.

NOTES

I am grateful to Rachel Douglas-Jones, Antonia Walford, Nick Seaver, Denielle Elliott, Erin Martineau, Tahani Nadim, Thomas Roiss, Sandra Widmer, and two anonymous reviewers for their insightful and generative comments on earlier versions of this essay. This research was supported by the Social Sciences and Humanities Research Council of Canada.

[1] In this essay, I do not attempt to represent the viewpoints of the Athabasca Chipewyan First Nation and the Mikisew Cree First Nation communities. As a non-Indigenous scholar, my research centres on critiquing settler colonial structures, epistemologies, and institutions that continue to inflict violence; it is not my right (nor is it my desire) to speak on behalf of Indigenous peoples.

[2] This is another reason why the 'Water is a living thing' report is methodologically distinct: it presents concrete evidence of TK on its own terms. As the Canada Research Chair in Indigenous Environmental Justice, Deborah McGregor (2020), has noted, it is difficult to find documentation of TK recorded in published reports because Indigenous voices and TK have been chronically disregarded by practitioners of Western science in the settler colonial context. TK has been excluded from official research and reports not only because it primarily takes the form of oral knowledge, but also because it has been viewed as antithetical to Western science.

[3] Bullard (1993) explains how the uneven distribution of environmental harm is exacerbated by policy-makers' dismissal of knowledge held by racialized and economically marginalized communities. These communities struggle to have their local and experiential knowledge recognized rather than discounted in the absence of external legitimation (Kimura & Kinchy 2019). The environmental justice movement draws attention to the systemic forms of discrimination that undergird the disproportionate levels of environmental contamination affecting marginalized communities (Cole & Foster 2001).

[4] Sally Engle Merry (2016) shows that quantitative data is increasingly demanded by the paradigm of evidence-based governance.

[5] It is important to avoid setting up a binary between TK and quantification. TK is not a static, unchanging entity; knowledge practices change over time and are not always imposed from the outside. Indigenous communities develop and adapt and alter ways of knowing intentionally and strategically. Likewise, quantified data is not always the opposite of TK; it can be messy and its meaning is dependent upon its interpretation.

[6] The methodology was also designed to meet Indigenous communities' desire and need for data sovereignty: that is, to possess and to control the uses of their data on their own terms. Despite the work carried out by the National Aboriginal Health Organization and the First Nations Information Governance Committee in developing principles of ownership, control, access, and possession (OCAP) for Indigenous self-determination in research and data management, the struggle for Indigenous communities to own and control their own data is ongoing, as many communities lack the structural and material resources that would enable data ownership. A broader discussion of OCAP is beyond the scope of this essay, but for more on OCAP and Indigenous Data Sovereignty, please see McGregor (2013) and Schnarch (2004).

[7] The idea that TK in narrative form could improve the accuracy of numerical measurement may sound counter-intuitive. However, as Annie McClanahan (2016) shows, credit reports were initially produced (and widely trusted) in narrative form, and only in the last century was numerical credit reporting developed. Furthermore, in his history of quantification, standardization, and bureaucratic demand for numerical measurement, *Trust in numbers: the pursuit of objectivity in science and public life*, Ted Porter (1995) argues that quantification emerged as a technology that would allow bureaucratic institutions to gain trust across vast cultural and epistemic differences, as numerical measurements could be presented as politically 'neutral' (and thus accepted and trusted) in a way that measurements and calculations presented in narrative form could not.

[8] Though TK held very little epistemic value under the Harper government, it has gained some standing in Canada following the 2015 publication of the Truth and Reconciliation Commission's Calls to Action, as well as through international pressure and support provided by UNESCO's Local and Indigenous Knowledge Systems Programme, which provides resources for the inclusion of Indigenous TK in science globally.

[9] It is also possible, however, that this critique was a deliberate attempt to limit the circulation of incriminating data on environmental contamination and its risks for human health. It may have been more effective for critics to devalue the study's methodology than to contend with the data itself.

[10] I find these studies to be emblematic of the ongoing structural violence enacted by the settler colonial state in its aim of delegitimizing TK. The studies can be understood as enacting what Walter and Russo Carroll characterize as the work of policy-making in colonizing nation states in that they are fuelled by data's 'limited scope, aggregate format, deficit focus and decontextualized framework'. Furthermore, these studies lack the ability to 'yield meaningful portraits of the embodied realities of Indigenous lives' that are most affected by this contamination (Walter & Russo Carroll 2021: 2).

[11] This insistence on framing the research as removed from political, social, and cultural considerations could be seen as an extreme case of what Steven Shapin and Simon Schaffer (1985) describe as the 'modest witness', who constructs boundaries delineating the phenomena that are thought to lie beyond the reach of their research methods. I thank Tahani Nadim for this insight.

[12] As Thom Davies notes on the politics of producing evidence of contamination in 'Cancer Alley', Louisiana, 'fly-in' scientists have also been known to plan their sampling visits to coincide with times when lower levels of contaminants might be measured. See Davies (2018) for a detailed discussion of industry's role in manipulating the temporality of toxins.

REFERENCES

AGRAWAL, A. 2002. Indigenous knowledge and the politics of classification. *International Social Science Journal* **54**, 287-97.

ALTMAN, R.G., R. MORELLO-FROSCH, J.G. BRODY, R. RUDEL, P. BROWN & M. AVERICK 2008. Pollution comes home and gets personal: women's experience of household chemical exposure. *Journal of Health and Social Behavior* **49**, 417-35.

BAKER, J.M. & C.N. WESTMAN 2018. Extracting knowledge: social science, environmental impact assessment, and Indigenous consultation in the oil sands of Alberta, Canada. *The Extractive Industries and Society* **5**, 144-53.

BARANDIARAN, J. 2015. Chile's environmental assessments: contested knowledge in an emerging democracy. *Science as Culture* **24**, 251-75.

BERLAND, J. 2015. Editorial: The politics of evidence. *Canada Watch* (**Fall**), 1-5.

BOYD, D. & K. CRAWFORD 2012. Critical questions for big data. *Information, Communication & Society* **15**, 662-79.

BRAUN, L. & H. KOPINSKI 2018. Causal understandings: controversy, social context, and mesothelioma research. *BioSocieties* **13**, 557-79.

BROWN, P. 1997. Popular epidemiology revisited. *Current Sociology* **45**, 137-56.

BULLARD, R.D. 1993. *Confronting environmental racism: voices from the grassroots*. Boston: South End Press.

BURANYI, S. 2015. The fight to unmuzzle Canada's scientists. *Vice*, 27 August (available online: *https://www.vice.com/en_us/article/qkv79v/the-fight-to-unmuzzle-canadas-scientists*, accessed 25 January 2021).

CALLISON, C. 2014. *How climate change comes to matter: the communal life of facts*. Durham, N.C.: Duke University Press.

——— 2020. The twelve-year warning. *Isis* **111**, 129-37.

CANTOX ENVIRONMENTAL INC. 2007. Assessment of the potential lifetime cancer risks associated with exposure to inorganic arsenic among indigenous people living in the Wood Buffalo region of Alberta. A report prepared for Alberta Health and Wellness.

CHEN, Y. 2009. Cancer incidence in Fort Chipewyan, Alberta. A report prepared for Alberta Health Services, the Nunee Health Board, and Health Canada.

COLE, L.W. & S.R. FOSTER 2001. *From the ground up: environmental racism and the rise of the environmental justice movement*. New York: NYU Press.

CREARY, M.S. 2018. Biocultural citizenship and embodying exceptionalism: biopolitics for sickle cell disease in Brazil. *Social Science & Medicine* **199**, 123-31.

DAVIES, T. 2018. Toxic space and time: slow violence, necropolitics, and petrochemical pollution. *Annals of the American Association of Geographers* **108**, 1537-53.

ELLIS, S.C. 2005. Meaningful consideration? A review of Traditional Knowledge in environmental decision making. *Arctic* **58**, 66-77.

ELLIOTT, D. 2019. Epidemiology, the media, and Vancouver's public health emergency: a critical ethnography. In *Thinking differently about AIDS* (eds) E. Mykhalovsky & V. Namaste, 302-31. Vancouver: University of British Columbia Press.

FRICKEL, S., S. GIBBON, J. HOWARD, J. KEMPNER, G. OTTINGER, D.J. HESS 2010. Undone science: charting social movement and civil society challenges to research agenda setting. *Science, Technology, & Human Values* **35**, 444-73.

GABRYS, J., H. PRITCHARD & B. BARRATT 2016. Just good enough data: figuring data citizenships through air pollution sensing and data stories. *Big Data & Society* **3** (available online: *https://journals.sagepub.com/doi/full/10.1177/2053951716679677*, accessed 25 January 2021).

GHOSH, P. 2013. Has Canada's government been muzzling its scientists? BBC News, Science & Environment, 2 April (available online: *https://www.bbc.com/news/science-environment-22005706*, accessed 25 January 2021).

HOOVER, E. 2013. Cultural and health implications of fish advisories in a Native American community. *Ecological Processes* **2**: 4 (available online: *https://doi.org/10.1186/2192-1709-2-4*, accessed 25 January 2021).

——— 2017. *The river is in us: fighting toxics in a Mohawk community*. Minneapolis: University of Minnesota Press.

HULL, M.S. 2012. Documents and bureaucracy. *Annual Review of Anthropology* **41**, 251-67.

KELTY, C. & H. LANDECKER 2009. Ten thousand journal articles later: ethnography of 'the literature' in science. *Empiria: Revista de metodología de ciencias sociales* **18**, 173-92.

KIMURA, A.H. 2016. *Radiation brain moms and citizen scientists: the gender politics of food contamination after Fukushima*. Durham, N.C.: Duke University Press.

——— & A.J. KINCHY 2019. *Science by the people: participation, power, and the politics of environmental knowledge*. New Brunswick: Rutgers University Press.

KINCHY, A. 2020. Contentious baselining: the politics of 'pre-drilling' environmental measures in shale gas territory. *Environment and Planning E: Nature and Space* **3**, 76-94.

———, S. PARKS & K. JALBERT 2016. Fractured knowledge: mapping the gaps in public and private water monitoring efforts in areas affected by shale gas development. *Environment and Planning C: Government and Policy* **34**, 879-99.

KOVACH, M. 2009. *Indigenous methodologies: characteristics, conversations and contexts*. Toronto: University Press.

KUCHINSKAYA, O. 2014. *The politics of invisibility: public knowledge about radiation health effects after Chernobyl*. Cambridge, Mass.: MIT Press.

LAVE R. 2012. Neoliberalism and the production of environmental knowledge. *Environment and Society* **3**, 19-38.

LAW, J. 2004. *After method: mess in social science research*. London: Routledge.

LI, F. 2009. Documenting accountability: environmental impact assessment in a Peruvian mining project. *PoLAR: Political and Legal Anthropology Review* **32**, 218-36.

LIBOIRON, M. 2021. *Pollution is colonialism*. Durham, N.C.: Duke University Press.

LUPTON, D. 2016. *The quantified self: a sociology of self-tracking*. Cambridge: Polity.

LYON, D. 2014. Surveillance, Snowden, and Big Data: capacities, consequences, critique. *Big Data & Society* **1**: **2** (available online: *https://journals.sagepub.com/doi/full/10.1177/2053951714541861*, accessed 28 January 2021).

MCCLANAHAN, A. 2016. *Dead pledges: debt, crisis, and twenty-first-century culture*. Stanford: University Press.

MCGOEY, L. 2019. *The unknowers: how strategic ignorance rules the world*. London: Zed Books.

MCGREGOR, D. 2013. Traditional Knowledge, sustainable forest management, and ethical research involving aboriginal peoples: an aboriginal scholar's perspective. *Aboriginal Policy Research Consortium International (APRCi)* **10**, 227-44.

——— 2020. Decolonizing global health research. Paper presented at York University, 30 September.

MCLACHLAN, S.M. 2013. Deaf in one ear and blind in the other: science, aboriginal Traditional Knowledge, and implications of the Keeyask hydro dam for the socio-environment. A report for the Manitoba Clean Environment Commission on behalf of the Concerned Fox Lake Grassroots Citizens. Submitted to the Clean Environment Commission, Winnipeg, Manitoba.

——— 2014. 'Water is a living thing': environmental and human health implications of the Athabasca oil sands for the Mikisew Cree First Nation and Athabasca Chipewyan First Nation in Northern Alberta. Environmental Conservation Laboratory, University of Manitoba. Phase Two Report, 7 July.

MATZ, J.R., S. WYLIE & J. KRIESKY 2017. Participatory air monitoring in the midst of uncertainty: residents' experiences with the speck sensor. *Engaging Science, Technology, and Society* **3**, 464-98.

MERRY, S.E. 2016. *The seductions of quantification: measuring human rights, gender violence, and sex trafficking*. Chicago: University Press.

MURPHY, M. 2006. *Sick building syndrome and the problem of uncertainty: environmental politics, technoscience, and women workers.* Durham, N.C.: Duke University Press.

———— 2017. Alterlife and decolonial chemical relations. *Cultural Anthropology* **32**, 494-503.

MYERS, N. 2015. Amplifying the gaps between climate science and forest policy: the Write2Know Project and participatory dissent. *Canada Watch* (**Fall**), 18-21.

———— & M. LIBOIRON 2015. Write2Know (available online: *http://write2know.ca/*, accessed 25 January 2021).

NATCHER, D., N. BRUNET, A.-M. BOGDAN & D. TCHIR 2020. Seeking indigenous consensus on the impacts of oil sands development in Alberta, Canada. *The Extractive Industries and Society* **7**, 1330-7.

OTTINGER, G. 2010. Buckets of resistance: standards and the effectiveness of citizen science. *Science, Technology, & Human Values* **35**, 244-70.

———— & B.R. COHEN 2011. *Technoscience and environmental justice: expert cultures in a grassroots movement.* Cambridge, Mass.: MIT Press.

PINE, K.H. & M. LIBOIRON 2015. The politics of measurement and action. In *Proceedings of the 33rd Annual ACM Conference on Human Factors in Computing Systems*, 3147-56. New York: Association for Computing Machinery.

PORTER, T.M. 1995. *Trust in numbers: the pursuit of objectivity in science and public life.* Princeton: University Press.

PROCTOR, R. & L.L. SCHIEBINGER (eds) 2008. *Agnotology: the making and unmaking of ignorance.* Stanford: University Press.

RILES, A. 2006. Introduction: In response. In *Documents: artifacts of modern knowledge* (ed.) A. Riles, 1-38. Ann Arbor: University of Michigan Press.

ROISS, T. 2019. *The limits of individual responsibility in the case of endocrine disrupting chemicals.* MA thesis, Technical University of Munich.

ROSE, N. & P. MILLER 2010. Political power beyond the state: problematics of government. *British Journal of Sociology* **61**, 271-303.

ROSS, M., A. DOS SANTOS PEREIRA, J. FENNELL, M. DAVIES, J. JOHNSON, L. SLIVA & J.W. MARTIN 2012. Quantitative and qualitative analysis of naphthenic acids in natural waters surrounding the Canadian oil sands industry. *Environmental Science & Technology* **46**, 12796-805.

SADOWSKI, J. 2019. When data is capital: datafication, accumulation, and extraction. *Big Data & Society* **6**: **1** (available online: *https://journals.sagepub.com/doi/full/10.1177/2053951718820549*, accessed 28 January 2021).

SCHNARCH, B. 2004. Ownership, control, access, and possession (OCAP) or self-determination applied to research: a critical analysis of contemporary First Nations research and some options for First Nations communities. *International Journal of Indigenous Health* **1**, 80-95.

SHADAAN, R. & M. MURPHY 2020. Endocrine-disrupting chemicals (EDCs) as industrial and settler colonial structures: towards a decolonial feminist approach. *Catalyst: Feminism, Theory, Technoscience* **6** (available online: *https://catalystjournal.org/index.php/catalyst/article/view/32089/26034*, accessed 25 January 2021).

SHAPIN, S. & S. SCHAFFER 1985. *Leviathan and the air-pump: Hobbes, Boyle, and the experimental life.* Princeton: University Press.

SLY, P.D., D.O. CARPENTER, M. VAN DEN BERG, R.T. STEIN, P.J. LANDRIGAN, M.-N. BRUNE-DRISSE & W. SUK 2016. Health consequences of environmental exposures: causal thinking in global environmental epidemiology. *Annals of Global Health* **82**, 3-9.

STAR, S.L. & J.R. GRIESEMER 1989. Institutional ecology, 'translations' and boundary objects: amateurs and professionals in Berkeley's Museum of Vertebrate Zoology, 1907-39. *Social Studies of Science* **19**, 387-420.

TALLBEAR, K. 2013. *Native American DNA: tribal belonging and the false promise of genetic science.* Minneapolis: University of Minnesota Press.

TECKLIN, D., BAUER C., PRIETO M. 2011. Making environmental law for the market: the emergence, character, and implications of Chile's environmental regime. *Environmental Politics* **20**, 879-98.

TENENBAUM, D.J. 2009. Oil sands development: a health risk worth taking? *Environmental Health Perspectives* **117**, A150-6.

TIMONEY, K. 2007. A study of water and sediment quality as related to public health issues, Fort Chipewyan, Alberta. A report prepared for the Nunee Health Board.

TODD, Z. 2016. An Indigenous feminist's take on the ontological turn: 'ontology' is just another word for colonialism. *Journal of Historical Sociology* **29**, 4-22.

———— 2018. Refracting the state through human-fish relations: fishing, Indigenous legal orders and colonialism in North/Western Canada. *Decolonization: Indigeneity, Education & Society* **7**, 60-75.

Tuhiwai Smith, L. 2012. *Decolonizing methodologies: research and indigenous peoples* (Second edition). Dunedin: University of Otago Press.

Tyas, M. & S. McLachlan 2014. *One river, many relations*. Documentary film, 62 minutes.

Walter, M. & S. Russo Carroll 2021. Indigenous Data Sovereignty, governance and the link to Indigenous policy. In *Indigenous Data Sovereignty and policy* (eds) M. Walter, T. Kukutai, S. Russo Carroll & D. Rodriguez-Lonebear, 1-20. London: Routledge.

West, S.M. 2019. Data capitalism: redefining the logics of surveillance and privacy. *Business & Society* **58**, 20-41.

Whyte, K. 2018. Settler colonialism, ecology, and environmental injustice. *Environment and Society* **9**, 125-44.

Une traduction stratégique : pollution, données et savoir traditionnel autochtone

Résumé

Cet article examine le rôle que jouent les pratiques autour des données dans la construction et l'opposition à la science de l'environnement colonisatrice. En enquêtant sur la contestation épistémique autour de la pollution générée par l'industrie pétrolière dans la province de l'Alberta (Canada), l'autrice aborde une approche alternative de la toxicologie : un programme communautaire de suivi utilisant une « triple » méthodologie afin de présenter les données sous trois formes différentes. En ayant recours à cette méthode, les communautés des Premières Nations ont entrepris une traduction stratégique, cherchant à équilibrer leur objectif de rendre le savoir traditionnel et les besoins communautaires lisibles auprès des décideurs politiques, avec leur souhait d'empêcher que leur savoir traditionnel soit assimilé dans le paradigme dominant des données. L'autrice avance que cette traduction incarne une forme de résistance en ces temps de donnéification impitoyable : la transformation des choses en données peut refléter une certaine force plutôt qu'une soumission à des pressions extérieures. Ainsi, cette triple méthodologie montre comment les communautés marginalisées peuvent se servir des capacités productives des données à leurs propres fins et contribuer aux connaissances scientifiques selon leurs propres conditions.

9
Bodies of data: doubles, composites, and aggregates

RACHEL DOUGLAS-JONES *IT University of Copenhagen*

In this essay, I describe three bodies of data, analysing how relations are drawn between physical, digital, and political composites. Following the phrase 'getting to know your data self', my aim is to draw out the kinds of relations people use data to make, and the versions of the body that I find codified in data imaginaries. Thematically, the stories give different accounts of control over data, as the data body is doubled, built out of composites, and aggregated into a body politic.

> The social body constrains the way the physical body is perceived
> Mary Douglas (2003 [1970]: 72)

In 2018, viewers of UK television, on a mild May evening, might, between segments of an entirely forgettable show, have been struck by a short advert for the credit company Experian. Created the year before by the advertising company Bartle Bogle Hegarty, the advert opens with Marcus Brigstocke, a well-known English comedian. Brigstocke is conversing with an almost double of himself on a wide green sofa. 'I'm Dan', says Brigstocke, 'And I'm his data self', says his (better-attired) double. The double appears in each scene, interfering in Dan's everyday life, as he wanders clumsily through the world, shopping, taking his partner out for dinner, moving house. The double is always visible, acknowledged, a third wheel in the relationship. The double makes (financial) life possible. Our protagonist introduces the double to the viewer: 'He's a physical manifestation of my financial history. He's made up of things like my transactions, phone contract. Stuff like that'. The double of Experian's advert is a cheerful, if cheeky, rendition of an otherwise felt or intangible presence, one way of communicating (in this case positively) the ongoing invisible collection of data. Viewers are exhorted at the advert's close to 'Get to know your data self, with Experian'.[1]

This essay interrogates the exhortation of 'getting to know your data self'. To understand the phrase, and the ideas it embeds, I work through three stories of data generation and use. I refract my thinking through the body, in order to bring forward often tacit assumptions about where data comes from, where it goes, how it is 'us' (or not us), and the ways in which it – as extension – is thought to be or stand in for

Journal of the Royal Anthropological Institute (N.S.) **27**, 159-170
© Royal Anthropological Institute 2021

larger wholes. My objective is not to ground data in the material, physical body, but rather to explore how movement and use of data gives it new meanings. In histories of biomedicine, the physical human body is placed as a site of debate – something that changed over time, had differing values depending on its physical integrity, and was imagined to have a 'relation' to a less tangible soul. In their edited collection *Beyond the body proper*, Margaret Lock and Judith Farquhar tell us that '[i]n medieval times debate about the body, its relation to soul, whether or not it has transcendental qualities, its incipient fecundity during putrefaction and in death, and its worth once fragmented, was ubiquitous' (2007: 19). Bodies have long been given the capacity to act as containers, sites for conceptualizing both plurality and completeness. The partibility of the body has given rise to a vast richness of literature on organs, donation, and commodification (Hogle 1995; Martin 1992; Scheper-Hughes & Wacquant 2003; Sharp 2000). But as Lock and Farquhar go on to tell us, with the beginnings of an era they call modernity, 'the body was gradually bifurcated, making an *object* body that became a *subject* for systematic investigation by the natural sciences' (2007: 19, emphasis added). By paying attention to how the body appears in bodies of data, I make space to explore the creation of today's object body as a subject for systematic investigation by data science. The sites of exploration are data doubles, bodies of aggregated data and government data, census data, statistics, and an exercise of state knowing (Kertzer & Arel 2002). This points in the direction I want to take my account: from a meditation on the remix of individual, person, and self that is taking place within personal data worlds, into the worlds of state knowledge, populations, and statistics. In the theoretical slippage already available in the legacies of political science thought, I argue for new compositional capacities for bodies politic.

In each of the stories I present, what is being pursued or sold are forms of control as a relation to a (changing) body of data. By keeping in mind a concern with control, I direct attention to what it is about data that is seen to need controlling. The sociologist Deborah Lupton (2013) has offered us an initial entry point through her observations of a language of fluidity around data, tending towards assumptions of data's unpredictability, the challenges of control and containment. She remarks how liquid metaphors 'evoke the notion of an overwhelming volume of data that must somehow be dealt with, managed and turned to good use' (2015: 107). While the stories I tell share a sense that data is everywhere (already collected or *in potentia*), they also hint it is in the control of 'others'. Where the stories diverge is in what is to be done about this. Building on my opening vignette with Dan, the first story offers a form of control generated through individual self-improvement, a simplified image of a data self who facilitates one's passage through the world, opening financial doors, or closing them. The second creates a corporate 'dividual' at the centre of data collection, composed of multiple data streams which are then hers for the using. It is a form of control over data intended to counter the sole use of data by large corporations. The final story also resists the collection and use of data, but it asks different questions about control by placing data within a history of colonial enumerations. As the self-as-body imaginary is deployed across these three accounts, I explore its self-evidence, emerging in comparison.

Dan's data self

Let us return to 'Dan', going about his everyday life. 'Dan' is an amiable but ultimately shallow character – the advert stands alone and we will never learn more about his everyday life or the role his 'data double' comes to take in it. But this double – described in the voiceover as a 'physical manifestation' of his financial history – is created precisely to prompt this imagining of a broader life. The viewer is invited to wonder what *their* 'data double' looks like, and enticed onto Experian's website to find out. This is the making-visible of credit scoring and creditworthiness – data that is collected by companies, and aggregated, on the basis of financial activities. While this is primarily a British (and English language) story, it is a visually legible idea of a double, made somehow of 'data', walking around with us, affecting our capacity to act in the world. The making of a cultural artefact like Experian's advert leaves professional traces. Laura McGovern, part of the advert's design team, writes that she and her colleagues introduced the idea of the data self for Experian because they 'liked the idea that we all have one, but it really became fun when we started to think about what kind of person they would be. Would they be helpful or a hindrance? It felt like the premise for a buddy comedy' (McGovern 2018). The advert is a newly colloquial form of something academics have been discussing for some time. Its presence as a social artefact, however, prompts reflection on the work that 'the data double' has been doing analytically. There are varying names for this sense of duplication, identified both by scholars and within the data industry. The 'data double' was described by Kevin Haggerty and Richard Ericson as far back as 2000, with more recent incarnations being the 'exoself' (Kelly 2012), 'duodividual' (Harcourt 2015), data proxy (Smith 2016), data doppelgänger (Watson 2014) and pixelated person (Greenfield 2016) (see Schüll 2019: 34-5 for a detailed discussion).

We could add Dan's data self – what Experian turn into his physical twin – to the catalogue of cases that put forward the idea of relating to 'oneself' through data. Digital tracking of daily life, such as steps walked, hours of sleep, weight, or food intake, has been widely documented as part of the Quantified Self movement. Formalized in 2008 as an international community, Quantified Self, or QS for short, 'supports every person's right and ability to learn from their own data' (QS 2020) and supports meetings and conferences internationally on methods and 'cultures' of tracking oneself. Scholars working ethnographically within QS have shown us the potential extensions of the idea that data is a better form of knowledge, from authenticity (Sharon 2017) to autobiography (Tamminen & Holmgren 2016) and the personal laboratory (Kristensen & Ruckenstein 2018). Here, data is routed through, but varyingly rooted in, the physical body as a means to then knowing and acting upon a self. The distinction is useful, as Ana Viseu and Lucy Suchman point out: the role given to data makes evident a gap it is perceived to mediate between 'the modern body and the knowing and acting self' (2010: 175).

The self as a 'growth industry' was prefigured long before it became possible to quantify sleep, or measure steps. In 1992, the anthropologist Elvi Whittaker embarked on an analysis of the emergence and marketability of the 'self'. As she pointed out, within scholarship this was a literal growth. She used numbers from the *Social Sciences Citation Index* to demonstrate her point: in 1974-5, there were 137 entries, by 1990-1991 there were 473, with new terms to be 'prefixed with "self"': acceptance, actualization, confidence, criticism, image, interest, respect, sufficiency, understanding …. Care, consciousness, help' (1992: 196). In what can only be taken as a deliberate pun, she remarks that the self has become an issue that is 'too often assumed to be self-evident' (1992: 198). Returning to Viseu and Suchman's point, the perceived gap between body and acting self allows the sense that 'the body may be increasingly controlled by reason'

(Ruckenstein 2014: 69). Experian's invention of Dan's data double serves as an entry point to this control, since his appearance in the advert is both associated with reason and yet slightly out of reach. The double is not wholly knowable, and it is precisely this doubt that makes the advert effective. More than this, despite being only his *financial* double, he nonetheless appears as a complete body generated from his financial history and transactions, debt and credit scores, fully capable of interfering in all of Dan's life. Life – in this reading – is what one can do financially, what one's double *lets* one do. What happens when the data records a person makes are given the agentive personhood evident in this advert? There are two points I would like to draw out concerning the role of the image of Dan's data double and its bodily form.

First, I suggest that Dan's 'double' relocates the metaphor for self-knowledge outwards. For a long time, ideas of surface and depth have shaped a Western, modern sense of where truth might lie: consider colloquial phrases such as 'hidden below the surface'. In material sciences, for example, a much-fetishized site of the authentic and its role as a placeholder for the true, favoured techniques are drilling, x-raying, sampling, 'looking beyond the surface to see what "truly" is' (Jones 2010: 188). Surfaces are suspicious. But why? Archaeologist Siân Jones has noted that these techniques 'involve investigation of an object's interior space or substance' (2010: 184), a practice she goes on to link to Western notions of a true, interior, self. While literature on this topic is vast and by no means in agreement, Jones lays out the markers through which authenticity took on overtly moral overtones, concluding that 'a new inward-looking notion of authenticity emerged in the modern era … linked to forms of social and physical dislocation on a grand scale and new ideas about the individual' (2010: 187). Yet as anthropologist Janelle Taylor would argue, 'practice makes surface' (2005: 744). As soon as a body had a surface, this generated the 'impulse to surface its interior', 'render what was hidden a spectacle for public view', with Taylor noting that surfaces 'emerged in tandem with new ways of configuring subjects and objects, representations and realities, bodies and collectivities in European modernity' (2005: 747).

Second, there is a competing logic here not of surface and depth but of overspill and disaggregation. In data collection, there is always an overspill, as Minna Ruckenstein has pointed out. Data use, she argues, 'frames the natural [physical] body as incomplete', with analytics 'thus firmly rooted in the externalization of nature as something that people are able to transform' (2014: 69). In Natasha Dow Schüll's ethnography of the QS movement, we meet Joshua, whom she describes as a 'bearded venture capitalist in his early thirties from California'. For Joshua, who has been tracking aspects of his daily life for years, 'the self can be overwhelming as an integrated, whole thing'. By doing projects of self tracking within the QS movement, and by sharing the progress and results, he says 'you can disaggregate various aspects of self, work on just those …, it takes an incredible burden off you' (Schüll 2019: 31). Elsewhere in her work, Schüll has described these data doubles and databases as 'informational self-containers', conceived 'in Heideggerian terms, as standing reserves of potential insight – ordered data archives ready to disclose hitherto hidden patterns of action at play in our day-to-day lives' (2017: 46). She explores the labour of self-curation, the sense of excess and archive that this work generates.

Lock and Farquhar describe their 'studies of objectifying practice' as part of a long struggle to 'rehabilitate the body as something other than an appendage to the mind' (2007: 19). What Dan's data self appears to do is reinvent objectification. However, what Dan is being offered is a form of self-knowledge already possessed by an other. The exhortation we set out to comprehend, 'get to know your data self', is that self as seen by a financial corporation. To bring these two points together, instead of the excess of unknowability being placed within unknown interior depths, beneath surfaces, it is placed in unknown exterior archives.

Composite citizens

The idea of data excess or overspill has been circulating for longer than Dan's data double, with data as a currency rapidly ceasing to be metaphorical through logics of both accumulation and extraction (Gregg 2015; Puschmann & Burgess 2014; Zuboff 2015). However, as Orit Halpern reminds us, 'there is nothing automatic, obvious or predetermined about our embrace of data as wealth. There is, in fact, an aesthetic crafting to this knowledge, a performance necessary to produce value' (2014: 4). In this performance, data becomes the means by which the transacting self comes into being. In 2013, the UK newspaper *The Financial Times* created and ran an online calculator promising a calculation of how valuable your data was (Steel, Locke, Cadman & Freese 2013).[2] At the time, the categories it used were broad. Criteria that produced greater financial value from your data were predicated on expensive upcoming life events, such as the prospective purchase of a car or the intention to become pregnant. The newspaper's objective with the calculator was twofold: first, to create another side to the by then already vast and still growing data brokerage industry; and, second, to make visible to the 'sources' of data – people – just how it could be turned into money. On offer was the monetization of everyday activities, meticulously and invisibly catalogued by digital technologies. 'You deserve more for your data', the potential clients of New York-based start-up Datacoup are told, 'if you connect data, you'll earn' (Datacoup 2019). In this section, I explore the composite body of data upon which such promises are based, drawing out comparisons with the double along the way.

Primarily based in Europe, MyData Global is a non-profit organization on a mission to 'empower individuals by improving their right to self-determination regarding their personal data' (MyData 2021). Founded in the wake of a series of conferences held every year in Finland or Estonia since 2016, the growing MyData network is primarily what Tuukka Lehtiniemi and Minna Ruckenstein, who work with it, call an 'infrastructure-level intervention' (2019: 5). In their terms, the network is made up of 'human-centric personal data proponents', set up to counter and contrast with corporate models. The group puts individual control of data at the heart of its 'mission', asserting both that 'individuals should be in control of data about themselves', and that this 'human-centric vision … has strong roots in the European value tradition' (Lähteenoja *et al.* 2020: 11). For the initiative, 'the right to decide on the uses of personal data collected by organizations – such as data on economic transactions, location, smart home appliances, occupational health check-ups or social media – should reside with the data subjects themselves, instead of being monopolized by the organizations' (Lehtiniemi & Ruckenstein 2019: 4). As a result, each year, founders of companies, government representatives, NGOs, and data activists gather to talk about data business models and use cases, 'proof points' and 'proof of concept', in a collective effort to counter the perceived hegemony of data harvesters or brokers, otherwise termed an 'organization-centric system' (Lehtiniemi & Ruckenstein 2019: 4). Out of this range of apps and approaches, let me walk through one example, which its CEO describes as similar to Experian, the creators of Dan's data double.

CitizenMe, an app-based start-up, was presented during the 2018 MyData conference by its CEO, StJohn Deakins. Deakins is a technology veteran, having developed booking systems, mobile data services, and a platform company over the last twenty-five years (Deakins 2020). His app CitizenMe is described variously online as an 'identity control service' (Deakins 2020), a 'personal identity management service' (Judge Business School 2020), and a 'customer insight' tool (CitizenMe 2020a). During the MyData Conference, Deakins laid out a vision of CitizenMe as 'Experian levels of data in real time, with ethics' (Deakins 2018). The 'ethics' here referred to the consent given by users of the app to share their data. The real-time data comes from users of the app, with Deakins (2018) arguing that as he researched the field, he found that what 'people wanted was a very simple application, where people could partake in different activities with their data'. Following the principles of an 'individual-centric' model of data control common at the conference, Deakins's presentation argued that individuals would have a 'very eclectic' range of data that they both owned and controlled. CitizenMe appears on Apple's App store with its name, and the tagline 'control, value, trust'. Through the app, Deakins promised in his conference presentation, it would be possible to 'do' many things with data.

What can one do, then? While the interface is evolving with each update, users of the CitizenMe app at the time Deakins was presenting his design would be faced with four buttons named Insight, Donate, Earn, and Fun. Insight, a lightbulb icon against a blue background, acts as an enticement to users and a medium of exchange for data sharing,[3] Deakins says, means 'you can get insights about yourself, anything from "How intelligent am I according to my Facebook picture", shallow, fun stuff, through to "Am I going to get diabetes in the next few years?"' Donate, a red heart, allows a user to 'donate' their data to organizations they want to. Earn, the green button, enables users to find out the value of their data to others and receive money via PayPal. 'It allows you', says Deakins (2018), 'to immediately transact data sets for cash. You get an immediate cash reward'.

At the conference, Deakins offers something closer to a pitch than a case study, but demonstrates, in his view, both the feasibility of an individual selling their answers and a model for a future of data less in the hands of 'big tech' and more locally held and transacted from a smartphone. The drama of his presentation rises about half-way through, when his slides show data sources multiplying, layering information for 'personal insight' (Deakins 2018). It is the combination of data that generates this insight: 'You can put in your step count information from your phone', he says, 'and combine that with how many hours a day you're watching Netflix, whether you're overweight, and that information is very valuable'. To a LinkedIn audience a few years after the conference, the proposition is seen from the other side: 'You can talk to millions of Citizens on their terms, who will anonymously share data including: beliefs, values, psychometrics, app usage, photos, a market-leading research Q&A – all delivered into a self-service dashboard with live, AI-driven clustering and segmentation' (CitizenMe 2020b). The app, while still current and available in the Apple and Android app stores, is arguably more substantially grounded in its vision of value around data than its enactment thereof.

There is much to unpack in CitizenMe, and again I focus on just two aspects. First, in Deakin's app, the user is invited to 'become a Citizen', yet the term is largely divorced from anything one might be a citizen 'of'.[4] Outward facing market-orientated webpages tell companies that they can connect with real people, 'Citizens' (always capitalized), some unspoken new order of digital capitalism. Yet looked at from within the app's data flows, the 'Citizen' acts as a container for (and manager of) data, where the (expandable) multiplicity is contained within. Through the rhetoric of control over one's own data, an app user is responsible for managing the options and opportunities for their data selves. At the heart of this hall of mirrors, where all the data gets reflected back, is a solitary self who decides. There is no sense in the mode of the 'Citizen' that the decision is collective. It is an atomized self who, managing 'flows of data', decides the ways already-captured data will get put to use.

So, second, and in contrast with the promise of Dan's *double* of the self (complete, all arms and legs, at the point of *financial* information), CitizenMe offers a *composite* image, built from seemingly endless sources of data. What Deakins calls 'power' comes from 'connecting up your disparate sources of data', an inferential practice already well utilized in industry. Here, inference takes on a greater social life, greater personal and commercial promise. With the person-as-data-point becoming a container for multiple potential traces, Lehtiniemi and Ruckenstein confirm that

> in order to avoid the legal debate on data ownership and property rights, MyData activists consciously employ the concepts of data management and control, focusing on individuals' practical capacity to make use of their data … [Activists] portray the individual as the 'operation centre', placed in the middle of the digital service ecosystem uniting data sources and endpoints; flows of data pass (either permission-wise or in actual transfers) through the central point (2019: 5).

What an individual-as-operation-centre model rests upon is a newly perceived relation between a person and their data. Whereas Dan's digital self was an image of a literal body, a self-same 'double', users of CitizenMe are encouraged to think of themselves as made up of and producers of multiple data *streams*, parts that can 'earn' on their behalf. Deakin's dashboard for a given user is a composite image of a self refracted back at the user through data. The actor at the centre of this 'operation centre' adjudicates between different data selves, explicitly partial, objectified in order to be managed.

From their critical position embedded within the MyData movement, Lehtiniemi and Ruckenstein invoke 'Our Data' against what they see as its individualizing tendencies. CitizenMe is but one kind of individualization, as they argue 'that developing data technologies for the individual and leaving it up to the market to correct the economic imbalances will hardly work alone'. As they point out, 'the very collection of data and not only subsequent uses of it, may have negative implications' (2019: 8). For all the focus on individual agency over data within MyData, Lehtiniemi and Ruckenstein are pointing to a return of the relations inherent in the production of these data flows that the individual may control.

Data sovereignty, data aggregation

Picking up on Lehtiniemi and Ruckenstein's invocation of 'Our Data', and the ideas of citizenship severed from CitizenMe, my final section shifts from the investigation of the individualized body double and individually controlled body of data to concern with data held on a body of people. This is not the individualized self-determination of MyData, but the self-determinism of Indigenous Data Sovereignty activists. How people are 'peopled' through data has been the subject of research for some time, possible through the collection of official statistics and 'data' (Cakici, Ruppert & Scheel 2020; Ratner and Ruppert 2019). By looking to data activist movements surrounding Indigenous Data Sovereignty in this closing section, I explore how data comes to be redefined in the service of projects seeking to reshape how knowledge is made on, and into, a body politic.

That the state is an actor seeking knowledge of citizens though data is the foundation of much scholarship on what kinds of data are collected, how, and why (Amoore 2011; Scott 1998). The task of describing collective bodies has long fallen to statisticians. Statistical units of measurement shape what is and can be known, even if, as the Wongaibon/Ngiyampaa epidemiologist Raymond Lovett and his colleagues point out, '[m]any of the assumptions underpinning old and emerging data ecosystems rest on Anglo-European legal concepts, such as individual privacy and ownership, which translate poorly into the big and open data environments' (Lovett *et al.* 2019: 34). Indigenous critiques of state data collection, statistical practice, and governance increasingly take issue with the individual as the starting point. In the introduction to their edited collection setting out an agenda towards Indigenous Data Sovereignty, Tahu Kukutai, a professor of indigenous demography, and John Taylor, an emeritus population geographer, tell us that '[t]he insistence on using the individual as the primary – often only – statistical unit of measurement is an embedded practice'. It produces a tendency to 'aggregate from that level (for example, to households)' and means policies are not 'responsive to the collective conceptions that inform indigenous aspirations and agendas'. The chapters of the collection show how starting with the individual and aggregating from that level limits governments in developing 'policies that are genuinely responsive to the collective conceptions that inform indigenous aspirations and agendas' (Kukutai & Taylor 2016: 13).

The Indigenous Data Sovereignty movement, which emerged in 2015, is a response to these conceptual inadequacies. Scholars, statisticians, researchers, and activists from North America, Aotearoa New Zealand, and Australia work together across different historical, census-based, administrative, and policy regimes. In contrast with the negotiations for individual control over already-collected data, or trying to tip a balance between individuals and companies, they are interested in a way of thinking data collection around a collective not encapsulated in existing state logics. At present, 'Big Data and Open Data', argue Indigenous Data Sovereignty methodologists, 'operate to further distance lived social and cultural realities from their database embodiment … Open Data, without specific Indigenous data protocols, just expands the number of Indigenous statistical analyses that are conceived and executed from non-Indigenous worldviews' (Walter & Suina 2019: 236).

Data that does exist may be as problematic as that which doesn't: different categories of collection afford different stories. In Maggie Walter's account, based on her work on indigenous statistical engagement and Australian National Government data, the stories that emerge from government data are based on the *kinds* of data collected (Walter 2016). They produce accounts of disparity, deprivation, disadvantage, dysfunction, and difference. Editors Kukutai and Taylor note that this 'dearth of data on indigenous peoples that present an alternative narrative' that Walter observes 'serves to cement a "deficit data-problematic people" correlation' (Kukutai & Taylor 2016: 7). As Victoria Tauli-Corpuz notes in her preface to *Indigenous Data Sovereignty*, in 2002 the UN Permanent Forum on Indigenous Issues 'already recognized that a key challenge faced by national and international bodies is the lack of *disaggregated* data on indigenous peoples' (2016: xxi, emphasis added). Data, argues Tauli-Corpuz, in the way it is currently collected by states and indeed in the way it is understood, is an *insufficient* means to the kind of knowledge Indigenous Data Sovereignty methodologists would like to generate. But knowing through data requires access to that data. Working in Aotearoa New Zealand, Rawiri Jansen, a GP working toward health equity, asserts that:

> Māori sovereignty is informed by knowing about ourselves. Knowing who we are, where we are, what we do, when we do it, how we do it or how much we do what we do – all of the data that describe who we are – are our data, and are likely to be useful and informative and amenable to our analysis (Jansen 2016: 208).

Control over data is figured here as both access and ownership: data is a means to knowledge for its capacities to tell stories that will inform, as Jansen puts it.

Data does more than inform and describe, however. Kirikowhai Mikaere, statistician and founding member of Te Mana Raraunga, the Māori Data Sovereignty Network also in New Zealand, describes data slightly differently. When asked in an interview *How do we understand and encapsulate the relationship people have with the data?* Mikaere responded: 'Data is not just numbers but comes from and represents people and the environment. Data is essentially a piece of you and describes places, things, and relationships' (Hazel & Martin 2018: 5). Between these two – between 'represents' and 'is a piece of' – lies a gap to which I would like to direct our present and ongoing attention. This is not a simple mapping of the individual body to the body of the state. Rather, the capacity of data to be simultaneously a piece of and a representation points to ongoing conceptual tensions in the concept and its capacity to shift as it is put to use.

Bodies of data and the ethics of inference

The epigraph opening this piece begins Mary Douglas's essay 'The two bodies'. In it, she is continuing her inquiry into natural symbols through a series of engagements with scholars interested in bodies, considering throughout the essay a correspondence between bodily and social control (2003 [1970]: 71). Bodies of data – doubles, composites, and aggregates – bring out a parallel dilemma in commentators and advocates alike. We might ask not how the social body constrains the physical body, but how ideas from the physical body shape imaginations for data that cannot be fully separated from 'us'. Martin Holbraad and Morten Axel Pedersen argue that 'the most basic methodological question for anthropology (as for any other "discipline") is how to bring this "plural" data under some kind of control [which] must involve deciding which data go with each other and which do not' (2009: 373). By data, they mean empirical materials ethnographers use in analysis. This is what I also mean; it just happens that the data in question *is an instance of the idea of data*.

Like theoretical work in the 'emergent' biosciences, where anthropological accounts also took on an 'emergent' quality, theorizing data risks being as anticipatory as its object: 'a conceptual frame for analyzing the emergent, the about-to-be, the evanescent' (Clarke, Shim, Mamo, Fosket & Fishman 2010: 40). As with forward-looking studies of life and the implications of new genetic understandings, the grammar of data is often in the future tense. Across these stories, the presence of data promises a new capacity for those with access to *know*. What this 'new depths yet to be explored', revelatory quality risks concealing, however, are the reworkings of (collective) personhood taking place under and through the heading of data. I suggest that data is an analytical challenge for the relations it creates: for its capacity to be thought of as something that is an 'us', that belongs to an 'us', and that constitutes an 'us'. The ease with which differences are elided should give us pause. The 'data' making up Experian's figure of 'Dan' is simply not doing the same work as the 'data' that Indigenous Data Sovereignty activists seek to generate.

The data sought for the 'self-knowledge' of the bearded venture capitalist and data that will constitute 'self-knowledge' for a people through reshaping statistical assumptions are not the same. An anthropology of data must attend to what data is made to do, in order to illuminate how this changes what it is.

NOTES

This essay was written as part of the 'Data as Relation' research project at the IT University of Copenhagen, 2017-20, supported by the Villum Fonden Denmark grant agreement 12823. I would like to thank Dr Haidy Geismar for insightful comments at the Anthropology of Data workshop, and the reviewers of the special issue for clarifying suggestions. Thanks are due also to my co-editors, Antonia Walford and Nick Seaver, for critical readings and endlessly inspiring conversation.

[1] The Experian adverts have also appeared on the London Underground and in Deborah Lupton's work. For a 'more-than-human' perspective on data selves, see Lupton (2019).

[2] They also promised to not collect any data you input into the calculator.

[3] A Facebook post on the CitizenMe page from 11 July 2019 comes with a shareable screenshot from the app: 'I just exchanged my data for an Insight about my Twitter personality on CitizenMe'.

[4] Judith Gregory and Geoff Bowker open one of their essays with a quote from the Pragmatist philosopher Arthur F. Bentley, and his now classic meditation on 'The human skin: philosophy's last line of defense' (Bentley 1941; see also Turner 1993 [1980]). They argue that a separation between 'the citizen' and the 'data about the citizen' is an equally misconceived separation. As they put it, '[T]o imagine a "citizen" as an ideal type who exists outside of data flows is conceptually flawed: s/he becomes a citizen because s/he is saturated with data flows, markers, indicators, analyses. We are constituted differently as data citizens at different technological moments' (Gregory & Bowker 2016: 220). In contrast with the 'Citizen' of CitizenMe, the skin is a site of mediation between the corporate self and the presumed companies in whom data collection originates. (Sofia [2000] provides a good overview of containership logics.)

REFERENCES

Amoore, L. 2011. Data derivatives: on the emergence of a security risk calculus for our times. *Theory, Culture & Society* 28: 6, 24-43.

Bentley, A.F. 1941. The human skin: philosophy's last line of defense. *Philosophy of Science* 8, 1-19.

Cakici, B., E. Ruppert & S. Scheel 2020. Peopling Europe through data practices: Introduction to the special issue. *Science, Technology & Human Values* 45, 199-211.

CitizenMe 2020a. For Citizens (available online: *https://www.citizenme.com/for-citizens/*, accessed 26 January 2021).

——— 2020b. About us. LinkedIN (available online: *https://www.linkedin.com/company/citizenme*, accessed 26 January 2021).

Clarke, A., J.K. Shim, L. Mamo, J.R. Fosket & J.R. Fishman 2010. Biomedicalization: a theoretical and substantive introduction. In *Biomedicalization: technoscience, health, and illness in the US* (eds) A. Clarke, L. Mamo, J.R. Fosket, J.R. Fishman & J.K. Shim, 1-44. Durham, N.C.: Duke University Press.

Datacoup 2019. Unlock the value of your personal data: introducing the world's first personal data marketplace (available online: *http://datacoup.com*, accessed 26 January 2021).

Deakins, S. 2018. Making MyData mainstream. My Data Conference, Global (available online: *https://www.youtube.com/watch?v=eREooiXXasg&feature=youtu.be*, accessed 26 January 2021).

——— 2020. About me (available online: *https://stjohndeakins.wordpress.com/about/*, accessed 26 January 2021).

Douglas, M. 2003 [1970]. The two bodies. In *Natural symbols: explorations in cosmology*, 72-91. London: Routledge.

Greenfield, D. 2016. Deep data: notes on the *n* of 1. In *Quantified: biosensing technologies in everyday life* (ed.) D. Nafus, 123-46. Cambridge, Mass.: MIT Press.

Gregg, M. 2015. The gift that is not given. In *Data, now bigger and better!* (eds) T. Boellstorff & B. Maurer, 47-66. Chicago: Prickly Paradigm.

Gregory, J. & G. Bowker 2016. The data citizen, the quantified self and personal genomics. In *Quantified: biosensing technologies in everyday life* (ed.) D. Nafus, 211-26. Cambridge, MA: MIT Press.

Haggerty, K.D. & R.V. Ericson 2000. The surveillant assemblage. *The British Journal of Sociology* 51, 605-22.

HALPERN, O. 2014. *Beautiful data: A history of vision and reason since 1945*. Durham, N.C.: Duke University Press.

HARCOURT, B.E. 2015. *Exposed: desire and disobedience in the digital age*. Cambridge, Mass.: Harvard University Press.

HAZEL, J. & W.J. MARTIN 2018. Māori data futures: Hui report. Science for Technological Innovation, University of Wellington, 9 May.

HOGLE, L. 1995. Standardization across non-standard domains: the case of organ procurement. *Science, Technology & Human Values* **20**, 482-500.

HOLBRAAD, M. & M. PEDERSEN 2009. The intense abstraction of Marilyn Strathern. *Anthropological Theory* **9**, 371-94.

JANSEN, R. 2016. Indigenous Data Sovereignty: a Māori health perspective. In *Indigenous Data Sovereignty: toward an agenda* (eds) T. Kukutai & J. Taylor, 193-213. Canberra: ANU Press.

JONES, S. 2010. Negotiating authentic objects and authentic selves: beyond the deconstruction of authenticity. *Journal of Material Culture* **15**, 181-203.

JUDGE BUSINESS SCHOOL 2020. The Psychometrics Centre, Cambridge Judge Business School (available online: *https://www.psychometrics.cam.ac.uk/client-showcase/citizenme*, accessed 26 January 2021).

KELLY, K. 2012. The quantified century (*http://quantifiedself.com/conference/Palo-Alto-2012*, accessed April 2019, no longer available online).

KERTZER, D. & D. AREL 2002. Censuses, identity formation and the struggle for political power. In *Census and identity: the politics of race, ethnicity and language in national censuses* (eds) D. Kertzer & D. Arel, 1-42. Cambridge: University Press.

KRISTENSEN, D.B. & M. RUCKENSTEIN 2018. Co-evolving with self-tracking technologies. *New Media & Society* **20**, 3624-40.

KUKUTAI, T. & J. TAYLOR 2016. Data sovereignty for Indigenous peoples: current practice and future needs. In *Indigenous Data Sovereignty: toward an agenda* (eds.) T. Kukutai & J. Taylor, 1-25. Canberra: ANU Press.

LÄHTEENOJA, V., A. POIKOLA, K. KUIKKANIEMI, O. KUITTINEN, H. HONKO & A. KNUUTILA 2020. MyData – an introduction to human-centric use of personal data (Third revised edition). White paper, MyData.

LEHTINIEMI, T. & M. RUCKENSTEIN 2019. The social imaginaries of data activism. *Big Data & Society* **6**: 1 (available online: *https://journals.sagepub.com/doi/full/10.1177/2053951718821146*, accessed 26 January 2021).

LOCK, M. & J. FARQUHAR 2007. Introduction to part I: An emergent canon, or putting bodies on the scholarly agenda. In *Beyond the body proper: reading the anthropology of material life* (eds) M. Lock & J. Farquhar, 19-24. Durham, N.C.: Duke University Press.

LOVETT, R., V. LEE, T. KUKUTAI, D. CORMACK, S. C. RAINIE & J. WALKER 2019. Good data practices for Indigenous Data Sovereignty and governance. In *Good data* (eds) A. Daly, S.K. Devitt & M. Mann, 26-36. Amsterdam: Institute of Network Cultures.

LUPTON, D. 2013. Quantifying the body: monitoring, performing and configuring health in the age of mHealth technologies. *Critical Public Health* **23**, 393-403.

——— 2015. *Digital sociology*. Oxford: Routledge.

——— 2019. *Data selves: more-than-human perspectives*. Oxford: Wiley.

McGOVERN, L. 2018. Experian (available online: *https://www.lauramcgovern.com/Experian*, accessed 26 January 2021).

MARTIN, E. 1992. The end of the body? *American Ethnologist* **18**, 121-40.

MYDATA 2021. Impact (available online: *https://mydata.org/impact/*, accessed 29 January 2021).

PUSCHMANN, C. & J. BURGESS 2014. Big data, big questions: metaphors of big data. *International Journal of Communication* **8**, 1690-709.

QS (Quantified Self) 2020. About (available online: *https://quantifiedself.com/about/*, accessed 29 January 2021).

RATNER, H. & E. RUPPERT 2019. Producing and projecting data: aesthetic practices of government data portals. *Big Data & Society* **6**: **2** (available online: *https://journals.sagepub.com/doi/10.1177/2053951719853316*, accessed 26 January 2021).

RUCKENSTEIN, M. 2014. Visualized and interacted life: personal analytics and engagements with data doubles. *Societies* **4**, 68-84.

SCHEPER-HUGHES, N. & L. WACQUANT (eds) 2003. *Commodifying bodies*. London: Sage Publications.

SCHÜLL, N.D. 2017. Digital containment and its discontents. *History and Anthropology* **29**, 42-8.

——— 2019. Self in the loop: bits, patterns and pathways in the quantified self. In *A networked self and human augmentics, artificial intelligence, sentience* (ed.) Z. Papacharissi, 25-38. New York: Routledge.

Journal of the Royal Anthropological Institute (N.S.) **27**, *159-170*
© Royal Anthropological Institute 2021

SCOTT, J. 1998. *Seeing like a state: how certain schemes to improve the human condition have failed*. New Haven: Yale University Press.

SHARON, T. 2017. Self-tracking for health and the quantified self: re-articulating autonomy, solidarity and authenticity in an age of personalized healthcare. *Philosophy and Technology* **30**, 93-121.

SHARP, L. 2000. The commodification of the body and its parts. *Annual Review of Anthropology* **29**, 287-328.

SMITH, G. 2016. Surveillance, data and embodiment: on the work of being watched. *Body & Society* **22**, 108-39.

SOFIA, Z. 2000. Container technologies. *Hypatia* **15**, 181-201.

STEEL, E., C. LOCKE, E. CADMAN & B. FREESE 2013. How much is your personal data worth? *The Financial Times*, 12 June (available online: *https://ig.ft.com/how-much-is-your-personal-data-worth/*, accessed 26 January 2021).

TAMMINEN, S. & E. HOLMGREN 2016. The anthropology of wearables: the self, the social and the autobiographical. *Ethnographic Praxis in Industry Conference Proceedings* **1**, 154-74.

TAULI-CORPUZ, V. 2016. Preface. In *Indigenous Data Sovereignty: toward an agenda* (eds) T. Kukutai & J. Taylor, xxi-xxiii. Canberra: ANU Press.

TAYLOR, J. 2005. Surfacing the body interior. *Annual Review of Anthropology* **34**, 741-56.

TURNER, T.S. 1993 [1980]. The social skin. In *Reading the social body* (eds) C.B. Burroughs & J.D. Ehrenreich, 15-27. Iowa City: University of Iowa Press.

VISEU, A. & L. SUCHMAN 2010. Wearable augmentations: imaginaries of the informed body. In *Technologized images, technologized bodies* (eds) J. Edwards, P. Harvey & P. Wade, 161-84. New York: Berghahn Books.

WALTER, M. 2016. Data politics and Indigenous representation in Australian statistics. In *Indigenous Data Sovereignty: toward an agenda* (eds) T. Kukutai & J. Taylor, 79-98. Canberra: ANU Press.

———— & M. SUINA 2019. Indigenous data, indigenous methodologies and Indigenous Data Sovereignty. *International Journal of Social Research Methodology* **22**, 233-43.

WATSON, S.M. 2014. Data doppelgängers and the uncanny valley of personalization. *The Atlantic*, 16 June (available online: *https://www.theatlantic.com/technology/archive/2014/06/data-doppelgangers-and-the-uncanny-valley-of-personalization/372780/*, accessed 26 January 2021).

WHITTAKER, E. 1992. The birth of the anthropological self and its career. *Ethos* **20**, 191-219.

ZUBOFF, S. 2015. The big other: surveillance capitalism and the prospects of an information civilization. *Journal of Information Technology* **30**, 75-89.

Corps de données : doubles, composites, agrégées

Résumé

Cet article décrit trois corps de données et analyse comment les relations sont établies entre les données composites physiques, digitales et politiques. En appliquant l'expression « connaître son double numérique », l'autrice se propose de déterminer les types de relations que les individus établissent grâce aux données, ainsi que les versions du corps codifiées dans les imaginaires des données. Thématiquement, différents cas de contrôle des données émergent, selon que la masse de données est faite de doubles, de composites, ou agrégée en corps politique.

Data forward: an afterword

BILL MAURER *University of California*

Abolition means the creation of something new.

Yeshimabeit Milner (2019)

Antonia Walford's contribution to this issue of the *Journal of the Royal Anthropological Institute* makes a provocative analogy between data and money – with which I cannot resist beginning this afterword. It is not just that data is a speculative source of limitless return: the new oil, the new gold, an all-encompassing resource that can be mined for insights and value. It is also, as Walford observes, that data is potential, and, in particular, transformative potential. Data is value(able) 'because it can be transformed into something else' – anything else.

   I will return to this key insight in a moment, but I also want to note the other harmonies between money and data that resonate from the essays in this thought-provoking issue. We can begin with Tahani Nadim's discussion of datafication of natural history collections and biodiversity projects, where we see that data – like money – mediates the abstract and the concrete, contributing to homogenization but dependent on the specificities of local workflows. Or Sarah Blacker's discussion of the tension between Canadian First Nations peoples' traditional knowledge and Western, objectified toxicology, in relation to which the former must mediate its claims about environmental contamination. Or Nick Seaver's analysis of the mathematical models devised to fix and map 'culture' as a Euclidean spatial field, a co-ordinate system of individual and cultural values translatable into monetary value, a 'conceptual space in which everything is measurable and quantified, controlled by central authorities in the service of capital'. And just as money's materiality matters – its stuff surfaces again and again in ethnographic accounts and in everyday practice – so, too, as A.R.E. Taylor shows us in a report on bunkered data centres, the materiality of data infrastructures matters for data's aggregation, configuration, and durability. And the latter is central: future-proofing data by securing servers in underground concrete bunkers is a means to do one of those things money also does so well – like other institutions, it 'forestalls loss' (Kockelman 2010: 406), carrying value across time into the indefinite future, a mediating infrastructure for value preservation. In this case, data's material infrastructure is a bridge across an undetermined and undeterminable timespace so that it will be able to realize its limitless potential in any number of possible futures.

Like money, data is about the authoritative determination and allocation of value(s). The contributors to this issue go beyond providing ethnographic 'context' to data and data worlds, and instead use data as a ground for anthropological theory. What emerges are theories that foreground the authorizing agents or forces determining and distributing value, theories of inequality, control, domination, and accumulation. This raises the question, however, of how to understand data in different systems of inequality (and my touchstone for the very idea of systems of inequality remains Yanagisako & Collier 1988). Does 'data' and all that it entails – its capture, categorization, cleansing, formatting, flow, infrastructure, insertion into other relations – always and only replicate structures of domination? Or instead, when does 'data' work more like 'the gift', varied in meaning and pragmatic, unfolding depending on the stakes of the games in which people are caught up? A shell valuable works differently in kula or a bridewealth presentation, even if it 'looks' similar (Collier 1988); a pig is never just a pig, interchangeable with all the others, but 'this' pig which sits in a system of relations among other pigs and people, making its transfer particularly commanding (Strathern 1988). Despite its etymology, data is never just a 'given', a point Rachel Douglas-Jones, Antonia Walford, and Nick Seaver make in their cogent introduction.

The challenge, it seems to me, is that in moving from ethnography to theory, from describing the sociotechnical milieux in which data and people and other agents are enmeshed to using data worlds to move theoretical conversations in anthropology, we have to contend with a social space in which machines 'are becoming anthropologists in their own right' (Kockelman 2020: 33). That is to say, a 'machine ethnography' (Kockelman 2020: 33) will be the study of the interpretative practices of datafication and algorithmic processes – as is on offer in this collection of essays – as well as a study of the machines themselves engaged in interpretative practices, engaged in theory-making. There is a taste of this in this collection, but much more work remains to be done.

In my graduate seminar in economic anthropology, I demonstrate 'data' by walking across the classroom and out the door. Then, returning to the classroom, I pick up my cellphone and walk out the door a second time. The first action represents mere social practice; the second represents the datafication of my social practice, the rendering into different forms of value of my physical movement in timespace. Walking is 'just' kinesics, interpretable by my students in our shared social space – peculiar, perhaps, insofar as it is a minor violation of the conventions or norms of the classroom ('What's he doing? Why did he just walk out the door?'). Walking with a device that records my movements, formatting them into data based on my location relative to multiple cellphone towers, together with radio signals received from satellites owned by the US military, is qualitatively different. It secures from my everyday activity 'data' that is translated into formats able to be used by any number of applications, which in turn may enclose it within their own proprietary data forms or formats. It enlists my motion in timespace into corporate and government sociotechnical systems; it becomes something new – and, thereby, so do I. (Of course, walking without the device is also data! One would have to imagine a world without such devices, or launch a programme of data abolition, to create zones of autonomy from data and datafication.)

By saying that we need to understand data in different systems of inequality, systems which include machines interpreting behaviour and participating with human agents in recursive projects of interpretation and sense-making, I want to challenge the familiarity of these systems of inequality. They might not even be 'systems' or intentionally devised to work systematically. All contemporary geolocation services use the Global Positioning System (GPS) of satellites because it's there, and is available for anyone or anything. Now, *why* it is openly available is an interesting story indeed: US President Ronald Reagan opened the network to global civilian use after Soviet fighter jets shot down Korean Airlines flight 007 in 1983 after that ill-fated flight strayed into Soviet airspace. There had been a perfect storm of human and machine error. Today, the fact that an Uber (shorthand for the whole machinic-human assemblage) can know my location and pick me up to drive me to my destination, or a food delivery app can recommend restaurants in my vicinity, or I can 'find my friends' using my cellphone is the effect of a happenstance of navigational error, human tragedy, and geopolitical competition that turned what had initially been top-secret technology into something much more mundane. My cellphone's GPS capability is not so much embedded in the military apparatus of the GPS satellite network as it is an effect of a path dependency caused by a series of errors that led to Reagan's political decision.

So, our 'systems' can be comprised of or set in motion by misfires, accidents, or turns of fate that create pathways channelling people and things in certain directions or towards certain aims they might not even have had at the outset of their collaborative journeys. This is part of their puzzle and the bewilderment they can inspire (see Guyer 2004). Sometimes they barely hang together. Or they hang together for now, but change a parameter or condition or input … and things fall apart.

One way of tackling this might be with help from Anna Tsing's (2015) notion of salvage capitalism. As with my walking experiment, salvage capitalism is a system of accumulation based on the extraction of value from natural and more-than-natural processes – the detritus of failed civilizational experiments, the flotsam and jetsam of ruined landscapes and sedimented histories in scarred lives. But one need not go to the logical, devastating ends of capitalist extraction to see such appropriation. Julia Elyachar (2010) shows how communicative practice – not even a specific utterance but the barest opening of a channel for such (the raised eyebrow, the insouciant grin, welcoming the gossip to follow) – creates social infrastructures of communicative pathways that can be harnessed for different value projects. Her case is women in Cairo who become subjects of financial empowerment projects.

Seen one way, such social infrastructures do indeed form the raw material for projects of capitalist accumulation no longer within Cairene women's control. You could easily imagine it all getting sucked into the project and platform of Facebook or Instagram if these women started posting their daily lives and interactions, which then would become part of the newly valuable data value chain. Seen another way, however – just out of focus, or from a side glance – such infrastructures allow people to continue along the tracks already laid towards ends of their own choosing, outside, to one side of, or just out of phase of those circuits of capital. This is a point I have made often (most recently Maurer 2019).

I make the point in this afterword because I want to suggest the contributors to this special issue are not solely presenting theories of state or capitalist domination or control ('now, through data!'). First, state and capitalist control has long been figured through data, from the first French government national accounts (Soll 2011) to the ledger books of the New World plantation (Rosenthal 2018). Unlike these systems, however, the data worlds described in these essays suggest something more nuanced than the creation of and accounting for fixed identities or a singular point of perspective for a state or colonial gaze. Vijayanka Nair's essay on the Indian government's biometric identification programme (*Aadhaar*) demonstrates the point. While, on the one hand, a project by the state to obtain surveillance and exert control, it also, by opening up the concept of the 'individual' identified by somatic features, presented ongoing challenges to the fiduciary relationship between a person and the data generated in relation to it. Far from fixing identity, *Aadhaar* leaves it in what Nair calls a 'state of becoming' – which implies it leaves the state in, well, an uncertain state too.

Second, if society has been conceptualized as a force pushing against the self-regulating market when the latter's excesses threaten social existence (Polanyi 2001 [1944]), and if the state has been conceptualized as the manifestation of society's sovereign will or else a means of social control, the data worlds described in these essays necessitate a re-theorization of society itself. Take Cori Hayden's essay on the figure of the crowd. How do we theorize society in systems that pre-empt it? Margaret Thatcher could proclaim, there is no society, only individuals and families. Hayden's 'more-than-human crowdings' add the corollary, there is no society, only disaggregated data, intensities, networks, patterns, contagions, and associations. And her point is that this is not new: it is a reminder that the era of crowds has always been with us – if, again, perhaps off to one side.

Paul Kockelman is my go-to for widening the scope of conversations in anthropology like those represented in this issue of the *JRAI*. In his musings on machine learning praxis, he asks why we should be surprised by seemingly new forms of algorithmic scrutiny given the basics of semiotic interaction: 'As long as there have been languages and minds, eyes and memories, people have watched the behavior of others, characterized the actions being undertaken, and thereby ascribed meanings to such actions, and motivations to such actors' (Kockelman 2020: 2). For Kockelman, this is not a matter of simple perception, but encompasses processes that are 'wily, epistemic, performative, and often violent' (2020: 3), algorithmically (re)producing racist, misogynistic, ableist, homophobic outputs of which digital critical race theorists Ruha Benjamin (2019) and Safiya Noble (2018) warn: 'male or female; white or black; straight or queer; rioting or queuing; citizen or alien; saluting or plotting; ethnic majority or ethnic minority; healthy or sick; critter or vermin' (Kockelman 2020: 10).

And this brings us back to systems of inequality, and the question of transformation with which I opened this afterword: why are *these* the foreordained outputs? Benjamin and Noble argue that the fact that algorithms fed 'big data' consistently spit out racialized and gendered bias couched as objectively derived ('the machine did it') should be a signal of the depth of the authoritative grounds with reference to which meaning-making human-machine agents' practices unfold.

I want to suggest that we bring the data *forward*, switch ground and figure, so that we can query the persistence of the differential and hierarchical valuation of persons, actions, things, utterances, on the authoritative grounds now cast as 'data'.

Hannah Knox's essay in this issue suggests how we can do this. If you can't unground the grounds, you can hack the channel through which the authoritative force flows that institutes them as the *only* grounds (for knowledge, for interpretation, for practice or meaning-making). You can take the data not just as a second-order representation of some reality, but as a response to imprecise and sometimes unknown relations, a 'just-so', the very instability of which provides an occasion for inviting others to join in the understanding and then hacking of the data and of the model-making which takes that data as its ground – again, bringing the data forward.

This can be frightening – for disciplinary authority, for political projects the ends of which we cannot yet quite discern. Yeshimabeit Milner (2019) of Data 4 Black Lives calls for an abolitionist movement for data:

> The prison abolition movement asks the question: how do we create solutions in our communities without recourse to prisons? With this call to action I apply the same lens to big data. How do we dismantle and reimagine industries that concentrate big data into the hands of a few? And how can [we] abolish the structures that turn data into a powerful and deadly weapon?

Abolition is both a 'mourning', she writes, for we have to give up the way of life to which we have become accustomed, or inured; and it is a 'celebration of life, of possibility, a new path full of uncertainty'. She concludes with a provocative metaphor: 'we make the road by walking'. Charting a new path by interfering with the established channels or path dependencies. Jumping the tracks. Cutting the cables. Or seizing the channels towards our own ends, together perhaps with our machinic model-making counterparts.

This would set in motion alternative values. A transformative current through the wires and networks subtending our data-saturated world.

REFERENCES

BENJAMIN, R. 2019. *Race after technology: abolitionist tools for the New Jim Code*. Cambridge: Polity.
COLLIER, J. 1988. *Marriage and inequality in classless society*. Stanford: University Press.
ELYACHAR, J. 2010. Phatic labor, infrastructure, and the question of empowerment in Cairo. *American Ethnologist* **37**, 452-64.
GUYER, J. 2004. *Marginal gains: monetary transactions in Atlantic Africa*. Chicago: University Press.
KOCKELMAN, P. 2010. Enemies, parasites, and noise: how to take up residence in a system without becoming a term in it. *Journal of Linguistic Anthropology* **20**, 406-21.
——— 2020. The epistemic and performative dynamics of machine learning praxis. *Signs and Society* **8**, 1-37.
MAURER, B. 2019. That touch of money. In *Being material* (eds) M.-P. Boucher, S. Helmreich, L.W. Kinney, S. Tibbits, R. Uchill & E. Ziporyn, 112-19. Cambridge, Mass.: MIT Press.
MILNER, Y. 2019. Abolition means the creation of something new: the history of big data and a prophecy for big data abolition. *Medium*, 31 December (available online: *https://medium.com/@YESHICAN/abolition-means-the-creation-of-something-new-72fc67c8f493*, accessed 27 January 2021).
NOBLE, S. 2018. *Algorithms of oppression: how search engines reinforce racism*. New York: NYU Press.
POLANYI, K. 2001 [1944]. *The great transformation: the political and economic origins of our time*. Boston: Beacon Press.
ROSENTHAL, C. 2018. *Accounting for slavery: masters and management*. Cambridge, Mass.: Harvard University Press.
SOLL, J. 2011. *The information master: Jean-Baptiste Colbert's secret state intelligence system*. Ann Arbor: University of Michigan Press.
STRATHERN, M. 1988. *The gender of the gift: problems with women and problems with society in Melanesia*. Berkeley: University of California Press.
TSING, A. 2015. *The mushroom at the end of the world: on the possibility of life in capitalist ruins*. Princeton: University Press.
YANAGISAKO, S.J. & J.F. COLLIER 1988. Toward a unified analysis of gender and kinship. In *Gender and kinship: essays toward a unified analysis* (eds) J.F. Collier & S.J. Yanagisako, 14-50. Stanford: University Press.

Index

4Chan 97
accounting 10, 11; energy accounting 114; Financial Accounting Standards Board 18
actor-network theory 64–5
advertisements 159, 160–2
algorithms 15, 34, 47, 51, 110, 174; biased 110
anthropology, and data 9–25, 45–8; and hacking 108–26; and reproductive technologies 10; cognitive 50–1; comparison 128, 138–9; cultural 45; data-driven 50; hacking 108–26; knowledge claims 109–10
anti-liberalism 35, 96, 97, 99
audit culture 10, 136

Barcode Index Numbers (BINs) 63
Barcode of Life Data System (BOLD) 65
Baudrillard, Jean 102
big data 9, 10, 14, 20, 76, 127–8, 174; and ethnography 12; and metaphors 127–8; and small data 64; and sociology 11
biodiversity 17, 63, 68, 171; crisis 72; data integration 72; Global Biodiversity Information Facility (GBIF) 65, 66–7, 69; surveys 68
biometric data 12, 14, 16–17, 26–42, 174
Blacker, Sarah 7, 19, 142–58, 171
Borch, Christian 96, 99
Bourdieu, Pierre 57
Brazil, data collection 129; Large-Scale Biosphere-Atmosphere project 18, 129–32; scientific data processing 128; stolen data 130
Brexit 97, 101
Broch, Hermann 100
Browne, Simone 14, 15, 32
Burton, Michael 46–7, 48

Cambridge Analytica 36, 97, 101
Canada, and Indigenous knowledge 19, 142–58; Harper government 145–6, 147, 153, 154; Health Canada 143, 149; oil pollution 142–58; restrictions on data 145–6; Write2Know campaign 146
Canetti, Elias 70, 96, 98, 99, 100
capitalism 45, 139; and data 18, 76, 139, 144; salvage 175
CitizenMe 164–5

classification 11, 28, 54, 56, 67

climate change 108, 114, 117, 124, 146; and activism 110; energy monitoring 111–16, 121; hacking energy 116–19; models 110–11, 123

cloud storage 76–9, 85, 95–6, 97; and materiality of data 90–1

Cold War 45, 76, 77, 81, 83; bunkers 76, 84, 85, 87, 91, 172

Coleman, Gabriella 31, 118

collaborative filtering 51, 55, 56

colonialism 11, 17–18, 21, 72, 143–5; bureaucracy 11; colonial science 143, 144; German 62, 67; violence towards Indigenous peoples 144

Coopmans, Catelijne 14, 49

covid-19 105; infection rates, 9; mortality rates, 9

crowd theory 19–20, 95–107; and social media 100–105; contagion 97, 98–9, 101, 103–5; heterogeneity 99; medium 99–100

data, aesthetics 16–17; and calculation 13–15; and disciplines 11–12; and money 129–30, 132, 171–2; and power 36; and resistance 16, 144; and value 11, 129–30, 132; as ends 131, 133; as means 131, 133; as potentiality 135–6, 138; as theory 12–13; bringing forward 171–5; census data 28, 160; collection 31–5; compositions 19–20; cultural data 43–61; definitions 10; economies 18–19; environmental 18–19, 148; ethnography 112–14; fieldsites 12, 13; form 15–16; formation 62–75; manipulation 108–26; material specificity 10–11; metadata 72, 73; 'moment' 128; open 127, 128, 135, 136, 138, 139, 153, 166; patterns 49–50, 51; 'raw' 34, 127–8, 130, 131; realities 108–11; security 87–90; sovereignty 19, 165–7; storage 76–94, 172; theorizing 167; 'thinking data' 95–107; times 17–18

data bodies 159–70; composite citizens 163–5; data doubles 9, 160, 161–3, 165; data self 159, 161; Quantified Self 12, 14, 116, 161

data bunkers 18, 76–94; and resilience 87

data processing, as reproductive labour 127, 132, 135

databases 26, 28, 62, 64, 67, 69, 71, 162; aesthetic 'surface' 16–17; customer 81; enrolment on 29–32; genetic 12; personal 9; public 135

digitization 62, 64, 68, 73; and museums 69–71, 73

disinformation 97

DNA sequencing 17, 62, 63, 108

documentation 10, 71, 150, 154

Douglas, Mary 159, 167

Douglas-Jones, Rachel 7, 9–25, 97, 159–70, 172

Durkheim, Émile 96

Earth BioGenome project 20

energy, hacking 116–19; monitoring 111–16, 121

environmental sciences 127–41; and genomics 128

ethnography, 13; and big data 12; and documents 145; and machines 172; digital data models 108–26

Facebook 97, 100, 101, 102–5

Fanon, Frantz 14

fingerprinting 33–5

Fort Data Centres 77, 79–91; deep-time data storage 85–7, 92; materiality of data 90–1; recovery services 87; security 87–90; upgrading 89

Freud, Sigmund 96, 105

future-proofing 76–94, 172; definition 78

Garrett, Bradley 85, 87

Geertz, Clifford 50

genomics 136–9; compared with environmental sciences 137–8; Human Genome Project 136; liberalism 137

geographers, and data 11
Global Earth Observation System of
    Systems (GEOSS) 135–6
GPS network 173
Group on Earth Observation (GEO)
    135–6, 138

hacking 108–26; anthropology 119–23;
    as model 118; definitions 111, 118;
    energy 116–19, 120, 121, 123; 'Hack
    Manchester' 117–18
Halpern, Orit 14, 15, 163
Hayden, Cori 7, 19–20, 95–107
historians, and data 11
humanists, and data 11
Hymes, Dell 45–6, 50

India, biometric data capture 32–5;
    biometric identity programme
    (Aadhaar) 16–17, 26–42; census 28;
    Central Identities Data Repository
    (CIDR) 26, 27, 32, 34; Constitution
    28, 39–40; democracy 28, 37;
    demographic data collection 31–2;
    Digital India 18, 26–42; elections 9;
    enrolment on database 29–31, 33–5;
    fingerprinting 33–5; individual and
    state 28–9, 37; legal challenge to
    datafication 36–8; political parties
    35; Unique Identification Authority
    of India (UIDAI) 26–7, 28, 29–32,
    34–5, 36, 37, 38; untouchability
    33, 34
Indigenous people 19, 142–58;
    Indigenous Data Sovereignty 19,
    165–7
    see also Traditional Knowledge
Indonesia, taxi drivers 9, 11
inscriptions 64, 65, 69, 71
Instagram 173

Jameson, Fredric 57
judicial systems 12

Kelty, Christopher 31, 95, 118, 145

kinship 10, 12, 13, 128, 133, 138, 139;
    spiritual 133–4, 135
Knox, Hannah 7, 18, 19, 108–26, 175
Konrad, Monica 133, 134, 135

Le Bon, Gustave 20, 96, 98–9, 100, 101,
    102, 105
Lefebvre, Henri 45
Linnaeus, Carl 63

machine learning 17, 44, 51, 52, 55, 56,
    58, 59, 174
matrix factorization 51–2; and movies 53
Maurer, Bill 7, 11, 20, 171–5
McLachlan, Stéphane 143, 145, 146,
    147–8, 152
measurement 143–5, 147, 171; accuracy
    154; incommensurability of data
    151–3; statistical practice 166, 167
memes 108
multidimensional scaling (MDS) 46–50,
    51, 52; and market research 54–5
museums, and taxonomic research 62–3,
    69; datafication of nature 62–75;
    digitization 69–71, 73; volunteers 66
MyData Global 163, 164, 165

Nadim, Tahani 7, 17–18, 62–75, 171
Nair, Vijayanka 8, 14, 16–17, 19, 26–42,
    174
nationalism 100
natural history, and digital data 62–75,
    171; naming practices 67–9
Nehru, Jawaharlal 28
Netflix Prize 52
New Reproductive Technologies (NRTs)
    10, 12–13

oil pollution 142–58; metrics 143–5

personhood 10, 12, 16, 27, 133, 135, 167
privacy 9, 92, 118, 166
proof of identity 26, 27, 33

QAnon 97

QR codes 68, 70, 71
quantification 10, 11, 13–14, 15, 43, 57,
    64, 139, 142, 147, 153, 154
Quantified Self 12, 14, 116, 161;
    quantitative autobiography 14

racialization 14, 103, 144, 154, 174
Reardon, Jenny 136–8
references, retracing 65–7
representation 109; and digital data
    models 109, 111; and reality 58, 116,
    122, 175
Riedl, John 52, 55, 57
Ross, Edward 100, 103
Russia, blacklisting 9, 11
Russo Carroll, Stephanie 143, 155

scale 64, 72, 101, 108–9, 121; and
    contexts 72
scaling 64; and psychology 50; cities 48;
    digital data infrastructures 121–2;
    fruit 49; occupation terms 47
Seaver, Nick 8, 9–25, 31, 95, 97, 101, 103,
    171, 172
Sebald, W.G. 87
securitization 13
self-tracking 16, 101, 161, 162
social media 95, 96, 97, 98, 100, 163; and
    incitement 101–3; as crowd media
    100–105; regulation 102
social scientists 15, 100, 104, 120; and
    data 11
sociologists 46, 50; and data 11
spatialization 17, 43–61; cyberspace 55;
    post-demographic hyperspace 55–7;
    proximity 48, 51, 56, 57; similarity
    44–5, 47, 49, 57, 58, 101
Stefflre, Volney 54–5

Strathern, Marilyn 20, 53, 128, 134

Tarde, Gabriel 96, 98–9, 100, 101
taxi drivers, booking apps 9
Taylor, A.R.E. 8, 18, 76–94, 171
tracking devices 19
Traditional Knowledge 142–58, 171; and
    data practice 142–58; collaborations
    with Western science 147–9
Trump, Donald 96, 97, 101
Tsing, Anna 85, 173
Twitter 97, 100, 102, 108, 114

United Kingdom, egg donation 127,
    133–4
United States 9; and terrorism 14;
    anti-liberalism 96; Centers for
    Disease Control and Prevention 97;
    music recommender systems 43–61;
    National Science Foundation 135;
    social scientists 100

value 10, 16, 104, 134, 163; financial 19,
    163, 171; of data 11, 16, 18, 109, 128,
    129–30, 132, 133, 135, 137, 138, 139,
    149, 151, 154, 163, 164, 171
Virilio, Paul 86

Walford, Antonia 8, 9–25, 45, 97, 127–41,
    171, 172
Walter, Maggie 143, 155, 166
WhatsApp 97
World Health Organization 97

YouTube 97, 100